# War, Torture and Terroris⌐

# War, Torture and Terrorism

## Ethics and War in the 21st Century

Edited by

David Rodin

**Blackwell**
Publishing

First published as Volume 23, Issue 3 of the *Journal of Applied Philosophy*.

BLACKWELL PUBLISHING
350 Main Street, Malden, MA 02148-5020, USA
9600 Garsington Road, Oxford OX4 2DQ, UK
550 Swanston Street, Carlton, Victoria 3053, Australia

First published 2007 by Blackwell Publishing Ltd

*Library of Congress Cataloging-in-Publication Data has been applied for*

War, torture, and terrorism : ethics and war in the 21st century / edited
by David Rodin.
     p. cm.
  Includes bibliographical references and index.
   ISBN 978-1-4051-7398-8 (pbk. : alk. paper)   1. War–Moral and ethical aspects.
2. Torture–Moral and ethical aspects.   3. Terrorism–Moral and ethical aspects.
4. National security.  I. Rodin, David.
  U22.W363 2007
  172′.42—dc22

                                            2007028756

A catalogue record for this title is available from the British Library.

Set in 9.5/12pt Plantin
by Graphicraft Limited, Hong Kong
Printed and bound in the United Kingdom
by TJ International, Padstow, Cornwall

The publisher's policy is to use permanent paper from mills that operate a sustainable forestry policy, and which has been manufactured from pulp processed using acid-free and elementary chlorine-free practices. Furthermore, the publisher ensures that the text paper and cover board used have met acceptable environmental accreditation standards.

For further information on
Blackwell Publishing, visit our website:
www.blackwellpublishing.com

# Contents

# Contributors

**David Rodin**
Oxford Uehiro Centre for
Practical Ethics
Oxford, UK.

**Rob Lawlor**
Research Fellow
Inter-Disciplinary Ethics Applied
A Centre for Excellence in
Teaching and Learning
University of Leeds
Leeds, UK

**Deane-Peter Baker**
School of Philosophy and Ethics
University of KwaZulu-Natal
South Africa

**Gillian Brock**
Philosophy Department
University of Auckland
Auckland, New Zealand

**David Mellow**
Philosophy Department
The University of Calgary
Calgary, Alberta, Canada

**Daniel Statman**
Department of Philosophy
University of Haifa
Haifa, Israel

**Michael L. Gross**
Department of International
Relations
The University of Haifa
Haifa, Israel

**Uwe Steinhoff**
Department of Politics &
International Relations
University of Oxford
Oxford, UK

**Vittorio Bufacchi**
Department of Philosophy
University College Cork
Cork, Ireland

**Jean Maria Arrigo**
Project on Ethics and Art in
Testimony
Irvine, CA, USA

# 1 Introduction
## The Ethics of War: State of the Art

DAVID RODIN

The ethics of war, as a sub-field of moral philosophy, is currently experiencing a remarkable period of development. There are obvious reasons for this: the last decade and a half have brought tremendous change in the character of war and international politics. All of these changes have significant implications for the ethics of war.

The end of the cold war and the collapse of the Soviet empire represented an epochal change in global politics. It cleared the way for an optimistic but short-lived attempt to create a 'new world order' in which the legal and institutional framework of the United Nations could finally be made authoritative. Even as this project dissipated, an ambitious doctrine of humanitarian intervention was developed as a counterpoint to the dominant doctrine of state sovereignty. The doctrine claimed some limited, albeit contested, successes (notably in Kosovo, Sierra Leone and East Timor), but was otherwise marked by failed intervention (Somalia) and catastrophic non-interventions (most clearly in Bosnia, Rwanda and the on-going genocide in Darfur). The 9/11 attacks changed the dominant mode of world politics once again. They convinced the United States and others that they are facing a fundamentally changed and threatening strategic environment and triggered a period of increased US military activity culminating in the wars in Afghanistan and Iraq. This post 9/11 environment has generated many extraordinary innovations: the prosecution of an apparently endless 'war on terror'; the emergence of 'asymmetric war' as the dominant form of combat operations; and the attempt to establish radical new norms of international conduct including a norm permitting preventive war and forcible regime change. In the domestic arena it has generated challenges to some of the most basic rights and liberties of liberal societies, including the right to be free from detention without trial and the right against torture. Any one of these changes would merit a careful re-appraisal of the ethics of war. Collectively they have served to place legal institutions and ethical concepts under more strain than they have faced in over a generation.

The philosophical community has been quick to respond to these challenges. Philosophers have fulfilled their traditional roles as gadflies to the powerful, clarifiers of policy-oriented concepts, and generators of substantive moral theory. The ethics of war, long dominated by Michael Walzer's particular construal of Just War Theory has begun to shift, evolve and take new directions. As one would expect, there has been a significant increase in the quantity of publications on the ethics of war. But what is striking is the quality and range of much of the work. Established philosophers who do not normally work in the field have begun to publish on the ethics of war. While most writers continue to locate themselves within some variant of the just war tradition, the basic assumptions and constructs of this approach are being tested, challenged and reformulated. In parallel with this academic work, there is a growing readiness to engage with moral aspects of war on the part of military organisations, policy makers, politicians and the media. The result is an extraordinarily exciting period for those interested in the ethics of war and political violence more generally. The essays in this book exemplify the dynamism and vitality of the field at the current time. They provide rich and varied discussion of a broad range of current issues, from high level issues of *jus ad bellum*, through to specific issues of operational tactics and *jus in bello*.

If one looks at current work in the ethics of war, what trends are we able discern? I would like to highlight six trends that seem to me significant. The first four consist in moral controversies that have been, to a greater or lesser extent, generated out of the experience of recent conflicts. The remaining two derive from larger shifts in moral theory and have the potential to generate more far-reaching revisions to the ethical theory of war.

The first trend concerns controversies about whether established elements of the ethics of war can be modified or even violated in response to exceptional forms of threat. Two questions have become central here. The first is whether the norm of national self-defence should be expanded to generate a right of preventive self-defence, that is to say a right to engage in a war against a potential future aggressor who does not currently pose an imminent threat. The Bush administration claimed such an expanded right in order to forestall emerging terrorist threats in the 2002 *National Security Strategy of the United States of America*, and arguably this policy informed the 2003 invasion of Iraq. But the doctrine of preventive war clearly contravenes long-standing legal and ethical norms and demands careful appraisal.[1] A second controversy surrounds the idea of 'supreme emergency' first proposed by Michael Walzer in the 1970s.[2] According to Walzer's argument, a state or nation is morally entitled to engage in grave violations of the ethics of war, including the widespread intentional killing of enemy civilians, if this is the only way to avert a catastrophe such as the destruction of a nation at the hands of an enemy. Although no state involved in the current 'war on terror' is claiming the permission intentionally to target civilians, the supreme emergency argument has obvious and disturbing connections with the way that terrorist groups typically conceptualise and justify their own attacks on civilians. In this volume, Danny Statman provides a subtle discussion of the supreme emergency argument and suggests that a seemingly promising way of making sense of the argument is not in fact sustainable.

Related to the question of exceptional permissions in war is the question of whether established civil rights and liberties may be curtailed or annulled on the grounds of national security and defence against terrorism. Britain has recently passed legislation that curtails the right of *habeas corpus* and criminalises speech acts that are deemed to incite terrorism. President Bush has claimed the authority to wire tap citizens without a judicial warrant. These measures, and others like them, seem open to question given that most experts agree that the current threat from terrorism remains small in objective terms. Terrorism certainly does not pose an existential threat to any of the western states, in the way that Nazi Germany or the Soviet Union did in the twentieth century. But most extraordinary of all has been the emergence of a debate about whether torture might be a legitimate tool in the war on terror. There is substantial evidence that the United States has engaged in torture or torture-like practices at Guantanamo Bay and other secret detention centres around the globe, and that it has knowingly rendered prisoners for torture in foreign jurisdictions.

The question of torture had been considered settled for over a hundred years in liberal societies and the absolute prohibition of torture has long been regarded one of the central achievements of modern international law. Much philosophical argument about torture revolves around the so-called 'ticking-bomb hypothetical', which asks us to imagine that a horrendous terrorist atrocity can only be averted by torturing a captured terrorist. In this volume, Vittorio Bufacchi and Jean Maria Arrigo powerfully criticise the logic and assumptions of this pro-torture argument from a consequentialist perspective. Uwe Steinhoff is more sympathetic to the arguments for torture in certain contexts, but still rejects proposals to institutionalise torture practices such as Alan Dershowitz's proposal for a torture warrant.[3]

The third set of controversies arises from the increasing prominence of asymmetric wars, such as the ongoing conflict in Iraq. In an asymmetric war one side, which is typically much weaker in conventional military terms, engages in practices such as targeting civilians and employing guerrilla tactics in which soldiers hide amongst and often disguise themselves as civilians. Such conflicts challenge traditional just war theory, because they have the effect of blurring the boundary between combatant and non-combatant, a distinction fundamental to the *jus in bello*.[4] Among the most important debates stemming from asymmetric war is the ongoing controversy over the definition and potential justification of terrorism.[5] A less developed but equally important question concerns the legal and moral status of so called 'unlawful combatants', including many of the detainees at Guantanamo Bay.[6] The question is difficult because these people are not clearly civilians since they were engaged in combat operations, but neither do they have the status of lawful combatants under current international law. What does seem clear is that it is unacceptable that they should have no determinate legal status, which seems to be the preferred position of the US government. Michael Gross examines a further important issue arising in the context of asymmetric war with his insightful discussion of the ethics of targeted killing. This has become an important feature of the Israeli and Palestinian conflict and the tactic has also been employed by US forces. By analysing targeted killing as an instance of 'named killing', Gross argues that there are strong reasons for rejecting the legitimacy of the practice.

A fourth trend is the increasing attention paid to issues of *jus post bellum* or justice after war. While the just war theory has long had a *jus post bellum* component, it has generally been much less developed than the *ad bellum* and *in bello* sides of the theory.

Experience in Iraq has made it clear to all that what happens after major combat operations have ended is critical to the success and moral justification of military operations. While this themed issue of the journal contains no dedicated discussion of *jus post bellum*, the question of how the consequences of a war affect its overall justification is central to Rob Lawlor's fascinating discussion of war and moral luck. Lawlor argues that Bernard Williams' influential conception of moral luck lies behind the way that many analysts have viewed the Iraq war, but that this conception rests on a confusion between two forms of justification — evidentiary justification and de facto justification.

All of these trends and issues can be seen as a response to recent experiences of conflict and associated political developments. But a different type of trend gains their impetus, not from military and political experience, but from broader developments in moral theory and practice. One of the most significant such developments in the last sixty years has been the articulation and widespread acceptance of a doctrine of universal human rights. The implications of the doctrine of human rights for the ethics of war are profound, though philosophers were at first slow to recognise this.

The most obvious and well-developed implication of human rights theory has been in grounding a doctrine of forcible humanitarian intervention. The link between human rights and humanitarian intervention is well understood, and by now generally accepted: if the basic unit of moral concern is the individual human person (as human rights theory insists), then the moral status of state sovereignty derives entirely from its role in protecting and furthering human rights and human interests. For this reason if a state fails to protect, or actively violates, the rights of its citizens, then its sovereignty can no longer function to rule out forcible intervention which is designed to secure those rights. In this volume Gillian Brock usefully contributes to mapping the content and limits of permissible humanitarian intervention by employing a contractarian thought experiment inspired by John Rawls. David Mellow's paper addresses the justice of the 2003 invasion of Iraq, and he challenges a significant consensus among lawyers and philosophers that this war was unjust. It is a measure of just how accepted the norm of humanitarian intervention has become amongst theorists that Mellow argues for the justice of the Iraq war, not on the basis of preventive self-defence, but on grounds of humanitarian intervention.

The argument for humanitarian intervention suggests an expansion of the acceptable causes for going to war. In this sense at least, the argument is parallel to the argument for preventive war that also proposes an expansion to the list of accepted just causes. But a wholly different consequence of the theory of human rights is to provide the basis for challenging some of the most basic elements of just war theory itself, and hence potentially to contract the scope of just cause to vanishing point. In my 2002 book *War and Self-Defense* I argued that a right to national self-defence cannot be supported on the basis of individual rights of self-defence. The argument poses a far-reaching challenge to just war theory because, from earliest times, most just war theorists have assumed that a right of national defence can be grounded in the individual right of self-defence, either on the basis of a strong analogy with individual self-defence or by simple derivation from the individual right. I suggested that both views are wrong.

Much of the content of this criticism derives from simply confronting the accepted tenets of just war theory with the requirements of a minimal account of human rights. For example just war theory has always held that soldiers in war who fight in compliance with *jus in bello* do no wrong, even if the war in which they fight is unjust. But if that is so then how can we justify attacking and killing enemy soldiers in a defensive war? It would seem that in doing so we attack the morally innocent as a means to securing our rights, and this seems to be incompatible with their basic human rights to be free of attack. Jeff McMahan has recently suggested abandoning the traditional just war commitment to symmetrical *in bello* rights for soldiers on both sides of a war, partly as a response to such concerns.[7] On his view we should not regard soldiers who fight on the unjust side of a war as morally innocent, even if they comply with the *in bello* laws of war. This amendment to traditional theory seems an inescapable consequence of the doctrine of universal human rights, but it has wide-ranging implications for many aspects of the ethics of war.

A more intractable problem is how we can give an account of the goods that are appropriately defended in a war of national self-defence. These goods must be sufficiently important that protecting them is able to render proportionate the killing of rights-bearing enemy soldiers. But there are grave difficulties in providing such an account. On the one hand wars of national self-defence do not always defend the lives of individual persons. On the other hand it is extremely difficult to provide an account of the moral status of collective entities such as states or nations that is both philosophically coherent and supports a recognisable right of national self-defence.[8]

It is this argument that Deane Baker attempts to refute in his stimulating chapter in this book. Baker believes that the sceptical problems I identify in the doctrine of national self-defence are symptomatic of what Charles Taylor calls the 'primacy of rights thesis' — the view that individual rights are normatively fundamental and have a coherence independent of social structures. Drawing on the philosophy of Taylor and Martha Nussbaum, Baker argues that our full moral capacities and 'humanness' can only be realised within an appropriately constituted political community. He proposes that the right of states to fight defensive wars be understood as deriving from the basic role that states play in sustaining the identity of their citizens as full moral beings.

What we think of this solution to the self-defence problem will in large measure reflect our view of the cosmopolitan ethics and 'ontology of the human' that lie behind it. Baker has given much thought to how such an account can be made to yield a morally and politically viable conception of national defence, including a right of humanitarian intervention that is sufficiently (but not overly) permissive. But serious concerns remain. Why should we accept that persons are only 'fully human' within the web of relationships constituted by a particular political community? It seems trivially true that persons can lose their political community (as citizens of failed states do) or change their community (as immigrants do) without ceasing to be fully human. Baker insists that the particular social framework provided by our community is 'inescapable' and 'essentially defines' our identity (p. 295). But can this really be true? And if it is true, then the account seems too rigid to yield what Baker wants. If our identity, once acquired, is really inescapable, then it is unclear how aggression against the community could threaten our personal identity in the relevant way, or how military defence of the community could be effective in preserving it.

Because it locates the grounds of national-defence in goods associated with the community, Baker's account is also vulnerable to a more generic problem. This is that rights of national-defence are normally attributed to states, but communities, even national communities, are not well aligned with the boarders of states. Instead they cross and interpenetrate states in numerous complex ways. There are two difficulties here. The first is how to ensure that the right to national-defence can be properly attributed to existing states, which might not be co-extensive with a unitary national community. The second is how to ensure that the right to collective military defence does not proliferate wildly to a multiplicity of non-state communities.

But the most basic concern is whether an account which views the moral status of persons as fundamentally dependent on their relationship to a political community can provide an adequate account of human rights, many of which explicitly function to protect individual interests against those of the broader political community. My suspicion is that it cannot, and that giving up on a robust account of human rights is too high a price to pay for rescuing the just war theory's conception of defensive war. But it must be noted that Baker's essay, and also Rob Lawlor's essay on moral luck, illustrate another very constructive trend, namely the way in which much recent work on the ethics of war is informed by, and contributing to an understanding of broader issues in moral philosophy.

The final trend is worth briefly noting. This is that philosophers working in the ethics of war are increasingly engaged with questions of institutional design and legal reform. The work of Alan Buchanan is exemplary in this regard, but it is also a notable concern of many of the authors represented in this special issue.[9] I see this as an extremely positive development. Sensitivity to institutional design helps preserve philosophical work from becoming too theoretical and otherworldly. What is more, it is my own belief that many of the most intractable moral problems of war and conflict can only be addressed by making structural changes to legal and international political institutions. But this is not a task for philosophers alone; it will require close collaboration with other disciplines (most obviously law and international relations) and active engagement with the worlds of policy and politics.

The essays in this book provide an excellent introduction to some of the best current work in the ethics of war. I hope that they will stimulate further interest in an important and thriving area of applied philosophy.

## NOTES

1 On the issue of preventive war see: *Preemption: Military Action and Moral Justification*, Henry Shue and David Rodin (Eds.), Oxford University Press, Oxford, 2007; Luban, David. "Preventive War", *Philosophy and Public Affairs*, Vol. 32, no. 3, 2004: 207–248.

2 See M. Walzer, *Just and Unjust Wars* (New York: Basic Books, 1977), ch. 16.

3 See Alan Dershowitz, *Why Terrorism Works* (New Haven, NJ: Yale University Press, 2002).

4 See David Rodin, 'The ethics of asymmetric war', in R. Sorabji and D. Rodin, *The Ethics of War: Shared Problems in Different Traditions* (London: Ashgate, 2005).

5 For some of the best recent work on terrorism see recent special issues of *Ethics* and the *Journal of Political Philosophy*: *Ethics* 114, 4 (2004); *Journal of Political Philosophy* 11, 2 (2003).

6 See Christopher Kutz, 'The difference uniforms make: collective violence in criminal law and war', *Philosophy and Public Affairs* 33, 2 (2005): 148–180.

7 Jeff McMahan, 'The ethics of killing in war', *Ethics* July (2004): 693–733.

8 Deane Baker spells out this argument in greater detail in his paper in this volume.

9 See Allen Buchanan, *Justice, Legitimacy and Self-determination. Moral Foundations for International Law* (Oxford: Oxford University Press, 2003); Allen Buchanan, 'Institutionalizing the just war', *Philosophy & Public Affairs* 34, 1 (2006): 2–38; Allen Buchanan and Robert O. Keohane, 'The preventive use of force: a cosmopolitan institutional proposal', *Ethics & International Affairs* 18.1 (2004): 1–22.

# 2  Luck, Evidence and War

**ROB LAWLOR**

In his paper 'Moral Luck', Bernard Williams argues that many actions cannot be rationally justified at the time of action, and concludes therefore that — in these cases — whether or not we act morally depends on luck. This, Williams argues, is because the justification of the act depends on the outcome, and the outcome itself cannot be known until after the event and is, to some extent, beyond the control of the agent. 'The justification', he claims, 'if there is to be one, will be essentially retrospective'.[1]

Williams explains the problem with the example of (a fictionalised) Gauguin. In this example, Gauguin turns his back on his family and other commitments in order to dedicate himself to the realisation of his talents as an artist. Gauguin is not a person who does not care about his family or his other commitments. Rather, he is someone who, despite these concerns, still opts for the life of a painter dedicated only to his art.

Williams writes, 'I want to explore and uphold the claim that in such a situation the only thing that will justify his choice will be the success itself'.[2] Thus, if Gauguin fails, he did the wrong thing, but if he succeeds, then he can claim that his actions were justified. Regardless of how carefully he reasons before making his choice, Gauguin cannot justify his action at the time of acting. In this sense, Williams claims that whether or not Gauguin did the right thing is determined, to a large extent, by luck. Thus, Williams calls this moral luck.

At this point, it is important to stress that Williams is arguing against a particular view, which he identifies with the Kantian conception of morality in particular, but which is pervasive in moral philosophy (and common sense morality) generally. That view is that moral judgements should be immune to luck. Or, to put it another way, whether or not I act morally should not be a matter of luck.

Williams writes:

> The idea that one's whole life can in some such way be rendered immune to luck has perhaps rarely prevailed . . . but its place has been taken by the still powerfully influential idea that there is one basic form of value, moral value, which is immune to luck . . .[3]

And also:

> The Kantian conception links, and affects, a range of notions: morality, rationality, justification, and ultimate or supreme value. The linkage between those notions, under the Kantian conceptions, has a number of consequences for the agent's reflective assessment of his own actions — for instance that, at the ultimate and most important level, it cannot be a matter of luck whether he was justified in doing what he did.[4]

In this paper, I will argue that Williams is not successful in demonstrating that whether or not our actions are justified can be a matter of luck.

First though, consider another example. It is very common to claim that whether or not a country was right to go to war cannot depend on luck. However, it is also common to point out that it is very difficult to avoid this conclusion when we consider our own judgements about particular cases. For example, Piers Benn writes:

> ... many people think the nuclear bombing of Japan in 1945, involving the deliberate killing of about 100,000 non-combatants, was morally justified because it actually caused the Japanese to surrender. If they had not surrendered, many people's moral judgements would have been different. It cannot be stressed enough that this is not just a psychological remark. Rather, such people believe that whether the deed was *morally* justified can only be determined later, by seeing what actually happened.[5]

Or, to put it another way, closer to Williams' account, when making the decision to bomb Japan, this action cannot be justified. The bombing can only be justified by an outcome — the Japanese surrendering — that cannot be guaranteed at the time of acting, and is (for that reason and to that extent) beyond the agent's control.[6]

Similarly, writing in The Guardian, Julian Baggini made similar comments in discussing the war in Iraq.

> ... the idea that luck can make a difference to the morality of our actions — and even our wars — strikes most people as deeply odd. Whether we act well or badly is surely not something that owes anything to chance.[7]

Referring to a poll that suggested the majority of Iraqi people were in favour of the invasion of their country, Baggini added:

> Some philosophers have thought otherwise, however, and the current situation in Iraq shows why they might be on to something.
> ... whether a course of action is right or wrong depends at least to some extent on its consequences, and sometimes the outcomes of our actions are impossible to predict with any certainty, and depend in part on luck.[8]

The idea here is that we could not predict that the majority of Iraqi people would be in favour of the invasion. But given that this is the case, this fact makes the war right. That is, the outcome *makes* the war right. And of course, if you think the poll does not vindicate the war, but rather think that the war cannot be justified unless — for example — weapons of mass destruction are found, then this argument can be made in the opposite direction. That is, the fact that no weapons of mass destruction have been found *makes* the war wrong. Either way, the argument would be that this is an example of moral luck, and is therefore in conflict with the intuition that luck cannot make a difference to the morality of our actions — or our wars.

Thus, we seem to have conflicting intuitions regarding luck and war. Either, we deny that a war can be made just or unjust as a result of luck, and accept that we should not, for example, take the fact that the Japanese surrendered as reason to claim that the bombing of Japan was justified. Or, we allow such judgements, but as a result we have to accept that luck *can* make a war just or unjust.

This can then be taken as the foundation for a second argument in favour of moral luck. Essentially, the argument is that we have two conflicting intuitions. Although both intuitions seem plausible when considered in isolation, when we consider the conflict, it is (so the argument goes) more plausible to give up the first of the two intuitions.

Thus, we have two arguments in favour of moral luck. We have Williams' argument, and we have the intuitive argument above. In this paper I will argue that both of these arguments are ineffective. In relation to the first, I will argue that Williams' argument is guilty of equivocation. In relation to the second, I will argue that there is, in fact, a third option which is more plausible than either of the two considered above.

It seems that we can summarise the core of Williams' argument in one of two ways:

The first version
Premise:    'The justification, if there is to be one, will be essentially retrospective'.[9]
Conclusion: It is false that: 'it cannot be a matter of luck whether he was justified in doing what he did'.[10]

The second version
Premise:    'the only thing that will justify his choice will be the success itself'.[11]
Conclusion: It is false that: 'it cannot be matter of luck whether he was justified in doing what he did'.[12]

Consider the first version of the argument. This argument is invalid, because it relies on equivocation. The sense of justification in the premise is different from the sense of justification in the conclusion. I will explain this in more detail presently.

The second version, on the other hand, is valid, but it is not clear why we should accept the premise. Indeed, it looks more like the conclusion that we are trying to reach (or deny) rather than a legitimate premise to start with. So let us concentrate on the first version of the argument, which does seem to be a better representation of Williams' argument. Essentially, the idea is that Gauguin cannot justify his actions until after he has succeeded as an artist, and therefore it simply is not true that 'it cannot be matter of luck whether he was justified in doing what he did'.[13]

In order to see where Williams went wrong, we must acknowledge that the word 'justify' is ambiguous. Contrast, 'I justified my actions to the police' with 'my actions were justified'. And consider the following situation.

I am walking down the street when a man attacks me with a knife. He clearly wants to kill me. I fight back to defend myself. In the struggle, I stab him with his own knife (killing him) but I also knock my head on the pavement, and as a result I lose my memory. I do not know what happened — and there were no witnesses. No one knows what happened. And then the police arrive. 'Hello, hello, hello', the policeman says. 'What do we have here? It looks like you killed this man. I think you should come with us'.

Now we can ask two questions. First, can I justify my actions? And the answer is: No. I can't, because I don't know what happened. But then we can ask a second question: were my actions justified? And this time the answer is: Yes. It was self-defence. So, in short, it does not follow from the fact that I cannot justify my actions that my actions were not justified. But this is precisely the sort of inference that Williams' argument relies on.

Before we continue, let me disambiguate between these two uses by referring to justification(e) and justification(f). I use justification(e) to refer to justification in the sense of justifying yourself to the police, and I use justification(f) in the sense of 'my action was justified'.

I use (e) for 'epistemological' or for 'evidence', because ultimately whether I am able to justify myself depends on what evidence I have (if I am trying to justify myself to others), or on what I know (if I am trying to justify my actions to myself). For example, Gauguin could not justify his actions — even to himself (Williams claims) — because he did not *know* that he was an artistic genius. Only his success as an artist could prove that he was.

I use (f) for fact, because whether or not I was justified in killing my attacker is simply a matter of fact, and does not depend on what knowledge or evidence I have, or on whether I am able to justify(e) my actions.

Having made this distinction, we can see the flaw in Williams' argument.

> Premise:    'The justification(e), if there is to be one, will be essentially retrospective'.[14]
>
> Conclusion: It is false that: 'it cannot be a matter of luck whether he was justified(f) in doing what he did'.[15]

Likewise, consider the quote from Piers Benn:

> . . . many people think the nuclear bombing of Japan in 1945, involving the deliberate killing of about 100,000 non-combatants, was morally justified(f) because it actually caused the Japanese to surrender. If they had not surrendered, many people's moral judgements would have been different. It cannot be stressed enough that this is not just a psychological remark. Rather, such people believe that whether the deed was *morally* justified(f) can only be determined later, by seeing what actually happened.[16]

Here Benn doesn't equivocate on 'justified'. In both cases, he uses it in the sense of justified(f). However, he *does* seem to move from claims about what gives us evidence or reason to believe it was right to what actually makes an action right. So, in the first sentence, the act is justified(f) because the Japanese surrendered. I take this to mean, it is the actual outcome (the Japanese surrendering) that *makes* the bombing right. But now consider the final sentence quoted:

> Rather, such people believe that whether the deed was *morally* justified can only be determined later, by seeing what actually happened.[17]

The important question now is, why? There are two possible answers. Either, because the outcome actually makes the bombing right (which I have argued is the claim made in the first sentence) or simply because the outcome provides *evidence* for the judgement that the bombing will make the Japanese surrender.

If the second answer is given, then the claim is merely epistemological: 'whether the deed was *morally* justified can only be determined later' not because it is made right by the outcome, but just because we won't have the evidence until after we have *seen* the outcome. But, in that case, there is no reason to move from this claim to the conclusion that 'the nuclear bombing of Japan in 1945 . . . was morally justified because it actually caused the Japanese to surrender'.

Rather, what we should say is: the nuclear bombing of Japan in 1945 . . . was morally justified(f) because it was sufficiently *likely* to cause the Japanese to surrender. And when the Japanese did surrender then this provided evidence that helped the Allies to justify(e) their actions, and to claim that the bombing was justified(f).

Furthermore, this analysis will also allow us to respond to the argument regarding conflicting intuitions. As we saw, the claim was that there are two options. Either, we deny that a war can be made just or unjust as a result of luck, but accept that we should not let the outcome of our actions influence our moral judgements. Or, we allow such judgements, but as a result we have to accept that luck *can* make a war just or unjust.

Traditionally, these have been taken to be the two forks of the dilemma. However, we should be able to see that there is a third option, according to which the success is merely *evidence* that the action was right, but — as a matter of fact — the action was right *before* we had this evidence. Therefore, the fact that we cannot *know* if an act was right or not before we act does not necessarily entail that there is moral luck.

Thus, I argue that the two options considered above are not the only two options available. Rather, we can appeal to the outcome of our actions without claiming that this is, in anyway, an appeal to moral luck. Rather, as I claimed above, it is *evidence*. Indeed, Baggini does seem to notice that it might be evidence that is important here, rather than luck, when he writes:

> . . . while it is true that the poll by itself does not completely vindicate the invasion, it provides at least some *evidence* for the case that Blair made the right choice.[18]

However, Baggini doesn't seem to consider these as two distinct accounts. Rather, Baggini mixes the two together, writing as if the fact that the poll provides evidence to support Blair is itself an example of moral luck. Essentially, this seems to be the same mistake that Williams makes when he moves from the claim that an action can't be justified(e) until after the event to the claim that it can't be justified(f) until after the event, and therefore whether we act morally or not is not immune to luck.

In order to clarify the difference between an appeal to moral luck and this new alternative account, consider two different cases both of which are subject to luck.

Scenario 1
An eccentric multi-millionaire has decided to play a one-off game. This game makes use of a standard pack of cards. The multi-millionaire will pick a single card from the pack. Beyond the obvious probabilistic calculation, you have no idea what card it will be. The aim of the game is to guess correctly whether the card will be an Ace or some other card — that is, any card other than an ace. You are not required to specify any further than that. If you guess correctly, £1m will be shared between a number of very worthy charities. As a result, a significant number of lives will be saved, and a further number of lives will be significantly improved. There are no tricks. There is no reason to say 'Ace', suspecting that the millionaire has fixed it so that an ace will come up. If an ace comes up, it will be by chance alone. The millionaire is waiting. All you have to do is give your answer. 'Ace', or 'other'.

You say, 'other'. Now consider the two possibilities that may follow. First, the card is turned over. It is not an ace. Everyone is happy that you did the right thing.

Alternatively, the card is turned over. As a matter of bad luck, it is the ace of spades. The outcome of your action is that many people die who would have lived if you had said 'ace'. Most people's intuition will be that this is just a matter of bad luck, and no one would blame you for saying 'other'. You did the right thing, but were unlucky. There is nothing more to say.

I am aware that there are philosophers who think that, in such cases, you *did* do the wrong thing, but claim that it is blameless wrong-doing.[19] However, I agree with W. H. Shaw that this account fails to do justice to the situation:

> If the unlucky utilitarian faced the same choice again (and the probabilities haven't changed), then it would be reasonable and right for her to make the same decision again.[20]

In short, it is hard to reconcile the thought that she did wrong (blameless or otherwise) with the thought that, if she finds herself in the same situation later, she ought to do the same thing again.

Now, suppose you say, 'Ace'. Remember, it is not a trick. You know the odds. The question is, given the odds, what do you do? We do not have to wait for the outcome in order to make a moral judgement. Given that there are many lives at stake, and given that the odds are clearly against you, you have done a terrible thing.[21] You made the wrong choice, and this judgement should not be altered by luck.

In summary then, this is a situation in which the outcome is beyond your control, and you have no way of influencing or predicting which card will be chosen. However, despite this — and contrary to Williams' arguments — you *can* justify(e) saying 'other' at the time of action. We do not need to wait in order to justify(e) the action retrospectively, and we do not need to wait to see if the action was justified(f). Given the odds, and given the stakes — the importance of what could be achieved — you *did* have a moral duty to say 'Other'. Even if the card does turn out to be an ace, your choice was still correct[22] and can be justified(e). Therefore, we have straightforward, moral responsibility which is not influenced by luck.[23]

But now consider a second scenario.

The scenario is similar to the previous one. Again, a multi-millionaire has decided to play a game of chance, and will give £1m to charity if you win. This time, however, it is not a card game, but a sporting event. Manchester United are to play West Ham in the final of the FA Cup. The millionaire will give the money to charity if you correctly predict who will win the FA Cup. All of the major bookies have Manchester United as the favourites, offering odds of 13 – 1 for West Ham.

At first, we might think that this scenario is essentially the same as the first. You ought to go for Manchester United, and you do wrong if you don't. Opting for West Ham in this case would be equivalent to saying 'ace' in the first scenario.

However, there is a significant difference. In the first scenario, if I say 'ace' I am either being capricious (which is morally wrong in the circumstances) or I am being irrational or superstitious. However, in the second scenario, it is less clear that I do wrong if I predict that West Ham will win. Imagine I am a very dedicated football fan. I acknowledge that Manchester United are higher in the league, and generally the better team. However, I really do believe that the bookies and the pundits have all got it wrong. Although United are the better team, I predict that West Ham will win. I don't merely think they can win, no one is denying that, but I really do think they are more likely to win. I believe the bookmakers have got the odds wrong. Perhaps I have noticed that Manchester United have struggled when they come up against a team that play in a certain way — the way West Ham play. Or, I might think that United will be complacent, that their mental attitude to the game is all wrong, and West Ham will take them by surprise. Whatever the reason, I sincerely believe West Ham will win, and this belief is not whimsical or superstitious.

Now I have a dilemma. Do I act on my own beliefs, or do I think the pundits and bookies can't all be wrong. I know that millions of people will never forgive me if I pick West Ham and they lose, but I also know that I won't be able to forgive myself if I chose United, and they lost. After careful deliberation, I decide on West Ham.

Whatever we think of my choice in this case, it seems clear to me that it is quite different from choosing 'ace' in the first scenario. If I choose ace, and an ace comes up, I see no reason to think this vindicates my choice. It gives us no reason to think that maybe we made a mistake when we calculated the odds. In the second scenario though, if West Ham do win (and especially if Manchester United *did* look complacent and *did* seem to struggle with West Ham's style of play) there is very good reason to suggest that the actual outcome does vindicate my choice.

However, this is not because my action was made right by luck, but because the actual outcome provides *evidence* for the claim that my judgement was right, while yours was wrong. It suggests that my understanding of the game is better than the pundits, and people should have listened to me, and not to them. And, of course, this is the vital difference between the two scenarios. If an ace came up in the first scenario, this would not give us reason to think that we underestimated the chances of the aces. But if West Ham do beat Manchester United this does give us reason to question whether our judgement was correct. Maybe we underestimated them.

So, to return to the issue of just wars, it seems clear that it is the second scenario and not the first that is most analogous to the war examples. We do not have knowledge of the odds. We have to rely on our judgement, and your judgement may not be the same as mine. Consider the bombing of Japan, but this time consider the debate *prior* to the bombing. Note that Benn is concerned with those who 'believe that whether the deed was morally justified can only be determined later'. Thus, Benn is excluding those who insist that the bombing would be impermissible *regardless* of the outcome. As such, to the extent that this example is relevant to this paper, the debate is precisely about which outcome is more likely. Those in favour of the bombing insist that it *would* cause the Japanese to surrender. At least, they insist that this is likely. Those against the bombing deny this. Clearly then, when the Japanese, as a matter of fact, do surrender, this clearly goes some way to *vindicating the judgement* of those in favour of the bombing, and, therefore, suggests that the action *was* permissible.

As described, this has nothing to do with luck. Rather, the outcome provides evidence in favour of one judgement and against another.

Of course, luck is not removed completely. Those opposed to the bombing can, quite reasonably, continue to insist that the bombing of Japan was rash, or reckless, and could easily have killed thousands of people without having *any* good consequences. They may continue to insist therefore that the action was impermissible, despite the outcome, and insist that the Allies simply got lucky.

Nevertheless, in cases where the action is a one off (such as bombing Japan), it seems natural to take the *actual* outcome as one of the most significant sources of information available in relation to the question of whether or not a particular outcome was likely.

In other cases, however, this line of argument is less convincing. Consider the following example. I have been to the pub with a friend and have drunk ten pints of lager. Leaving the pub at closing time, I get my keys out and stagger towards my car. My friend protests, insisting that I should not drive while drunk, but I insist that alcohol does not affect my ability to drive safely. 'Furthermore', I say, 'I will prove it by driving home now, without crashing'. My claim that alcohol doesn't effect my driving is unconvincing in the face of scientific research, *regardless* of whether or not I make it home safely on this particular occasion.

The fact that we take the actual outcome as relevant to our moral appraisal in the case of bombing Japan, but not in the case of drink driving provides further support for my claim that, when the outcome effects our moral appraisal of an action (or a war), this is because we take the outcome as *evidence* for or against the claim that a person's judgement was correct.

Thus, I conclude:

1) To the extent that the outcome depended on luck, the outcome should not effect our moral appraisal, and
2) To the extent that the outcome *does* legitimately effect our moral appraisal, this is not a case of *luck* effecting our moral appraisal, but a case of the outcome providing *evidence* (after the event) for the claim that the war was or was not just.

On this account, what should we say about Williams' Gauguin example? My two conclusions can be applied as follows: first, to the extent that the outcome depended on luck, the outcome should not effect our moral appraisal. So if Gauguin's success (or failure) was only a matter of luck, it should *not* effect our appraisal. Second, to the extent that the outcome *does* legitimately effect our moral appraisal, this is not a case of *luck* effecting our moral appraisal, but a case of the outcome providing evidence.

Thus, if we think that his success does justify(e) his actions, this is because we don't think he was just lucky. Rather, we conclude that his judgement was right. Gauguin made the following judgement: my talent is so great that I would be justified(f) in turning my back on my family and other commitments in order to realise my talents. Whether or not he was justified(f) depends largely on whether this judgement was right — that is, whether his talent was as great as he thought. And, finally, the success of his venture then provides evidence for the claim that his judgement was right: he was as talented as he thought he was, and he did create the masterpieces he expected to.

On the other hand, if Gauguin's success or failure was merely a matter of luck, we should not let this influence our moral judgement. To clarify this, consider two alternative versions of the Gauguin case, the first of which is suggested by Williams himself.

Variation 1
Suppose that 'Gauguin sustains some injury on the way to Tahiti which prevents his ever painting again'.[24] This 'certainly means that his decision (supposing it now to be irreversible) was for nothing, and indeed there is nothing in the outcome to set against the other people's loss'.[25]

Variation 2

Gauguin has no talent. After twenty years he has not created anything of any worth. He is, in fact, the worst artist in the world. Then, one day, he is bitten by a radioactive spider. Gauguin feels a strange energy spread through his body and, in that instant — as well as being endowed with spider powers — he becomes an artistic genius. Furthermore, this was not some act of God, and thus he cannot claim that he knew that God would help him. It was just a matter of luck, and could not have been predicted by anyone.

On my interpretation, we should say of the first variation that Gauguin's choice may or may not have been justified(f), but we could never know this. All chances of our finding any evidence either way have been destroyed. And we should say of the second variation that Gauguin was not justified(f). This is because, although Gauguin did succeed in becoming an artistic genius, the nature of the success is such that it does not provide any evidence to suggest that Gauguin's judgement about his own potential was correct. In fact, until the radioactive spider bit him, twenty years of failure provided strong evidence to the contrary.

In fact, Williams seems to come very close to recognising this. Indeed, some readers might wonder to what extent — if any — my account really differs from Williams'. Williams writes:

> . . . it matters considerably to the thoughts we are considering, in what way the project fails to come off, if it fails.[26]

Discussing the first variation considered above, he continues,

> . . . that train of events does not provoke the thought in question, that after all he was wrong and unjustified.[27] He does not, and never will, know whether he was wrong.[28]

This statement seems right, but it doesn't seem to be consistent with Williams' project. As I have argued, Williams' point doesn't seem to be a merely epistemological one. It doesn't look like he is making the modest and fairly uncontroversial claim that sometimes we have difficulty knowing what is right. Rather, he is objecting to the idea that moral value could be immune to luck.[29] It seems that he is arguing that, in some cases, the outcome actually *makes* an act right or wrong.[30] And it is here that we disagree. I am arguing that Williams' arguments are not sufficient to show that moral value cannot be immune to luck. And this is the crucial point.

Thus, in the Gauguin case, Williams should not claim that we will never *know* if his decision was wrong. Rather, if the claim is that the outcome actually justifies(f) an act — because moral value is not immune to luck — then the conclusion should be much stronger than that. The conclusion should be that his decision was wrong — because he failed. Or, if this is the wrong sort of failure, as Williams argues, he should conclude that the decision is neither right nor wrong. If it was the success itself that justified(f) it, and the failure (of the right sort) that made it wrong, then the case that Williams describes would indeed be one in which the decision was neither right nor wrong. On my interpretation, however, we do not have acts or decisions that are neither right nor wrong. Rather, the problem is merely epistemological. We lack evidence. There is a fact of the matter, regarding whether or not the act was right or justified(f), but it is a fact that we cannot know. This seems far more plausible.

In summary, people often suggest that there are two forks of the dilemma, regarding whether or not the actual (but unexpected) consequences should count in our moral judgement.

The first fork is to say yes, they always do, which leads us to conclude that whether or not we do the right thing depends largely on luck. The second fork is to insist that we should only consider the expected consequences, or the reasonably expected consequences, and insist that the actual consequences should not influence our moral judgement at all.

The second option allows us to avoid the conclusion that whether or not we do the right thing depends on luck. However, it doesn't appear to be consistent with the common-sense moral judgements that we do in fact make.

The purpose of this paper has been to offer a third possibility, according to which we are primarily concerned with expected consequences, but nevertheless the actual consequences are not irrelevant. In cases where people *disagree* about what we should expect — or what could reasonably be expected — the actual consequences provide evidence after the event, which can then vindicate the judgement of those whose predictions are supported by the outcome.

**Acknowledgments**

I would like to thank Peter Goldie, Brad Hooker and two anonymous referees from the *Journal of Applied Philosophy* for comments on previous drafts of this paper.

## NOTES

1  B. Williams, 'Moral luck' in his *Moral Luck* (Cambridge: Cambridge University Press, 1981), p. 24.

2  Williams, op. cit., p. 23.

3  Williams, op. cit., p. 20.

4  Williams, op. cit., pp. 21–22.

5  P. Benn, *Ethics* (London: University College London Press, 1998), pp. 103–4.

6  This account of the bombing of Japan, and the moral luck involved, is largely based on the suggestions of an anonymous referee for this journal.

7  J. Baginni, 'If you can't be moral, be lucky', *The Guardian* 17th March, 2004. Also on line: http://www.guardian.co.uk/g2/story/0,3604,1170754,00.html.

8  Baginni, op. cit.

9  Williams, op. cit., p. 24.

10  Williams, op. cit., pp. 21–22. Also see p. 20.

11  Williams, op. cit., p. 23.

12  Williams, op. cit., pp. 21–22. Also see p. 20.

13  Williams, op. cit., pp. 21–22. Also see p. 20.

14  Williams, op. cit., p. 24.

15  Williams, op. cit., pp. 21–22. Also see p. 20.

16  Benn, op. cit., pp. 103–4.

17  Benn, op. cit., pp. 103–4.

18  Baginni, op. cit. (my italics).

19  See W. H. Shaw, *Contemporary Ethics, Taking Account of Utilitarianism* (Oxford: Blackwell Publishers, 1999), pp. 27–31. (I am grateful to Brad Hooker for reminding me of this issue.)

20 Shaw, op. cit., p. 29.

21 Not everyone agrees with my claim that you have done a terrible thing just by saying 'Ace'. For many, because I have not violated anyone's rights etc. it may be hard to see that I have done anything wrong. I suggest it is terrible because people's lives are at stake and you sacrifice nothing by choosing the 'other' rather than 'ace'. Compare this with Tim Mulgan's Magic Game in T. Mulgan, *The Demands of Consequentialism* (Oxford: Clarendon Press/Oxford University Press, 2001) p. 131.

22 That is, justified(f).

23 This summary of the card game example is largely based on the suggestions of an anonymous referee for his journal.

24 Williams, op. cit., p. 25.

25 Williams, op. cit., p. 25.

26 Williams, op. cit., p. 25.

27 Unjustified(f), I suggest.

28 Williams, op. cit., p. 25.

29 See Williams, op. cit., pp. 20–22.

30 Or if this is not the case, and Williams is merely making an epistemological point, such that he and I are in agreement, we should realise that his arguments *don't* lead to the conclusion that luck can make a difference to the morality of our actions.

# 3    Defending the Common Life: National-Defence After Rodin

DEANE-PETER BAKER

## 1. Overview

In a prize-winning[1] recent book, *War and Self-Defense* David Rodin addresses the central ethical question relating to military action — when is it right to go to war? As Roger Barnett points out,[2] since Just War Theory first began to be systematised the reasons justifying the recourse to military force have been whittled down until only one — self-defence, or what Rodin calls national-defence — has remained uncontentious. David Rodin, however, contends that the seemingly unassailable position of national-defence is unjustified, at least as that notion is understood in contemporary Just War Theory and international law.

Part one of *War and Self-Defense* is dedicated to detailing a workable model of defensive rights that adequately accounts for cases of personal self-defence. Rodin begins his analysis with an account of the nature of rights. Using the framework of the jurist Wesley Newcomb Hohfeld, Rodin sees rights as consisting in the interrelationship of a number of distinct yet related deontic concepts — duty, claim (and no-claim), and liberty. From this platform Rodin goes on to build a model of defensive rights. This model, rightly, treats defence as a derivative right, and one that is limited by the features of necessity, imminence, and proportionality. He then goes on to argue that consequentialist and 'forced choice' explanations of self-defence cannot adequately account for this concept. More successful, Rodin argues, is the rights based theory he develops to explain the 'moral asymmetry' between the aggressor and the defender in cases of legitimate personal self-defence (i.e. the reason the defender is within his rights to kill the aggressor, but the aggressor may not justifiably kill the defender, even though both lives are in imminent danger).

Rodin moves on in Part II of the book to offer an analysis of the applicability of the account of self-defence that he develops in Part I to the case of a state responding with force to military aggression by another state, what he calls national-defence. After a brief but thorough account of the role of national-defence in international law, Rodin moves on to consider the two main justifications of national-defence. Both, he argues, lean heavily on the moral legitimacy of self-defence. The first does so by means of a reductive argument — that is, that national-defence is, in effect, the 'collective form' of self-defence. This can be understood either as the claim that national-defence is 'simply an application, *en masse*, of the familiar right of individuals to protect themselves and others from unjust lethal attack'[3] or as the claim that 'the state has an obligation (and therefore a right) to defend its citizens in much the same way that a parent has the right to defend his or her child'.[4] The second justification for national defence that Rodin addresses is what he calls the 'analogical strategy', which is most famously articulated as Michael Walzer's 'domestic analogy' in which 'the rights and duties of states can be understood on the model of the rights and duties of individual persons'.[5] After giving close attention to both of these approaches to justifying national-defence, Rodin concludes that '[n]ational-defense cannot be reduced to a collective application of personal rights of self-defense, and it cannot be explained as a state-held right analogous to personal self-defense. Because the right of national-defense has always been the central "just cause" for war within the Just War Theory, and because the analogy with self-defense has always been its central justification, this result must be seen as a serious challenge to the traditional Just War doctrine of international morality'.[6]

Recognising that this conclusion is, to say the least, somewhat disconcerting, Rodin offers his own solution to the dilemma created by his analysis. He contends that the way out of the dilemma is to view just war as a form of law enforcement. For this justification to work, however, what is required is the establishment of a global state or something similar. Even those with less jaundiced views of this sort of idea than that held by Paul Cornish — 'Fat chance'[7] — must nonetheless acknowledge that such a response to the question of national defence is at best problematic, and that some more immediately to hand solution is desirable.

It is the central claim of this paper that the counter-intuitive conclusion this book reaches points not so much to weaknesses in Rodin's arguments as to the problematic nature of a key presupposition on which his analysis is based, what Charles Taylor calls 'the primacy of rights thesis'. In the last part of the paper I apply Taylor's critique to Rodin's Hohfeldian framework, and offer an alternative account in which national defence regains its place as the chief justification for nations to engage in armed conflict.

## National-Defence and The Common Life

Before turning to critique, it is however necessary to give an account of Rodin's response to the attempt to justify national-defence on the basis of the defence of the common life. It is also important that we note that Rodin's project is essentially apologetic in nature and must therefore necessarily be restricted to attempts to develop an account of the right to national-defence that is 'substantially co-extensive with the way that right is understood in modern international law and the best interpretation of the Just War Theory'.[8] In particular, such an account must establish a right to national-defence that is held by all sovereign states, regardless of their particular forms of government. This is a critical consideration, as we shall see later.

As I have said, the second approach to justifying national-defence (after the reductive strategy) that Rodin considers, is what he calls the 'analogical strategy', an approach that attempts to discover in the state itself sufficient moral grounding for a right of national-defence that is analogous to the personal right of self-defence. The idea of 'the common life' is central to this approach, in which 'national-defence is a right held by states and grounded principally in the end, not of defending the lives of individual citizens, but of defending the common life of the community'.[9] Rodin identifies four interpretations of the common life as a potential end of national-defence, though he rejects one outright and concentrates his attention on the remaining three. The rejected interpretation is that which comes to light in one reading of the work of Hegel, namely the view that 'the common life is a source of value independent of its value for individual persons'[10] in which the rights and value of individuals are derived from the community to which they belong. Put another way, the claim here is that the value inherent in the community itself stands independent of, and prior to, the value that community might have for individual persons. Rodin rejects this view on the grounds that moral explanations (of which the pursued justification of national-defence is one) must derive their legitimacy from their contribution to individual human life.

The three remaining interpretations of the common life are given closer attention. Firstly, there is the approach that is rooted in Hobbesean social contract theory and which is based on the legitimacy of a state that arises out of its ability to provide order in the affairs of its citizens, who thereby escape the inconveniences of the state of nature. Rodin responds that this cannot provide grounds for a right to national-defence against aggressors whose goal is to substitute their own rule for the order provided by the home state. What is needed, he points out, is 'a moral reason not simply to defend order, but to defend a particular form of order; to defend *our* order'.[11]

This leads Rodin to consider the second approach to grounding national-defence in the common life. This is an approach that recognises that our identity is in some sense partially defined by the particular cultural and linguistic background provided by our community, and that we locate our lives within the history of that community. Both of these are things we recognise as goods of the first order, and therefore, supporters of this approach claim, the particular character of the common life can properly function as the end of the right of nation-defence, for the state's role is to protect and foster the unique character of the common life, as well as to embed the values and commitments of the community in its structures.

The main problem here, according to Rodin, is that such a view fails to achieve the level of objectivity required to support a universal right of national-defence. The value of any particular form of common life is evident only to those within that common life, not to those beyond it. '[I]t is not apparent why someone who is not a participant in that particular common life should recognize its distinctive form as a good and a value'.[12] Rodin points out, further, that states which show a clear disregard for human rights, but which fall below the currently-accepted threshold for human-itarian intervention (a disregard which, we may assume, runs contrary to the common life of the people in those states), are nonetheless clearly possessors of the right of national-defence in international law and under most interpretations of the Just War Theory. One attempt at getting around this problem of the subjectivity of the common life is through a relativisation of value in which it is impossible for us to judge the value of a mode of life that is not ours. This approach functions by claiming that this rela-tivism means that we cannot legitimately judge across boundaries and therefore must abstain from intervening in other communities. This, therefore (it is argued), gives rise to a right to national-defence that is the flip side of this duty of non-interference. But this approach, Rodin argues, requires accepting a relativism of value in all cases except for the case of non-intervention, which must be objectively valuable in order for the argument to succeed. Rodin dismisses this as hopelessly ad hoc.

The failure of the 'subjective' view brings into view the final interpretation of a common-life-based right of national-defence. In this approach what is needed is 'a value that is both objective and particular — it must be objective and recognizable as valid across cultures, yet still provide a reason for defending a particular state or community'.[13] Freedom, autonomy, and particularly self-determination seem to some thinkers, most notably Michael Waltzer, to fit the bill here. These seem to be objectively valued goods that underpin all particular notions of the common good. Furthermore, the argument goes, these goods can only be protected if state sovereignty is respected, and so from this a universal right to national-defence arises.

The obvious objection here, as Rodin rightly recognises, is that only democratic societies truly provide the opportunity for self-determination, and so this sort of argument could only apply to democratic states. But this, of course, is insufficient to the task of finding a basis for the near universal possession by states of the right to national defence. Michael Waltzer attempts to avoid this by arguing that in all states there is a process of 'working out' what form of political regime is in place, and that this process is one of collective self-determination. Rodin contends, however, that this is a case of stretching the notion of self-determination beyond all recognition, and concludes, therefore, that this final view is also an inadequate justification for the right of national-defence. And so he concludes that, despite our strong intuitions to the contrary, national-defence as it is understood in contemporary Just War Theory and in international law cannot be a justification for resorting to war.

David Rodin's project, if successful, undermines the usual justifications given for national defence, leaving actual actions of this kind in a morally-tenuous position. This is clearly a most undesirable situation. If the only way of getting around this moral problem is, as Rodin suggests, the creation of a universal state, then this ought to be urgently pursued. On the other hand, the unappealing conclusion of Rodin's thesis provides a strong impetus to find ways to resist that conclusion. In what remains of this paper I intend to elaborate an alternative account of the 'common life' strategy, one that I believe offers a way to justify national-defence without presenting a view of that notion that is radically at odds with Just War Theory or international law.

## The Common Life, The Primacy of Rights Thesis and National-Defence

A book as articulate, well-argued, and which reaches as contentious a conclusion as *War and Self-Defense* will inevitably stimulate defenders of the various arguments Rodin analyses to respond vigorously, and have indeed already begun to do so.[14] My response here will not be a direct response of this kind. Instead I intend to set out an alternative account of the common life as a potential end of national-defence, one not considered by Rodin because, I will argue, of an implicit commitment to what Charles Taylor calls the 'primacy of rights thesis'. It seems to me that an account such as the one I will here articulate offers the potential to avoid the skeptical conclusion Rodin reaches, and though this may not be the only way of doing this, it seems one worthy of consideration.

This approach, as I will describe it here, can be found in the social philosophy of Charles Taylor as it is, for our purposes, most usefully articulated in his classic paper 'Atomism'.[15] The impetus for the emergence of this view comes from Taylor's attack on what he calls 'the primacy of rights thesis' and the view of the self that underlies it, which he views as endemic to social contract approaches to political theory. This approach is to blame, according to Taylor, for the difficulty of resisting political arguments whose conclusions 'lie far outside the common sense of our society'.[16] He describes the primacy of rights thesis as follows:

> Theories which assert the primacy of rights are those which take as the fundamental, or at least a fundamental, principle of their political theory the ascription of certain rights to individuals, and which deny the same status to a principle of belonging or obligation, that is a principle which states our obligation as men [sic] to belong to or sustain society, or a society of a certain type, or to obey authority or an authority of a certain type. Primacy-of-right theories in other words accept a principle ascribing rights to men as binding unconditionally, binding, that is, on men as such. But they do not accept as similarly unconditional a principle of belonging or obligation. Rather our obligation to belong to or sustain a society, or to obey its authorities, is seen as derivative, as laid on us conditionally, through our consent, or through its being to our advantage.[17]

This primacy of rights thesis rests on a view of human selfhood that conceives of the individual as fundamentally self-sufficient, a view Taylor refers to as 'atomism'. It is easy to see why Taylor links atomism with social contract theory — such an approach is assumed by the very idea of humans existing as independent agents in a state of nature, from which they escape by way of voluntary contract. Against this view, Taylor argues in favour of a range of theories that posit humans as fundamentally social beings:

> The claim is that living in society is a necessary condition of the development of rationality, in some sense of this property, or of becoming a moral agent in the full sense of the term, or of becoming a fully responsible, autonomous being. These variations and other similar ones represent the different forms in which a thesis about man as a social animal have been or could be couched. What they have in common is the view that outside society, or in some variants outside certain kinds of society, our distinctively human capacities could not develop.[18]

In this view, rights are not separable from an essential conceptual background defining the specific forms of human flourishing those rights are intended to protect. It soon emerges that Taylor's own view is that our specifically human potential requires not the mere existence of any society but rather the existence of certain specific kinds of society — he is explicit, for example, in his belief that authoritarian societies hinder the development of our distinctly human capacities. While not made explicit in 'Atomism', it seems clear from some of Taylor's other writings that what underlies his view here is a commitment to a specific ontology of the human.[19] There are, Taylor thinks, particular non-contingent features of the human self that can be developed or denied. That Taylor believes that such development depends crucially on societal institutions such as the state is explicitly clear:

> [T]he free individual or autonomous moral agent can only achieve and main-tain his identity in a certain type of culture [which incorporates certain facets and activities]. But these and others of the same significance do not come into existence spontaneously each successive instant. They are carried on in institu-tions and associations which require stability and continuity and frequently

also support from society as a whole — almost always the moral support of being commonly recognized as important, but frequently also considerable material support. These bearers of our culture include museums, symphony orchestras, universities, laboratories, political parties, law courts, representative assemblies, newspapers, publishing houses, television stations, and so on. And I have to mention also the mundane elements of infrastructure without which we could not carry out these higher activities: buildings, railroads, sewage plants, power grids, and so on. Thus [the] requirement of a living and varied culture is also the requirement of a complex and integrated society, which is willing and able to support all these institutions.[20]

For our purposes, then, this approach can be sketched as follows. At its foundation is the claim that there are specific and non-contingent features of the identity of humans that are essential to true humanness, and that these features are not always already there but rather can and must be developed and worked out. But this process can only take place within a social context. For that reason full-blown human development is dependent on the existence of a specific range of societies (for not all societies will be conducive to the development of the relevant features of humanness), which in turn will usually require the existence and support of specific sorts of institutions such as (or paradigmatically) states (for not all regimes will be conducive to the support of the relevant sorts of societies). On this view humans will often be dependent on institutions such as states both for *attaining* and for *maintaining* their fundamental humanness. Because of their fundamental nature, the attributes of full humanness are such that they can legitimately be defended with lethal force under the right of (individual) self-defence. Furthermore, under the right of self-defence the right to defend x extends to the right to defend the necessary conditions of x.[21] Thus, because the state (or equivalent institution) is a necessary condition for the achievement and maintenance of the attributes of full humanness, persons have the right to defend their state (or equivalent institution) with lethal force. On the other hand, states that fail to adequately nurture, or which actively undermine, the conditions necessary for their citizens or the citizens of another state to achieve true humanness, have no such right to national-defence. Furthermore, it may well be argued that other nations (or the international community) have a duty to intervene in a proportionally appropriate way in order to see those conditions set in place.

This is, of course, only a sketch, and some fleshing out is needed to show its feasibility. Firstly to the claim that there exist specific and non-contingent features of the identity of humans that are essential to true humanness, features which are not always already there but which can and must be developed and worked out. An important distinction here is between holding those capacities or potentialities that make us human, on the one hand, and the fulfilment of those potentialities on the other. It is constitutive of humanness that these capacities exist; we have them just in virtue of being human. Even where a certain society or set of circumstances might prevent us from fulfilling those potentialities, they don't cease to exist for want of fulfilment. So for example slaves, or those who are oppressed in some other way, are no less human for the fact that their circumstances make them unable to flourish. Thus, in the terms we have been setting out above, they remain rights bearers, even if those rights are being denied.

The philosopher who has arguably developed this view most explicitly is Martha Nussbaum, who applies this 'capabilities approach' to the arena of development (in the economic/social/political sense of that word). As she writes, 'the intuitive idea behind the approach is twofold: first, that certain functions are particularly central in human life, in the sense that their presence or absence is typically understood to be a mark of the presence or absence of human life; and second . . . that there is something that it is to do these functions in a truly human way, not a merely animal way'.[22] Nussbaum goes further than most in setting out a specific list of central human capabilities, as follows:

1. **Life**. Being able to live to the end of a human life of normal length; not dying prematurely, or before one's life is so reduced as to be not worth living.
2. **Bodily Health**. Being able to have good health . . . to be adequately nourished; to have adequate shelter.
3. **Bodily Integrity**. Being able to move freely from place to place; having one's bodily boundaries treated as sovereign . . .
4. **Senses, Imagination, and Thought**. Being able to use the senses, to imagine, think and reason — and to do these things in a 'truly human' way, a way informed and cultivated by an adequate education . . . Being able to use one's mind in ways protected by guarantees of freedom of expression with respect to both political and artistic speech, and freedom of religious exercise. Being able to search for the ultimate meaning of life in one's own way. . . .
5. **Emotions**. Being able to have attachments to people and things outside ourselves . . . Not having one's emotional development blighted by overwhelming fear and anxiety, or by traumatic events of abuse or neglect. . . .
6. **Practical Reason**. Being able to form a conception of the good and to engage in critical reflection about the planning of one's life . . .
7. **Affiliation**. **A**. To be able to live with and towards others, to recognise and show concern for other human beings, to engage in various forms of social interaction; . . . (Protecting this capability means protecting institutions that constitute and nourish such forms of affiliation, and also protecting the freedom of assembly and political speech.) **B**. Having the social bases of self-respect and non-humiliation; being able to be treated as a dignified being whose worth is equal to that of others. . . .
8. **Other Species**. Being able to live with concern for and in relation to animals, plants, and the world of nature.
9. **Play**. Being able to laugh, to play, to enjoy recreational activities.
10. **Control over one's environment**. **A**. **Political**. Being able to participate effectively in political choices that govern one's life; having the right of political participation, protections of free speech and association. **B**. **Material**. Being able to hold property . . . having the right to seek employment on an equal basis with others; having the freedom from unwarranted search and seizure.[23]

Nussbaum is explicit in her desire to link her account of capabilities with a particular, Rawlsian, form of political liberalism. Such a connection is not, however, an inescapable one — Nussbaum points out that Amartya Sen (with whom she has regularly collaborated on forming this capabilities approach to development) makes no such explicit connection (though he is undoubtedly a supporter of political liberalism), and makes use of the capabilities approach for more modest purposes. She explicitly accepts that '. . . we may use this approach in this weaker way, to compare one nation to another, even when we are unwilling to go further and use the approach as the philosophical basis for fundamental constitutional principles establishing a social minimum or threshold'.[24] Still, Sen has not set out an explicit list of capabilities, so it is Nussbaum's list that we must work with here.

For the purposes of my argument in this paper, it is necessary to make two amendments to Nussbaum's list, by making one point stronger and another weaker. The first amendment is to point 7 listed above, the idea of 'affiliation'. This is the point that I wish to make stronger, and it relates to what I have said earlier about Taylor's view of the nature of human identity.

Taylor is a communitarian, who believes that we are never outside of some community, and that we each live continually within a 'web of interlocution', a network of others with whom we relate. Even those who shun human contact are not exempt — '[i]n the case of the hermit the interlocutor is God. In the case of the solitary artist, the work itself is addressed to a future audience, perhaps still to be created by the work itself. The very form of a work of art shows its character as *addressed*'.[25] More than that, our frameworks are value-laden as a result of our community, in the sense that as we interact with individuals and institutions we take on board the understanding of the good that each of those points of contact have. 'No one acquires the languages needed for self definition on their own. We are introduced to them through exchanges with others who matter to us — what George Herbert Mead called 'significant others'.[26] It is this framework of goods that stands behind the strong evaluations that make sense of our lives.

By contrast, Nussbaum's view as outlined in point 7 above looks far more like the classical liberal individualist view of the self, something that Taylor explicitly rejects. If we read Taylor's view into Nussbaum's list at this point, we are able to strengthen it by adding that what must be protected is not only our capacity to affiliate with others, but also the particular webs of relationships that underpin our very identities.[27] This is important in that it provides a reason why there is some justification for defending this particular community (and therefore any political arrangement, such as a state, that provides the framework for the existence of that community).

Point 10A, on the other hand, if left as it stands, restricts the type of political arrangement that would support capacities so defined to some form of democracy. And of course, for my purposes here, that is too limited, for, given that many states remain undemocratic, this cannot justify a generally-held right to national defence.[28] What is needed here is a loosening of the description, but one that does not undermine the essence of the capacity being described. One way this might be done is to describe this point negatively rather than positively.[29] What is perhaps better here is the idea of being free from oppressive political influence or domination that undermines the individual's ability to exercise any or all of the other capabilities listed. One achievement of this amendment is that it avoids the implication that all people living before the advent of democracy, or beyond the reach of a modern state, must, by definition, not be or have been flourishing human beings. This is clearly an undesirable implication — one would be hard pressed, for example, to view the Israelites under King Solomon's supernaturally wise rule to have fallen short of some standard of flourishing.[30]

This amendment goes some way towards opening this capabilities approach up to a pluralism of political arrangements that might possibly satisfy the requirements of the approach. But there remains the point[31] that if we consider people to have a right to a society that supports human flourishing, then if that right extends to the maximal development of human flourishing that would suggest a convergence towards a single model of society. This of course then undermines the openness to pluralism that I am attempting to get going here. However we need not cast around for some way of shoring up the capabilities approach in this respect, for Nussbaum has already addressed this issue through her idea of 'a threshold level of each capability, beneath which it is held that truly human functioning is not available to citizens'.[32] Chapters 3 and 4 of *Women and Human Development* contain extended discussions of how to define and secure such a threshold level of capability. As it is not my intention here to defend this particular account, only to show that something *like* this account provides a way out of the predicament Rodin's incisive arguments leave us in, there is little to be gained from rehearsing Nussbaum's account here. It is sufficient to my purposes that this notion of a threshold be a reasonable one, which I think it clearly is. The non-rigid nature of Nussbaum's account helps here too — she writes that 'the list remains open-ended and humble; it can always be contested and remade. Nor does it deny that the items on the list are to some extent differently constructed by different societies. Indeed, part of the idea of the list is its *multiple realizability*: its members can be more concretely specified in accordance with local beliefs and circumstances. It is thus designed to leave room for a reasonable pluralism in specification'.[33] In terms of enforceability, then, it seems that a central test would be whether there exists, within the society or community concerned, clear and broadly-supported calls for change or outside help on issues directly related to human flourishing as defined by something like Nussbaum's list.

It seems that something like the view I have articulated here provides an account of what is fundamentally human and which shows the dependence of the individual's basic flourishing on the existence of a certain community. Though such communities have obviously not always depended on the existence of modern states, it is equally obvious that in most cases today such a dependence does exist. This therefore provides both a general justification, derived from the individual's right to self-defence, for states to use armed force in self-defence, as well as a specific justification for particular states to defend themselves even where the invading state intends to put in place some form of social order (a specificity that is lacking from the standard Hobbesian defence of the right of states to defend themselves, something that Rodin shows to be problematic). Of course there remains the possibility, as Rodin points out,[34] that a neighbouring state might be in a better position to support the community in question than the state under threat of invasion, and that this might, in terms of the account given here, undermine that state's right to self-defence. In response to this point I refer back to Nussbaum's list, in particular the part of point 5 that reads 'not having one's emotional development blighted by overwhelming fear and anxiety'. If we make use of a notion of rights based on something akin to Nussbaum's list of capacities, as I suggest here, then a state that exists to protect those rights must also protect its citizens as far as possible from having to live with overwhelming fear and anxiety. It seems almost certain that living under the occupation of some other nation is a condition, even in the most benign cases, that is likely to cause significant levels of fear or at the very least anxiety. A second, and perhaps more important strand of response here relates to point 6, that of Practical Reason. The point here is that though another state might be in a position to provide or realise the conditions necessary for us to exercise our capabilities, it would not do so in the same particular way. It would thus undermine the exercise of practical reason that has led to the particular arrangement of things in that particular society, thereby undermining an important aspect of human flourishing as defined by Nussbaum's list.[35]

One further point must be addressed here before moving on. It is of course true that presenting an account of national-defence that is based on human flourishing is in some way misaligned with the individual right to self-defence. As Rodin points out in correspondence, 'I have the right to defend my life with lethal force, but arguably not the right to defend certain conditions for perfecting my capacities with lethal force'. That is certainly true as the right to self-defence is generally conceived and as described in Rodin's book. What must not be forgotten, however, is that the very limited circumstances in which one may exercise the right to use lethal force in defence of one's life are defined against the presumed background of the existence of a state, to which all other right to use lethal force, and all other responsibility for rights-enforcement, is deferred. If, however, we imagine something akin to a Hobbsean state of nature, presumably the right to use defensive lethal force would extend somewhat further to cover some or all of those conditions on which the existence and flourishing of one's life depends.

It is perhaps worth pausing here to make clear just how the account I'm giving differs from Waltzer's approach, as outlined above. Both offer objectively valued goods as the basis for deriving a right to national-defence, and both face the obvious objection that taking this approach restricts justifiable national-defence to a limited set of states, which is at odds with the way the right is conceived in Just War Theory and international law. The essential difference between the two approaches is that the objectively valued goods in the Nussbaum/Taylor-inspired account are far more specific than Waltzer's notion of 'self-determination'. Self-determination, at least as Walzer conceives of it, is a fairly broad and nebulous notion. It is because of this that Waltzer escapes the objection, whereas it seems to have more bite for Nussbaum/Taylor. The price is that his notion is so nebulous that it is a hardly an account of self-determination at all. The Nussbaum/Taylor view I'm arguing for here, on the other hand, is based on an ontology of the human, and therefore provides an objective and reasonably narrowly defined basis from which the right of national-defence is derived.

From another angle, on the other hand, the account I have given here account might be viewed by some as being uncomfortably close to the Hegelian view that Rodin unconditionally rejects.[36] Certainly both views strongly emphasise the individual's inescapable connection to her community. But though Taylor rejects the primacy of rights thesis, this is not to say that the view I'm outlining here is one that treats rights as of secondary importance. The point, rather, is that the rights of the individual and the value of the community are inseparable — viewing either as having primacy over the other leads inevitably to distortion.

So, then, the account I have outlined here successfully fulfils the requirement that an account of national-defence be grounded in values that are 'objective and recognizable as valid across cultures'. Of course there is likely to be some dispute as to what conditions are necessary for the development of the 'forms or qualities of life which are properly human',[37] or indeed what those forms or qualities are. Certainly much depends on the metaphysical account of the self that lies behind such a view. While I am here drawing on arguments from Taylor and Nussbaum to set out the defence of a 'common-life' based justification for national-defence, I do not wish to restrict this line of response to any particular account of how human flourishing is inextricably linked to certain specific forms of society. Many of the views of those that fall under the rubric of the 'neo-Aristotelian revival' would probably fit here. Even a view of the rational self as held by someone like Davidson, as articulated in a recent book by Pedro Tabensky,[38] might, from another angle, be used to build a case for national-defence along the lines that I have developed here. And it is not only Western philosophy that offers resources of this nature. Arguably the most central notion in African philosophy is that of *Ubuntu*, which, at its most fundamental level, is the notion that humans are essentially social beings. The classic statement of Ubuntu is that 'a person is a person through other persons'.[39] Thus, developing and defending a particular metaphysical account of this sort any further here would, I think, distract from the central purpose of this paper. Enough has been said, I hope, to show that there is real potential here for some such account to be the basis of a theory of national-defence that is based in the common-life and is at the same time unaffected by the spectre of cultural relativism.

What this approach manifestly does not do, however, is satisfy the requirement that the state *qua* state has an inalienable right to national-defence. Waltzer's self-determination requirement at least provided some opportunity to put forward an argument (albeit a weak and unconvincing one) to the effect that every state fulfils the requirement. No such argument is even conceivable regarding the account I have outlined here.

What, then, must we conclude? Is the Taylor-inspired account doomed to failure? I wish to contend that it is not. Instead, I wish to challenge the requirement that the right of national-defence be understood as held unequivocally by every sovereign state. In its place I put forward the claim that, as a matter of principle, every state must be taken to have the prima facie right to national-defence, but that under certain conditions it may be justifiably concluded that a particular state does not, in fact, have that right. Here the principle is similar to, and can be derived from, Taylor's 'starting hypothesis' with respect to the evaluation of cultures other than one's own — 'the presumption of equal worth'. 'As a presumption the claim is that all human cultures that have animated whole societies over some considerable stretch of time have something important to say to all human beings'.[40] What this presumption does not amount to however, is an *a priori* commitment to the value of all cultures. The value of a culture can only be established by investigating it. To value it otherwise would be an insulting form of homogenisation, and would amount to an arrogant belief that there is nothing to be learned from that culture. The flip side of this, however, is that some cultures may fall beyond the pale, and a line will have to be drawn. Taylor thinks that liberalism of the sort he outlines (a non-procedural and non-primacy of rights variant) should not balk at this conclusion: 'Substantive distinctions . . . are inescapable in politics, and at least the nonprocedural liberalism [to which Taylor is committed] is fully ready to accept this.'[41] This is because, in Taylor's memorable phrase, 'Liberalism is also a fighting creed'.[42] We are now in a position to see more clearly why the Taylor/Nussbaum view is preferable here to that offered by Waltzer. Though Waltzer's notion of 'self-determination' is broader than the view I have outlined above, it is nonetheless more restrictive in its application to actual societies. For, if we accept Rodin's argument against Walzer's attempt to justify his claim that all societies are self-determining, then it becomes clear that only a specific range of political regimes in fact support this objectively valued good — primarily, or perhaps exclusively, democratic forms of government. A sophisticated version of the approach that I have outlined here, on the other hand, will be able to recognise that for peoples embedded within differing cultures, some forms of non-democratic government (a benign monarchy, for instance) may in fact still foster the conditions for the development of the essential humanness of those peoples. This may of course turn out not to be true, but something like the approach I have described here at least leaves this possibility open. By focusing on the 'forms or qualities of life which are properly human'[43] rather than on one particular political good, the suitability of differing political regimes for different cultures remains an open question.[44]

It might be argued that in proposing this approach I have gone beyond the boundaries of Rodin's project (to develop an account of the right to national-defence that is 'substantially co-extensive with the way that right is understood in modern international law and the best interpretation of the Just War Theory')[45] and that I have instead offered 'a theory which generates deeply revisionary conclusions about the right of national-defence',[46] something that Rodin recognises as an interesting and legitimate area of enquiry, but which he expressly refrains from engaging in. It is possible that this is true, but I think that the following consideration suggests that it is not.

It seems to me that the emerging doctrine of humanitarian intervention as a justification in international law and in terms of Just War Theory, is important here. Rodin himself recognises this emerging doctrine, or at the very least the potential emergence of this doctrine, which 'permit[s] intervention in states that engage in widespread violations of human rights against their own citizens'. He however goes on to dismiss this doctrine as irrelevant to the question in hand on the grounds of its severely limited nature — involving only 'abuses of human rights which are so severe that they 'shock the conscience of mankind', typically involving genocide, mass expulsion, or starvation'.[47] This, however, strikes me as an irrelevant consideration. The fact that humanitarian interventions are only justified in particularly extreme situations seems to me to be simply a consequence of the doctrine of proportionality — a recognition that often a military intervention will result in greater hardship than the original offence that it aimed to rectify. Like self-defence, humanitarian intervention by means of military force is only one of a range of possible interventions that may be justified in proportion to the appropriateness of their deployment. And of course we *do* feel that nations are justified in intervening in all sorts of ways in the light of some deeply held views of the nature of human development — take for example the positive intervention of pouring funding for the education of women into a country where this is not something that has generally been valued.

The relevant point is that emerging international law and international relations theory (which, like the Just War tradition, is a constantly evolving entity) arguably treats the right to national-defence (and the corresponding duty of non-intervention) as a conditional rather than an inalienable right. A salient example is the recent report by the International Commission on Intervention and State Sovereignty, which deliberated on the issue of humanitarian intervention in the light of recent experiences in places such as Rwanda, Kosovo, Bosnia and Somalia, and concluded that the following basic principles ought to be applied:

A. State sovereignty implies responsibility, and the primary responsibility for the protection of its people lies with the state itself.

B. Where a population is suffering serious harm, as a result of internal war, insurgency, repression or state failure, and the state in question is unwilling or unable to halt or avert it, the principle of non-intervention yields to the international responsibility to protect.[48]

In his report to the United Nations General Assembly of March 2005, entitled 'In larger freedom: towards development, security and human rights for all', the UN Secretary General, Kofi Annan, endorsed the Commission's findings as follows:

> The International Commission on Intervention and State Sovereignty and more recently the High-level Panel on Threats, Challenges and Change, with its 16 members from all around the world, endorsed what they described as an 'emerging norm that there is a collective responsibility to protect'. . . . While I am well aware of the sensitivities involved in this issue, I strongly agree with this approach. **I believe that we must embrace the responsibility to protect, and, when necessary, we must act on it.** This responsibility lies, first and foremost, with each individual State, whose primary raison d'être and duty is to protect its population. But if national authorities are unable or unwilling to protect their citizens, then the responsibility shifts to the international community to use diplomatic, humanitarian and other methods to help protect the human rights and well-being of civilian populations. When such methods appear insufficient, the Security Council may out of necessity decide to take action under the Charter of the United Nations, including enforcement action, if so required.[49]

If Annan's comments reflect an emerging consensus regarding the applicability of the idea of humanitarian intervention, and I believe there is good reason for thinking that they do,[50] then in breaking with the notion of the inviolability of state sovereignty that was established at the Westphalia Conference (at which, crucially, the Just War doctrine was entrenched in international law for the first time), international law and its cognate, the Just War tradition, is already seeing a radical revision in the recognised justifications for the deployment of military force, a revision that is entirely compatible with the theory of national-defence that I have outlined here. True, this view may not correspond to the way Just War Theory was conceived of in, say, Anscombe's classic 1939 piece on the topic,[51] but as Rodin himself says it is rather difficult to establish exactly what Just War Theory *is*, and that 'it is more accurate to talk of the 'just war tradition' . . . for it includes a large number of diverse yet related positions'.[52] Rodin's own approach is to see the formulation of Just War Theory as it exists in international law as definitive. But of course international law is no monolith, and so the changes that are leading to a doctrine of humanitarian intervention must, following this approach, be considered to be changes to the accepted view of Just War Theory. One might even argue that this change is in some sense a partial return to an earlier formulation of Just War Theory. As James Turner Johnson points out, the classical Just War tradition included among the accepted reasons for going to war the just cause of 'the punishment of evil'.[53] While it is unlikely that this particular formulation would find too much favour in contemporary discourse, there seems nonetheless to be a significant dose of this in contemporary humanitarian interventions, which are at the very least aimed at the prevention of further evils and often also involve bringing to justice those who have perpetrated evil. Accordingly, it seems eminently arguable that the view I have outlined here must, at the very least, be on the cusp of correspondence with the accepted view of Just War Theory.

In a response to a critique of *War and Self-Defense* by Fernando Tesón,[54] who makes similar points about the relevance of the doctrine of humanitarian intervention, Rodin worries that taking this sort of approach opens up an 'implausibly permissive' view of humanitarian intervention. This is a particular problem, Rodin argues, for Tesón's account,

> . . . in which the right of national defense is grounded in the presence of just (that is, liberal) institutions, and the right of humanitarian intervention is grounded in their absence. Many, if not the majority, of the world's states are illiberal, and we may be uncomfortable with the implication that all such states are potential objects of humanitarian intervention. Such a view is certainly a substantial deviation from the emerging consensus in international law that humanitarian intervention is limited to cases of governmental abuse that 'shock the conscience of mankind.[55]

This may be a problem for Tesón, but it is not clear that it afflicts the account I have proposed here. As I've said above, a sophisticated version of the Taylor/Nussbaum-inspired account would not be wedded to any particular form of government, and would be theoretically able to recognize as valid non-liberal states where such forms of government were culturally appropriate means of achieving human dignity and development.[56]

Another concern that Rodin has in this regard is that 'viewing national defense and humanitarian intervention as integrated in this way makes it extremely difficult to make sense of the obvious thought that any right of forcible humanitarian intervention must be *balanced against* the defensive rights of the state in question'.[57] But this seems an unnecessary requirement, for cases in which forcible humanitarian intevention is appropriate are exactly those cases in which the state has forfeited its prima facie right to non-intervention, and therefore also the corresponding right of national-defence.

In conclusion, then, it seems that a doctrine of national-defence based in the protection of the common life, described in the way I have sketched here, does indeed offer real potential for providing a valid justification for going to war that is compatible with contemporary Just War Theory and international law.

## Acknowledgements

An earlier version of this paper was presented at a seminar hosted by the ANU branch of the Centre for Applied Philosophy and Public Ethics in 2004. I am grateful for comments received on that occasion, and grateful to CAPPE for helping fund my visit there. My colleagues at the University of KwaZulu-Natal have also helped me enormously in developing this paper. David Rodin kindly made numerous very helpful comments on the paper along the way, for which I owe him a real debt of thanks. And finally I am indebted to an anonymous referee for the Journal of Applied Philosophy who made a number of insightful observations about an earlier draft. As always I remain responsible for all remaining shortcomings in this paper.

## NOTES

1 The American Philosophical Association Frank Chapman Sharp Memorial Prize.
2 R. Barnett, *Asymmetrical Warfare: Today's Challenge to US Military Power* (Dulles, VA: Brasseys, Inc., 2003), p. 64.
3 D. Rodin, *War and Self-Defense* (Oxford: Clarendon Press, 2002), p. 127.
4 Rodin 2002, op. cit., p. 129.
5 Rodin 2002, op. cit., p. 141.
6 Rodin 2002, op. cit., p. 162.
7 P. Cornish, 'Nations must connect reality to morality before they arm themselves to the teeth', *The Times Higher Education Supplement*, 30 January 2004. Online version (www.thes.co.uk) accessed 16 April 2004. p. 2.
8 Rodin 2002, op. cit., p. 142.
9 Rodin 2002, op. cit., p. 142.
10 Rodin 2002, op. cit., p. 143.
11 Rodin 2002, op. cit., p. 149.
12 Rodin 2002, op. cit., p. 151. This claim is, of course, contestable — it is entirely feasible that a case can be made that one does not need to be a participant in any particular common life in order to have a general recognition that that particular common life has value for those who do participate in it. I am grateful to Deborah Roberts for this point.
13 Rodin 2002, op. cit., p. 155.
14 For good examples of such responses see the symposium on *War and Self-Defense* that appeared in *Ethics & International Affairs* 18, 1(2004).
15 C. Taylor, 'Atomism', in *Philosophy and the Human Sciences: Philosophical Papers 2* (Cambridge: Cambridge University Press, 1985).
16 Taylor 1985, op. cit., p. 189.
17 Taylor 1985, op. cit., p. 188.
18 Taylor 1985, op. cit., pp. 190–191.
19 For a developed account of how Taylor maintains this commitment in the face of the collapse of enlightenment fundamentalism and against the ontology-denial of postmodernist 'weak hermeneutics', see N. Smith, *Strong Hermeneutics: Contingency and Moral Identity* (London and New York: Routledge, 1997).
20 Taylor 1985, op. cit., pp. 205–206.
21 As David Rodin has helpfully pointed out (in a private communication), a useful analogy here might be that if I have the right to defend my life from unjustified attack with lethal force, then I have the right to defend with lethal force the necessary conditions of my continued survival from wrongful attack, for example in preventing the theft of my last food.
22 M. Nussbaum, *Women and Human Development: The Capabilities Approach* (Cambridge: Cambridge University Press, 2000), pp. 72–73.
23 Nussbaum op. cit., pp. 78–80.
24 Nussbaum op. cit., p. 6.
25 C. Taylor, (1991) *The Ethics of Authenticity* (Cambridge, MA: Harvard University Press, 1991), pp. 34–5.
26 Taylor 1991, op. cit., p. 33.
27 Rodin, in a private communication, has raised the case of immigrants as a counter to this point — such people clearly do not lose their fundamental humanness by leaving behind the communities that originally defined them and becoming part of some other community. Two points seem relevant here. Firstly, immigrants seldom leave behind their original communities and cultural identities entirely. Secondly, immigration is a voluntary act, and as such is an exercise of practical reason. The disruption caused by war is significantly different, as can be observed by the trauma experienced by refugees from conflict zones.
28 See also Rodin's response to Fernando Tesón's critique of *War and Self-Defense*, discussed below.
29 I am indebted to my colleague Douglas Farland for this point.
30 This of course presumes the accuracy of the biblical description. Readers will doubtless be able to think of other examples if this particular one does not satisfy. Nussbaum emphasises that her list is modern, not

timeless (Nussbaum 2000, op. cit., p. 77), but even so there seems no reason to assume that some society, perhaps one cut off from the modern state, might nonetheless still be considered to be one that supports human flourishing, even without having in place a politically liberal form of government.

31  Raised by David Rodin in a private communication.

32  Nussbaum 2000, op. cit., p. 6.

33  Nussbaum 2000, op. cit., p. 77.

34  In a private communication.

35  I am grateful to my colleague Deborah Roberts for this point.

36  Rodin 2002, op. cit., pp. 143–144.

37  Taylor 1985, op. cit., p. 201.

38  P. Tabensky, *Happiness: Personhood, Community, Purpose* (Aldershot: Ashgate Publishing, 2003).

39  N. Makhudu, 'Cultivating a climate of co-operation through Ubuntu', *Enterprise*, 68 (1993): 40–41.

40  C. Taylor, 'The politics of recognition' in A. Guttman, (ed.) *Multiculturalism* (Princeton, NJ: Princeton University Press, 1994). p. 66,

41  Taylor 1994, op. cit., pp. 62–3.

42  Taylor 1994, op. cit., p. 62.

43  Taylor 1985, op. cit., p. 201.

44  John Rawls argues for a similar point in his book *The Law of Peoples*, where he claims that though 'liberal constitutional democracy is, in fact, superior to other forms of society' (J. Rawls, *The Law of Peoples* (Cambridge, MA: Harvard University Press, 1999), p. 62), nonetheless 'decent' non-liberal societies are still deserving of respect.

45  Rodin 2002, op. cit., p. 142.

46  Rodin 2002, op. cit., p. 142.

47  Rodin 2002, op. cit., p. 152.

48  International Commission on Intervention and State Sovereignty, *The Responsibility to Protect* (Ottowa: International Development Research Centre, 2001), p. XI.

49  K. Annan (2005), *In larger freedom: towards development, security and human rights for all*, Report of the Secretary General to the 59th Session of the United Nations General Assembly, 2005 (http://daccessdds.un.org/doc/UNDOC/GEN/N05/270/78/PDF/N0527078.pdf?OpenElement), p. 35.

50  For another account of the ground-breaking nature (in terms of international law) of the NATO intervention in Kosovo, see G. Prins, *The Heart of War: On Power, Conflict and Obligation in the Twenty-First Century* (London: Routledge, 2002), chapter 5. From a legal perspective, Fernando Tesón (F. Tesón, *Humanitarian Intervention: An Inquiry into Law and Morality*, 2nd edn. (Irvington-on-Hudson, NY: Transnational Publishers Inc.,1997). pp. 173–174), argues that: 'The human rights imperative underlies the concepts of state and government and the precepts that are designed to protect them, most prominently article 2(4). The rights of states recognized by international law are meaningful only on the assumption that those states minimally observe individual rights. The United Nations purpose of promoting and protecting human rights found in article 1(3), and by reference in article 2(4) as a qualifying clause to the prohibition of war, has a necessary primacy over the respect for state sovereignty. Force used in defense of fundamental human rights is therefore not a use of force inconsistent with the purposes of the United Nations'.

51  G. E. M. Anscombe, 'The justice of the present war examined' republished in G. E. M. Anscombe, *Ethics, Religion and Politics: Collected Philosophical Papers vol. III* (Oxford: Blackwell, 1939/1981).

52  Rodin 2002, op. cit., p. 103.

53  J. Johnson, *Morality and Contemporary Warfare* (New Haven and London: Yale University Press, 1999), p. 29.

54  F. Tesón, 'Self-defense in international law and rights of persons', *Ethics & International Affairs*, 18, 1 (2004).

55  D. Rodin, 'Beyond national defense', *Ethics & International Affairs* 18, 1(2004): 94.

56  An additional benefit of this approach which is perhaps worth mentioning in passing, is that it also offers a way of accounting for why communities might be justified in defending themselves (through the formation of liberation movements and the like) against states that systematically undermine the basic conditions of human flourishing for those communities, even where outside intervention is not forthcoming or likely. Writing in the context of post-apartheid South Africa this strikes me as an important test of the value of any particular account of Just War.

57  Rodin 2004, op. cit., p. 94.

# 4 Humanitarian Intervention: Closing the Gap Between Theory and Practice

GILLIAN BROCK

When, if ever, is humanitarian intervention morally defensible? That is, when, if ever, may it be morally appropriate for action to be taken against a state or its leaders without its consent, for the purpose of protecting people in those other states?[1] Addressing this question has taken on some urgency in the last decade in particular in the wake of calls for more humanitarian intervention in places such as, Rwanda, Bosnia, Kosovo, and Somalia, and in view of the way appeals to humanitarian considerations are being used in an attempt to legitimate other interventions.[2]

Some think that action on behalf of those needing humanitarian assistance in cases where the consent of the government is not forthcoming would involve a violation of sovereignty, that is a violation of the right enjoyed by states to exercise authority over people occupying the territory of the state.[3] They argue that appropriate regard for the sovereignty or equality of states (or perhaps even tolerance of difference) militate against intervention. Much as we may want to help those in need, there is an important tension between respecting sovereignty and intervention to assist victims of humanitarian crises that must be appreciated and resolved in favour of non-intervention, according to them.

It looks like we get conflicting messages on this issue from examining current United Nations charters and agreements, since there seems to be considerable tension here concerning the permissibility of humanitarian intervention. On the one hand, there is much talk about promoting peace or avoiding war, but there is also much in these documents that involves firm commitment to human rights and their protection.[4] In the case of humanitarian intervention it would seem we have a conflict in these documents themselves over whether we should favour avoiding military intervention or rather restoring or protecting human rights.

Apparently, then, there are at least two important tensions that must be confronted in grappling with the issue of the permissibility of humanitarian intervention. First, there is the tension between respecting sovereignty and responding to the plight of the needy, that is, there is tension between respecting governments' authority and desire for non-interference, and respecting the individuals who suffer under their leadership. Second, there is tension between the goal of promoting peace, avoiding conflict and war, and engaging in military operations for protective purposes, which by definition involves conflict. How are we to resolve these tensions?

I argue that in both cases the tensions should be resolved in favour of protecting the individuals who suffer in these humanitarian crises, though the way to do this defensibly requires that we put in place many safeguards against abuse. My main theoretical argument is one that emerges from a model of global justice that I develop. A normative thought experiment provides a useful way of thinking through these issues and can give us an excellent framework for resolving issues concerning global justice in general, and humanitarian intervention in particular. In the second section, I examine recent reports on intervention and state sovereignty compiled by an international commission in order to show that consensus is building about the permissibility of military intervention to protect fundamental human rights for vulnerable populations in certain cases. Consensus is building about the nature of sovereignty such that the tension, strictly speaking, disappears in certain cases warranting humanitarian intervention. Some important public policy proposals are evolving in the direction of protecting individuals over states, but there are still some important gaps that remain between what is theoretically desirable and the public policy or international law which it is proposed that we adopt. I show where some of those gaps are and how we can close them.

## I. The Moral Argument

### A. *How to Think Through Matters of Global Justice: Some Background*

I begin by sketching a normative thought experiment that models ideal deliberating conditions.[5] I take my inspiration for the thought experiment from John Rawls,[6] though crucial details of my view are quite different from Rawls' account as should become quite clear soon enough.[7] Rawlsian-style thought experiments are well suited to examining what an ideal world might require of us.[8] These thought experiments, when properly set up, are a good way of fleshing out what we can reasonably expect of one another in a way that avoids inappropriate partiality: if people do not know what positions they might find themselves in during the lottery of life, they will pay more attention to what would constitute fair arrangements.[9]

An easy way to enter the thought experiment is to imagine a global conference has been organized. You have been *randomly selected* to be a decision-making delegate to this conference.[10] You are to participate in deciding what would be a fair framework for interactions and relations among the world's inhabitants. Though you have been invited to the decision-making forum, you do not know anything about what allegiances you have (or may have after the conference concludes), but you do know that whatever decisions are made at this conference will be binding ones. It may turn out that you find you belong to a very poor, overpopulated developing nation, with few natural resources, or you may discover you live in an affluent developed nation, for instance. You may discover you live in a state that includes many ethnic groups with a long history of conflict, especially conflict over territory and resources. You may find you live in a state that is ruled by a brutal dictator that allows the expression of only one religion. Given these sorts of possibilities, you are provided with reasons to care about what you would be prepared to tolerate in all sorts of cases.

You can have access to any information you like about various subjects (such as, history, psychology, or economics), but so far as possible, very little (if any) information about subjects like the demographics of world population should be made available. The idea is that you should not have access to information which could lead you to deduce odds, since (for instance) if you know that over 1 billion of the 6 billion people alive today are Indian, some might be tempted to gamble that they are going to turn out to be Indian, and so try to ensure Indians get better treatment than others. I want to eliminate scope for this sort of gambling.[11]

More positively, certain information will be made available to all delegates. This information pack includes material about our urgent global collective problems and how we will have to co-operate to solve them. For instance, delegates will have information about various threats to peace and security, including threats we face as a result of the increasing number of people who have access to weapons (especially weapons of mass destruction), and the activities of terrorists and drug traffickers.[12] As I discuss in more detail later, they will also have information about the history of the world and how it has sometimes produced brutal dictators who have oppressed their citizens unchecked for decades. They will also know that powerful states have sometimes meddled inappropriately in the affairs of less powerful states, supposedly with the intention of helping them. Some of the information will highlight the ways in which a humanitarian crisis in one state may have regional, and indeed sometimes global implications for security, stability, or economic prosperity. History shows that failing or failed states, or states that maintain order by grossly violating human rights, can be a considerable risk to everyone. Some of this material will therefore maintain that the people of the world are in a state of interdependence and mutual vulnerability, they rely on each other crucially if they are to achieve any reasonable level of peace, security, or well-being both now and in the future.

The main issue delegates must entertain concerns what *basic* framework governing the world's inhabitants we can reasonably expect to agree on. What is the *minimum* set of protections and entitlements we could reasonably be prepared to tolerate? Since individual contractors have no particular knowledge of how they will be positioned, who each will be once the conference adjourns, delegates would agree only to those policies that did not have unbearable effects on people, since they might end up being on the receiving end of such policies. More positively, delegates would find it reasonable for each person to be able to enjoy the prospects for a decent life and much discussion would be about the (minimum) content of such a life. I submit we would centre discussion towards the terms of agreement around at least two primary guidelines of roughly equal importance, namely, that everyone should enjoy *some* equal basic liberties, and everyone should be protected from certain real (or high probability) opportunities for serious harms.[13]

Reasonable people will care, at least minimally, about enjoying a *certain* level of freedom. Freedom may, of course, not be the only thing they care about and often they may not care about it very much when other issues are at stake about which they care more deeply. Nevertheless, reasonable people will care at least a little about enjoying *some* freedoms. Many kinds of freedoms will be of interest, but importantly, they would include freedom from assault or extreme coercion (such as slavery) and *some* basic freedoms governing movement, association, and speech. We need to be permitted to evaluate and revise the basic organizing ideas of our lives should we chose to do this. Delegates should recognize that it is possible they could find themselves in a society with whose major organizing values, principles, and commitments they disagree. In such situations, it would be reasonable that some might want to have the scope to question and revise the values operative in the society, or at least a certain freedom to live their lives in accordance with values they find more congenial. Recognizing this they would, therefore, endorse a certain freedom of dissent, conscience, and speech.[14]

In addition to caring about protecting freedom, rational decision-makers will also want protection from real opportunities for serious harms to which they would be vulnerable (and potentially powerless to resist) in certain cases. Under some kinds of arrangements there could be enormous opportunities to inflict harms. For instance, multinational corporations operating in unregulated market economies can threaten people's abilities to subsist in various ways, (say) by polluting so severely that they poison the soil and water such that crops are no longer able to grow properly. Indeed, people considering what arrangements to adopt would be vigilant to ensure that meeting their needs is within their reach and so importantly protected, since being unable to meet our basic needs must be one of the greatest harms that can ensue. Reflecting on the gravity of such a harm in particular,[15] more positively but in a similar vein, we would find it reasonable to have certain guaranteed minimal opportunities and those would be strongly coloured by what is necessary to be enabled to meet our basic needs for ourselves.[16]

My claim is that the minimum package it would be reasonable to agree to in the ideal choosing situation I have identified is that we should all be adequately positioned to enjoy the prospects for a decent life, as fleshed out by what is necessary to be enabled to meet our basic needs and those of our dependents (but with provisions firmly in place for the permanently or temporarily disabled to be adequately cared for) and certain guarantees about basic freedom. We would use this as a baseline and endorse social and political arrangements that can ensure and underwrite these important goods.

I should say a brief word here about what I take our basic needs to be since this has relevance further along. On my account, a need is basic if satisfying it is a necessary condition for human agency. This link to human agency helps us derive a list of our basic needs which can circumvent concerns about how an account of such needs could be sufficiently 'objective', non-arbitrary, and enjoy widespread cross-cultural support. If basic needs are those things the satisfaction of which is necessary for human agency, by examining the pre-requisites of human agency, of what being a human agent is like, we can derive a more specific list of such conditions, and so basic needs. For instance, by definition, to be an agent one must be able to deliberate and choose. In order to deliberate and choose one will need at least a certain amount of (1) physical and mental health, (2) sufficient security to be able to act, (3) a sufficient level of understanding of what one is choosing between, and (4) a certain amount of autonomy. Because of its important role in developing (and maintaining) (1)–(4), I also add a fifth basic need which underlines the importance of our social needs, namely, (5) decent social relations with at least some others. It may be that in some cases meeting our basic needs (1) and (2) take on special salience if physical life is to be sustained, so among our basic needs, (1) and (2) might be given special significance in certain emergency situations, as we later see.[17]

The minimum package endorsed will have implications for most spheres of human activity, especially economic activity and political organization. For instance, economic activity must be sensitive to everyone's prospects for a decent life and regulations must be devised to ensure this. Extensive sets of rules would need to be outlined to make plain for all just what would constitute important threats to people's prospects for decent lives. Organizations that can monitor and enforce these rules must be established (or empowered).

What sort of governance structure would we endorse? There are many kinds of arrangements we could choose, but two key guiding principles would operate: we would want our vital interests (such as, our ability to subsist) protected and it can be anticipated that we would want to retain as much control over affairs that directly affect us as is consistent with protection of those vital interests. Any governing authorities we endorse will have as a high priority that they are to protect our vital interests and the legitimacy of governing bodies will rest on their ability to do an adequate job of this. Mixed forms of governance might reasonably be chosen such that in some matters local bodies have complete control, in others — for instance, where protection of vital interests can only be secured if there is widespread co-operation across states — joint sovereignty might reasonably be chosen. At any rate, whatever governing structures we endorse would have as the central part of their mandate to protect people's vital interests, to ensure that people are so positioned that meeting their basic needs is within their reach and their basic liberties are protected.

As discussed, delegates are aware that all entitlements chosen need to be financed and so generate financial obligations. Resources will need to be forthcoming to fund the arrangements that are chosen as minimally acceptable. We will need to address the issue of what counts as fair ownership of resources, but whatever account of fair ownership of resources we endorse, cannot be such that it effectively blocks funding reasonable arrangements necessary to underwrite the basic framework, since obligations to set up and do our part in supporting the basic framework are more fundamental.[18]

### B. More Specific Application to the Case of Humanitarian Intervention

With this as some general background to the kind of basic framework that would be endorsed, what more specifically might be chosen on the issue of humanitarian intervention? Recall that delegates have information about the history of the world and that sometimes citizens have been oppressed by tyrants for many years, with no one coming to their assistance. They know that powerful states have sometimes meddled inappropriately in the affairs of less powerful ones, supposedly for their own good. They also know that a humanitarian crisis in one state may spill over into an entire region or even further afield, and can often have global implications for security and prosperity. Recall that delegates do not know anything about the allegiances they have or will have after the conference concludes, but since they realize they could find themselves significantly affected by the situation (whether directly or indirectly through the spill over effects of impaired economic prosperity or undermined security in the region), they would all have an interest in equitable solutions to humanitarian crises.

Delegates could find themselves very badly off in several kinds of ways. They would be aware of at least two central kinds of situations that would be abhorrent, both involving considerable abuse of power. The first kind of situation is one in which basic threats to life, liberty, and the prospects of a minimally decent life were widespread, for instance, a situation in which genocide, ethnic cleansing, large-scale killing, torture, or violence persisted, and either the government is actively engaged in causing the situation, or else fails to take action to remedy it. The second highly undesirable situation is one in which powerful states (or other actors) are able to interfere in people's lives, supposedly on humanitarian grounds, though the connection was tenuous and simply provided a thin veil of alleged legitimacy for what was basically an abuse of the situation for the intervening parties' own purposes. People would not want the rhetoric of humanitarian intervention to provide a mechanism for powerful states to simply muscle their way into other countries for their own reasons, with no real intention of alleviating the suffering, or of doing so only as a means to furthering their own ends.

Besides these two central kinds of dire cases, several other kinds of cases show that considerable caution is warranted. The history of intervention has not always been entirely happy: sometimes foreign interventions have been on the wrong side, or made things worse, or come back to haunt the interveners. Our records of intelligence gathering have sometimes been poor, so that interventions have been based on misleading or even false information. Despite this sorry history, let us focus on these two central dire cases, since as I aim to show, the protection that should be put in place to ensure interventions are warranted should allay many of the concerns that arise in reviewing this history.

Though delegates might have in mind to protect the vulnerable through some humanitarian intervention provisions, they would be just as concerned that any policies they endorse as permitting humanitarian intervention not be subject to abuse.[19] Indeed, some delegates might reasonably be more concerned with the latter situation than the former. Given these legitimate concerns, what kinds of policies might reasonably be endorsed?

Discussion might usefully start off by reminding delegates of their previous agreement on the kinds of governance structures it would be reasonable to endorse: any governing authorities we endorse have as a high priority that they are to protect our vital interests and the legitimacy of governing bodies will rest on their ability to do this. Where governing authorities are not able to protect vital interests, the governing authorities lose their legitimacy and alternative arrangements that can secure vital interests must be considered. It was previously thought reasonable to establish or empower some organization that would have the power to protect vital interests to deal with such situations. It might be useful for us to name this organization for later ease of reference. Let us call it the 'Vital Interests Protection Organization', or VIPO. The organization is concerned with ensuring that *individuals* are adequately situated such that they are able to enjoy the prospects for a decent life as fleshed out by what is necessary to be enabled to meet our basic needs and certain guarantees about basic freedom. This provides the mandate for the organization. The VIPO is concerned with protecting the five basic needs earlier identified (roughly, health, security, understanding, autonomy, and decent social relations), but with special concern being given to the first two basic needs, concerning health and security in special emergency situations. (Since the VIPO is concerned with the *needs and interests of all individuals equally*, interests such as advancing the geopolitical interests a particular nation might have in a region are automatically excluded from consideration here, using the cosmopolitan framework I have outlined. It is *individuals* that are the unit of moral concern, and they are *equal units of moral concern*. Things like the geopolitical interests one nation may have in a situation are not the relevant sorts of interests that come into our moral orbit here. If they come in, they come in equally for all people, and so these concerns are essentially neutralized or expunged from the moral picture.)

Under what conditions might the VIPO authorize the use of force to ensure that relevant vital interests are adequately protected? Delegates might usefully think through these issues by considering the just war theoretical framework, which after all purports to offer long-standing guidance on the legitimate use of force in situations not entirely dissimilar. It may be that it can serve as a useful starting point for discussion, and with suitable modifications, may be made to fit the situation of humanitarian intervention quite well. The just war framework at least presents several core factors which deserve consideration, namely, what constitutes a sufficiently just cause to warrant intervention, the intentions of the interveners, whether interventions are a 'last resort', the appropriate (or proportionate) use of force, who and what might be a legitimate target of force, reasonable prospects for success, and proper authorization.[20]

First of all, the issue of just cause must be addressed. Whatever else they might think constitutes severe suffering warranting help, threats to vital interests, such as the large scale loss of life, ethnic cleansing, torture, rape, and displacement of people from their homes and livelihoods, would surely count as significant threats to people's prospects for decent lives. When such activities are widespread, and the state either perpetrates these injustices or does nothing appropriate to end the suffering, it would be reasonable to suggest the just cause threshold has been reached. (Since delegates have legitimate fears about abuse, they might understandably be very cautious about sanctioning the use of force in cases where the level of harm is not grave and substantial. For now, I leave it as an open question whether or not they would endorse a lower threshold of harm as constituting just cause, satisfied for now, that there are at least some cases which would unambiguously count as just cause.) We see how large scale loss of life, ethnic cleansing, torture, rape and displacement of people from their homes and livelihoods are all the sorts of situations in which people's prospects for decent lives are significantly undermined. The very basic needs to a certain rudimentary level of health and security are significantly impaired.

Given their defensible fears about abuse, delegates will understandably be very cautious about sanctioning the use of force, and so might require several other conditions to be in place before action is warranted, or even eligible for appropriate authorization. Because delegates are (rightly) concerned with abuse of power, and therefore have a certain mistrust of powerful states, delegates might put heavy weight on the idea of interveners having the right intentions, namely, that would-be interveners are seriously concerned to put an end to the suffering and ensure the vital interests (previously outlined) are protected. But how are they reasonably to judge intentions, somewhat inscrutable at the best of times? Perhaps requiring the vital interests protection organization, VIPO, to be composed of representatives of all nations will provide some way to keep states with questionable intentions in check. If a unanimous decision is reached by such a body, fears about abuse of power can be somewhat allayed, especially if it puts heavy weight on consultation with the alleged victims and what the overwhelming majority of them want the international community to do. At any rate, the fears about abuse do point towards further desirable features for the composition of the authorizing organization that will manage the intervention (to which we return later).

Would all delegates really be so concerned with intentions of would-be interveners? Some of the delegates, projecting themselves into the position of those who are victims of genocide and ethnic cleansing, might adopt a more consequentialist line. They might argue that, intentions of the would-be interveners do not matter as much as how effective they are at ending the suffering. Some interveners may have the worst intentions in the world, but put an end to the suffering. Other interveners might be very well intentioned, but be completely unable to stop the suffering. Surely if you were a victim of the genocide, you would care a lot more about consequences here than intentions? Although this line of reasoning has a certain plausibility to it, two further points could be made, in response. First, further conditions still need to be reviewed before the account of defensible intervention is finalized. Second, it cannot be true that victims would care very little about would-be interveners' intentions in such cases. If interveners alleviate suffering in the short-term, but extend it in the longer term, victims would and should care very much. So it would be reasonable for delegates to have some assurance about intentions, at least as much as would be offered if the intervention were a strongly multilateral one, or at least authorized by an organization with wide representation.

Given that military interventions are sometimes fairly costly — both in terms of human lives and the use of resources — delegates might reasonably insist that military interventions should only be contemplated after more peaceful methods for resolving the situations have been explored. Whether or not military options should be a last resort, strictly speaking, in the sense that all possible other options have been exhaustively explored, they should not be undertaken lightly. It is better to explore a full range of diplomatic options first.

Delegates might also reasonably insist on guidelines that urge would-be interveners to use only the level of force needed to secure the explicit objectives — the level of force should be in balance with, or proportional to, the ends to be secured. So delegates might reasonably adopt a 'proportionality' requirement about the use of force. Projecting themselves into the position of civilians — that is, those not connected with the leadership and the offending actions — delegates might also reasonably stipulate that civilians, should not be targets of force, and that situations in which it can be predicted that civilians are to bear heavy burdens are to be avoided.

What would delegates do with the traditional notion of requiring a reasonable chance of success? Delegates might not put much weight on this criterion in certain situations. Rather, projecting themselves into the position of the very badly off — say, potential victims of genocide — they might put more weight on trying to alleviate the suffering, no matter if chances of success are expected to be low. On the other hand, they would surely not want it to be the case that the expected consequences of any proposed interventions are worse than the expected consequences of doing nothing. Here we have found a criterion the significance of which does seem to vary with the nature of the harm at issue. From the perspective of the potential victims of genocide, what could be worse than being an actual victim of genocide? If delegates really do this imaginative exercise properly they will want interventions to occur, even if chances of success are not great. So, the weight they might put on this criterion might well vary in accordance with the kinds of suffering at issue. Less weight might be placed on it in the case of genocide; more weight might be placed on it if the level of suffering is less severe.

We have already seen that proper authorization for any proposed intervention is critical if it is to allay concerns about abuse and appropriate intentions. Since there is likely to be a fair amount of evaluation and weighing up of evidence, probabilities, and anticipated consequences, these are further reasons to have such deliberations be conducted in a body that has very wide representation, with many different perspectives getting equal input into the making of the final decision.

On my model of global justice, the VIPO has a significant role to play in protecting individuals' vital interests. As we have already seen, delegates would agree to the existence of a VIPO that is appropriately resourced. Resourcing such an organization adequately so that it can operate effectively will be key. Reasonable delegates will agree to the necessary financial arrangements to make this happen — for instance, through specific taxes or dues — so as to spread the cost equitably amongst everyone.

What other provisions might delegates arrive at during the hypothetical conference? Recognizing that an ounce of prevention is worth more than a pound of cure (so to speak), they might insist on there being responsibilities not just to respond, but also to prevent conflicts where possible — to tackle underlying causes of conflict and to avert conflict before it escalates. The responsibility to respond militarily to crises should have as its aim to restore or ensure protection of vital interests is in place, so a certain amount of rebuilding and assistance with reconstruction and reconciliation may also be necessary. They might also quite reasonably want the arms trade much more heavily regulated than it currently is.

What kind of normative weight can be put on the results of a thought experiment such as this? It seems to me there are two main functions a normative thought experiment of this kind can serve: First, there is the 'negative value' — the thought experiment rules out certain situations as untenable because it would not be reasonable for delegates to choose or tolerate them, when in an appropriate situation that models impartiality. Second, there is the 'positive value' — the thought experiment shows us certain situations as morally desirable because it can be expected that delegates would reasonably choose them, when suitably situated. We can put substantial weight on the negative outcomes, on what would not be chosen or tolerated, since it has been shown that it would not be reasonable to choose to live with such a situation, under morally salient conditions. Situations that it would not be reasonable to choose are situations we can confidently say are morally undesirable — they are not ones we would choose under certain morally relevant conditions.

Perhaps, someone might object, we can put less weight on the positive outcomes — on what I specify *would* be chosen, since this is a function of our imagination and to some extent on what we think is possible, for instance. However, since the positive view I outline is so thinly developed, we can actually put some normative weight on it too. The positive view developed here outlines a framework and structure so thin it is hard to believe that its broad outlines would not feature in any positive solution we would choose as a solution to the situation. That has anyhow been my goal — to provide a framework or set of considerations that would feature in any positive policies and plans we would endorse as an ethically defensible way of resolving the issue of when intervention may be permissible. Having made my case, I now put the burden of proof on those who want to argue that the features of my basic framework would *not* be chosen to come up with plausible arguments as to why not.[21]

At any rate, whatever the specific contours of the positive choices delegates make, certain negative choices would not be made: delegates would not find it reasonable to choose to tolerate a situation in which, say, large scale ethnic cleansing and genocide are allowed to take place though it is overwhelmingly clear that an appropriate body which has engaged in peaceful means to resolve the situation could authorize an effective intervention which can be very clearly expected to cause minimal harm, and all involved in the intervention are genuinely concerned with the human tragedy rather than furthering their own interests. The main value of such a thought experiment can be to yield conclusions such as this 'negative' one, a conclusion about what would not be chosen. But I have also suggested that the imaginative thought experiment can also supply the contours for constructing something morally preferable, a positive account of what we would reasonably choose as better policy in guiding resolution of such cases. Some of those contours may get further support when we look at the results of certain kinds of efforts, such as efforts to consult a wide range of audiences with multiple interests and seeing whether consensus could be reached on a policy framework. It is to an important report of that kind that I turn next.

## II. The Report by the International Commission on Intervention and State Sovereignty

In this section I examine the report compiled by the International Commission on Intervention and State Sovereignty which concerns the issue of humanitarian intervention, that is, the question of when, if ever, it may be appropriate for states to protect people who are at risk in another state. The report articulates core principles on which the commission reached consensus, and more importantly, which it believes to be 'politically achievable in the world as we know it today'.[22]

The basic principles the commission endorsed are these: 'State sovereignty implies responsibility, and the primary responsibility for the protection of its people lies with the state itself'.[23] However, 'where a population is suffering serious harm, as a result of internal war, insurgency, repression or state failure, and the state in question is unwilling or unable to halt or avert it, the principle of non-intervention yields to the international responsibility to protect'.[24]

The basis for the responsibility to protect is argued to lie in at least four sources. First, the responsibility to protect is inherent in the concept of sovereignty itself. The report emphasizes that sovereignty is very important, but we must properly understand what sovereignty entails. Sovereignty is not best thought of in terms of control but rather in terms of responsibility. State authorities are responsible for protecting the safety of citizens and for promoting their welfare. They are responsible to the citizens, so they are internally responsible. But they are also externally responsible — state authorities are accountable for their acts to the international community. The commission notes: 'what has been gradually emerging is a parallel transition from a culture of sovereign impunity to a culture of national and international accountability'.[25] Frequently, human rights norms are the point of reference for such accountability, and enforcing rights is becoming more effective too, with the introduction of new international criminal tribunals.

Contrary to a popular misconception, the commission did not find widespread support for a view that sovereignty entails having unlimited state power to do whatever the state wants to its own citizens. Rather, it was widely acknowledged 'that sovereignty implies a dual responsibility: externally — to respect the sovereignty of other states, and internally, to respect the dignity and basic rights of all the people within the state'.[26] Indeed, it is noted that 'sovereignty as responsibility has become the minimum content of good international citizenship'.[27] Internal sovereignty does entail the ability to make authoritative decisions with respect to people or resources in the territory of the state, but that authority is not absolute; rather it is regulated internally, for instance, by constitutional power sharing arrangements.

The three other sources discussed for this responsibility to protect are, Article 24 of the United Nations Charter, specific legal obligations articulated in, for instance, human rights declarations or treatises, and finally, the commission argued that substantiation for the responsibility to protect can be found in the emerging and 'developing practices of states, regional organizations and the Security Council itself'.[28]

The general responsibility to protect involves three more specific responsibilities. First, it entails a responsibility to prevent, that is, to tackle underlying causes of conflict that put people at risk of needing humanitarian intervention. (Tackling root causes might involve, for instance, tackling poverty, political repression, and the inequitable distribution of resources.)[29] Second, it entails a responsibility to react, that is, to respond appropriately when there is compelling human need. Appropriate responses may include sanctions, international prosecutions or military interventions. Third, the responsibility to protect also entails a responsibility to rebuild that means appropriate help with recovering, reconstruction, and reconciliation should be forthcoming.

The principles that are developed for military intervention are strongly coloured by the long tradition of just war theory, but are modified to deal with the specific case of humanitarian intervention. As you might expect, before military intervention is appropriate, just cause must exist. They say, 'military intervention for human protection purposes is an exceptional and extraordinary measure. To be warranted, there must be serious and irreparable harm occurring to human beings, or imminently likely to occur, of the following kind: Either 'large scale loss of life, actual or apprehended, whether carried out by killing, forced expulsion, acts of terror or rape'[30] or 'large scale "ethnic cleansing", actual or apprehended, whether carried out by killing, forced expulsion, acts of terror or rape'.[31] They specifically do not endorse military intervention in cases involving other kinds of massive human rights abuse, such as in the case of rights to freedom of speech being systematically violated.

Just cause constitutes a necessary but not a sufficient condition for intervention. In addition, a number of other factors are relevant including these 'precautionary principles':[32] First, proper intentions must be in place. The intervention's primary purpose must be to avert human suffering, 'whatever other motives intervening states may have'.[33] They note that the right intentions are more likely to be assured 'with multilateral operations, clearly supported by regional opinion and the victims concerned'.[34] Second, military intervention may only be justified after all non-military options for peaceful resolution of conflicts have been explored. Third, proportional means should be used: the 'scale, duration and intensity of the planned military intervention should be the minimum necessary to secure the defined human protective objective'.[35] Fourth, the planned intervention must have reasonable prospects, that is, it must have a reasonable chance of stopping the suffering and it must not be the case that anticipated consequences of the intervention would be worse than the consequences of not intervening.

The committee then turns its attention to the issue of proper authorization for interventions. In the view of the committee, 'there is no better or more appropriate body than the United Nations Security Council to authorize military intervention for human protective purposes. The task is not to find alternatives to the Security Council as a source of authority, but to make the Security Council work better than it has'.[36]

To this end, they maintain that authorization for military interventions should always be sought from the Security Council before proceeding with interventive action. The Security Council has an obligation to deal promptly with any requests for such authorizations, especially when they involve urgent large-scale crises. Interestingly, they add that 'the Permanent Five members of the Security Council should agree not to apply their veto power, in matters where their vital state interests are not involved, to obstruct the passage of resolutions authorizing military intervention for human protection purposes for which there is otherwise majority support'.[37]

If the Security Council fails to deal with the request promptly or rejects the request, a number of other options are available. First, under the 'Uniting for Peace' procedure, the proposed intervention may be considered by the General Assembly in an Emergency Special Session. Alternatively, under Chapter VIII of the Charter, regional or sub-regional organizations may authorize interventions. A note of caution is raised that if the Security Council 'fails to discharge its responsibility to protect in conscience-shocking situations crying out for action, concerned states may not rule out other means to meet the gravity and urgency of that situation — and that the stature and credibility of the United Nations may suffer thereby'.[38] A number of operational principles are also articulated, such as that clear objectives be set (and resources to match their achievement be allocated); and that a common military approach should exist among intervening partners.

### III. Closing the Gaps Between What is Morally Desirable and the Current Situation, and Concluding Remarks

If the public policy proposals recommended by the International Commission on Intervention and State Sovereignty are endorsed and become international law, we would go quite some way towards narrowing the gap between what is theoretically desirable and what becomes the current practice backed by international law. However, there still would be some significant gaps and the normative thought experiment provides a useful tool for critically analyzing current arrangements. For instance, we noted what we want from a well-functioning and morally defensible VIPO, and there are obviously gaps between this ideal and the current arrangements. In particular, the UN and the Security Council do not currently function well as good VIPO organizations. The Security Council and its various mechanisms for ensuring security are not consistent with equal respect all parties should show each other, especially since the Security Council is not a body truly representative of all the people of the world. We must ensure that (at least) all nations have a say in interventive decisions, rather than just a sub-set, and no nation should be given veto powers over a decision which has the overwhelming support of other nations.

Further gaps are notable. Ideally, the VIPO should have more systematic powers, should be better supported financially, and have more means at its disposal to bring about necessary changes. The United Nations is still not adequately resourced to bring about some of the necessary measures to ensure people's basic needs are met. Arguably, this focus on basic needs can address more of some of the fundamental issues people actually care about. Clearly, reform of the United Nations is needed and the arguments presented here constitute further evidence as to the areas needing urgent reform.

However, for all the gaps that would remain, if the recommendations of the International Commission on Intervention and State Sovereignty became international law, we would have a considerable moral advance over the status quo. We would have some clear guidelines on when action should be taken against a state or its leaders without its consent for the purpose of protecting people in those other states. We would also have some clear international law that could resolve the two sets of tensions outlined in my introduction. Recall the two sets of tensions I referred to there. I indicated how some thought there was tension between the goals of respecting sovereignty and responding to the victims who suffer in these crises, that is, a conflict between respecting sovereignty and respecting the individuals who suffer. Second, it was noted that there is tension between the goal of promoting peace or avoiding conflict and engaging in coercive operations for protective purposes. In both cases I argued that the tensions should be resolved in favour of protecting the vulnerable individuals who suffer in humanitarian crises, though the way to do this defensibly required that we needed several safeguards to be put in place to protect against those who might abuse these provisions. I argued from a contractarian model of global justice why the resolutions I propose should have force. I also argued that the gap between theory and practice is likely to diminish if we make the recommendations proposed by the Commission on Intervention and State Sovereignty international law. Gaps would still remain, as my theoretical model reveals, and we should work on closing those gaps in the future. However, we would make some highly notable progress were we simply to implement the recommendations without any adjustments.

## NOTES

1 Interventions can include not just military interventions, but may also include sanctions and criminal prosecutions. I focus here on the case of military interventions, though, since these are thought to be hardest to justify. For more on defining the specific area covered by the now widely used term 'humanitarian intervention', see, for instance, Deen Chatterjee and Don Scheid (eds.), *Ethics and Foreign Intervention* (Cambridge: Cambridge University Press, 2000), especially pp. 1–4.

2 For charges of abuse see for instance, Noam Chomsky, *A New Generation Draws the Line: Kosovo, East Timor, and the Standards of the West* (New York, Verso, 2001); and Julie Mertus, 'Legitimizing the use of force in Kosovo', *Ethics and International Affairs* 51, 1 (2001): 133–150, especially p. 134.

3 See, for instance, Jovan Babic 'Foreign armed intervention: between justified aid and illegal violence' in Aleksander Jokic (ed.) *Humanitarian Intervention: Moral and Philosophical Issues* (Peterborough, Ontario: Broadview Press, 2003), pp. 45–69; J. Bryan Hehir, 'Intervention: from theories to cases', *Ethics and International Affairs* 9 (1995): 7; and Stanley Hoffman, *The Ethics and Politics of Humanitarian Intervention* (Notre Dame: Notre Dame University Press, 1996).

4 For example, see the Charter of the United Nations; even Chapter 1, articles 1 and 2 are in tension. More generally, compare Chapter VI on the Pacific Settlement of Disputes (e.g. article 33) and compare with the Universal Declaration of Human Rights adopted by the General Assembly of the UN in 1948, especially article 28.

5 Elsewhere I have focused on how the experiment can supply us with an excellent framework for settling matters of global distributive justice, but here I want to explore how it offers a systematic way for thinking through another issue concerning global justice, namely, the issue of humanitarian intervention. See Gillian Brock, 'Egalitarianism, ideals, and cosmopolitan justice', *The Philosophical Forum* 36 (2005): 1–30.

6 John Rawls, *A Theory of Justice* (Cambridge, MA: Harvard University Press, 1971).

7 As should become obvious, my account also differs from that developed by others who use a global original position as a device for thinking through what justice requires internationally, such as the positions developed by Charles Beitz *Political Theory and International Relations* (Princeton: Princeton University

Press, 1979) and Thomas Pogge *Realizing Rawls* (Ithaca: Cornell University Press, 1989). Some notable differences include that I use random sampling rather than the idea of representatives to assemble my delegates, that I do not endorse a Global Difference Principle, and more generally I argue that different choices would be made at my hypothetical conference to those emphasized by these other theorists.

8 I say 'Rawlsian-style' rather than 'Rawlsian' as I think there is much of value in the method Rawls employs, but much less of value in the assumptions he makes and the conclusions he thereby endorses, as discussed in *The Law of Peoples* (Cambridge, MA: Harvard University Press, 1999). Significantly, the method I describe provides a way we can try to help people think through what it would be reasonable to agree to in the choosing situation I go on to outline.

9 Many people raise questions of the following kinds when talk of social contracts is introduced: Is the contract supposed to be actual or hypothetical? If only hypothetical then why does a purely hypothetical contract have any binding force anyway? And if it has no binding force, then why adhere to it? I see talking in terms of social contracts as a way to specify what expectations various parties to the contract may reasonably have of each other: it is simply a way of fleshing out what those reasonable expectations might be. So, in answer to the questions listed: no, the contract developed assuming the ideal world presupposition is neither an actual contract nor a purely hypothetical one. It is a way to sift through what (actual) parties might reasonably expect of one another, by imagining a certain (hypothetical) choosing situation. Talking about social contracts is a way to talk about, and so uncover, the reasonable expectations people might have of one another in ongoing cooperation.

10 I prefer to have my delegates randomly selected rather than being representatives for a range of reasons having to do with the problematic nature of representation, especially in this context. The notion of representation does, and can do, no real work here.

11 I contend that if a rational individual does not know the odds, it is not rational to gamble (under at least certain conditions, especially the ones described). She will have to think more seriously about what 'the strains of commitment' will really involve and what she will honestly be prepared to tolerate.

12 Delegates will also have information about other problems including various environmental threats we face, such as, the destruction of the ozone layer and the current state of knowledge about global warming. Information about threats to health such as the spread of highly infectious diseases will also be included. Some of this information will make clear that these problems have global reach and require global co-operation if they are to be resolved.

13 Perhaps someone may wonder whether there is only one important principle at issue here, the principle concerning protection from real opportunities for serious harms, since the freedoms highlighted are important because being deprived of them can lead to serious harm? I prefer my formulation because it brings into better view two key features that would be selected in the normative thought experiment.

14 Delegates would want certain minimum guarantees about what counts as permissible treatment. Heading the list of guarantees we would choose would be guarantees against assault, torture, imprisonment without trial or sufficient warrant, extreme coercion of various kinds (such as slavery) and so forth. But as I have also suggested, it would be reasonable for them to add some freedoms governing dissent, conscience, speech, association, and movement, contrary to what Rawls suggests in *Law of Peoples*.

15 Indeed, what could be a more fundamental harm than being deprived of one's livelihood or the ability to eke out a livelihood for oneself and one's dependents?

16 Furthermore, delegates should consider the possibility that they are permanently disabled and they should also consider the actual periods of extreme dependence that naturally occur in the human life-cycle. Having contemplated these issues, delegates would want adequate protections to be guaranteed should/ when the need arises. Clearly-thinking individuals behind an appropriate veil of ignorance should be strongly motivated to choose not only to ensure certain minimal opportunities to meet our needs for ourselves are available, but also that persons should have adequate provisions to be assisted with need-satisfaction, should they not be in a position to meet their needs themselves.

17 These ideas are developed in 'Needs and global justice' (forthcoming in *Philosophy*, 2006).

18 I have suggested that a rough guiding principle we would choose is to have social and political arrangements that allow reasonable opportunities for us to be enabled to meet our basic needs. But would we not want more? Would we find it reasonable to endorse something like a Global Difference Principle, or more substantive equality? Elsewhere I argue that it is not the more reasonable choice, on both theoretical and empirical grounds. See Gillian Brock, 'Egalitarianism, ideals, and cosmopolitan justice' op. cit.

19 By 'the vulnerable' I mean those whose prospects for decent lives are significantly shattered from the causes here under review.

20 These are the essential elements from both *jus ad bellum* and *jus in bello*.
21 The main concern an opponent might have to my framework would probably be fears about the power the VIPO would have and whether the VIPO could abuse this power. If the VIPO is constituted by representatives of all nations of the world (not just states), and at least supermajority was needed for all decisions to be binding on the VIPO, it is not clear to me that it would be able to do anything it wasn't duly authorized to do. Of course, human beings can always find ways to abuse institutions, but that should not stop us advocating for certain just institutions, and doing what we can to limit opportunities for abuse.
22 *Ibid.*, p. viii.
23 *Ibid.*, p. xiii.
24 *Ibid.*
25 *Ibid.*, p. 14.
26 *Ibid.*, p. 8.
27 *Ibid.*
28 *Ibid.*
29 *Ibid.*, p. 23.
30 *Ibid.*, p. xii.
31 *Ibid.*
32 *Ibid.*
33 *Ibid.*
34 *Ibid.*
35 *Ibid.*
36 *Ibid.*
37 *Ibid.*, p. xiii.
38 *Ibid.*

# 5 Iraq: A Morally Justified Resort to War

DAVID MELLOW

For argument's sake, let us assume the following in regards to the US led war in Iraq:

1. Saddam Hussein's regime neither possessed weapons of mass destruction (WMD) nor was actively engaged in developing or intending to develop such weapons.
2. Given a further amount of time, the UN inspectors would have gathered sufficient information to confirm the first assumption.
3. The Bush and Blair governments intentionally deceived their citizens regarding the likelihood that Saddam Hussein's regime possessed weapons of mass destruction.
4. Based on international law, the war represented an illegal act of aggression against the state of Iraq, and furthermore, was not justified in light of the negotiated agreement reached at the end of the earlier Gulf War.

Admittedly many of these assumptions are debatable. Nonetheless, I propose we grant all these assumptions to the opponent of the war. In this paper I will argue that even if all these assumptions are true, the resort to war was still morally justified.

My argument will proceed on the assumption that the just war tradition (so called 'just war theory') provides the correct understanding of the morality of war.[1] I begin by offering the following list of criteria that must be met for the resort to war to be morally justified:

1. There must be a sufficient just cause.
2. Only a legitimate authority may undertake the war.
3. The war must be undertaken with the right intention.
4. The war must be undertaken as a last resort.
5. The war must pass the test of proportionality.[2]

While different just war theorists may propose different lists of criteria, the list presented here encapsulates the criteria that most commonly and consistently appear in such lists. Furthermore, it is in the context of the criteria listed that most of the moral criticisms of the resort to war in Iraq have been raised. It is, therefore, in reference to these criteria that I will make the case that the resort to war in Iraq was morally justified.[3]

## Sufficient Just Cause

According to just war theory, a morally justified decision to go to war requires the presence of a just cause of sufficient moral importance. The crucial task is to identify precisely what counts as 'sufficient'. More precisely, we need some account of what sorts of causes are not only just, but also of sufficient importance to defeat the prima facie presumption against the use of direct, forceful, and violent military means that intervene in the cultural and political affairs of another people, nation or state.

With respect to Iraq, at least three considerations have been offered as constituting (individually or collectively) a possible sufficient just cause. The first, which was arguably the main focus prior to the war, was removing the threat posed to other nations by Iraq's possession of, or attempts to acquire, WMD. The second was that Iraq, by failing to fully cooperate with the inspectors, was violating the legal terms agreed to at the end of the earlier Gulf War. The third was putting an end to the ongoing grave humanitarian injustices suffered by the Iraqi people.

While the first two considerations lead to some much discussed questions regarding if and when wars of prevention are justified, I will, in light of the assumptions granted at the start of the paper, accept for arguments sake that neither of the first two considerations provides a sufficient just cause, and instead, will argue that the humanitarian injustices provided such a cause. I begin by describing the two general moral considerations that ground humanitarian sufficient just causes.[4]

First, there is the value attached to a people being self-determining. This value lies both in the *collective right* that a people have to be politically and culturally self-determining and in the *basic good* of a people engaging in a collective process of self-determination. When a people's ability to be self-determining is ruthlessly suppressed, with no reasonable hope that the people themselves can overthrow the tyranny, this generally provides third party states with a sufficient just cause.

The claim that a sufficient just cause may be grounded (in part) in violations of a people's prima facie right of collective self-determination is not uncontroversial.[5] In particular, Richard Norman rejects this claim. Norman contends that that '[n]ations do not have an automatic right to be defended' and that 'we cannot escape the need to make *qualitative* judgements about its [a nation's] cultural and political life'.[6]

While I agree with Norman that we do need to make qualitative judgements about a nation's cultural and political life, this recognition is, *contra* Norman, compatible with nations having a prima facie right of self-determination that is often a central consideration in determining whether there is a sufficient just cause. A comparison with individual autonomy rights should help.

In the case of individuals, the generally held view is that each and every individual possesses prima facie autonomy rights. Autonomy rights are intimately tied to our concept of what it is to be a person. One does not have to do anything to earn either those autonomy rights or the right to defend them. Though one can do things that, in certain situations, will undermine the moral case for exercising and defending autonomy rights — and which might even, in a hard to define sense, result in the forfeiture of those rights — autonomy rights exist and carry moral weight prior to any qualitative judgements regarding a person's actions, plans and character.

Similarly, the collective right of self-determination is intimately tied to our concept of what it is to be a nation or a people. Each nation or state possesses the prima facie right of collective self-determination. A nation or people is not required to do certain things, or act in certain ways, to gain either that right or the right to defend it. While certain actions or political and cultural features may, in certain contexts, undermine the moral case for exercising that right, and even result in the forfeiture of the right, the right exists and carries moral weight prior to any judgement about such actions and features. In other words, one starts with the presumption that a people or a nation has the right to be self-determining.

A common argument raised against some or all humanitarian military interventions is that even if such interventions are grounded in just causes, those just causes are usually not sufficient to justify interfering in a people's process of self-determination. However, this argument loses much (and arguably all) of its force when a people are *severely* oppressed because they are then not engaged, or are engaged only very minimally in a process of self-determination. To put this last observation in slightly different terms, when people are severely oppressed there is a significant lowering of the bar with respect to what just causes count as sufficient.

The second set of moral considerations that underlie humanitarian sufficient just causes are systematic violations of *individual* human rights and the existence of widespread *individual* human suffering. Sometimes the violations of individual rights or the experiences of human suffering are on such a scale and of such a degree that it provides third parties with a sufficient just cause. While this consideration has historically not always been given its due, there is now widespread recognition that it is an important moral consideration in determining whether military intervention is justified.

In summary, there are both collective and individual grounds for the use of military force. Furthermore, such grounds may justify not only first party but also third party use of military force.

What then about the people of Iraq? In Iraq, the ruling regime clearly was repressive. The severity and systematic nature of the oppression was, perhaps, most obvious in the case of the Shiites and Kurds, but even amongst the Sunnis there was a systematic reign of terror that made any significant assertion of collective will a practical impossibility. Thus it is clear that the peoples of Iraq could only very minimally exercise a process of collective self-determination. Furthermore, the oppression involved massive systematic individual human rights violations — killing, gassing, torture, rape, forced displacement, campaigns of terror, and severe religious restrictions. The numbers killed, maimed, tortured and displaced, though imprecise, are staggering — at the very minimum involving hundreds of thousands in a population of twenty-two million.

While it is sometimes contended that the large-scale human rights violations mainly occurred prior to and immediately after the 1991 Gulf War, this is not the case. First, the severe oppression of any meaningful collective process of self-determination was clearly an ongoing reality. Furthermore, even in regards to individual human rights violations there was strong evidence of ongoing systematic violations. In January 2003 Human Rights Watch documented the 'ongoing campaign . . . against the Ma'dan or so-called Marsh Arabs whose numbers, at the time of writing had been reduced from some 250,000 people as recently as 1991 . . . to . . . fewer than 40,000 in their ancestral homeland'.

Additionally, reports and statements presented throughout the 1990s by Max Van Der Stoel, Special U.N. Rapporteur of the Commission on Human Rights on the Situation of Human Rights in Iraq, indicate ongoing large-scale and systematic violations of human rights. As recently as March 1999, he addressed the U.N. Commission on Human Rights stating that it is his 'sad duty yet again to report: allegations of numerous and systematic arbitrary executions, interferences with the independent religious practice of the Shi'ite community, continuing internal deportations of ethnic Kurds, violations of the rights to food and health, violations of the rights of the child . . .'. The Special Rapporteur also goes on to document the assassination of religious leaders and the broader humanitarian suffering and deaths caused by the government's unwillingness to either work with the U.N. de-mining program or take full advantage of the food-for-oil program. Of course, one may have hoped that the future under Saddam Hussein and his likely successors (e.g. his sons) would not continue past practices, but the serial ongoing actions of the regime give us no reason to think this likely. Again quoting the Special Rapporteur: 'Regrettably, the situation of human rights has not improved in Iraq, nor does it show any sign of improving'.[7]

The crucial question, of course, is whether the oppression, suffering and rights violations were systematic and grave enough to ground a sufficient just cause. There is (rightly) now substantial agreement that stopping an act of genocide against a people represents a sufficient just cause. But surely if stopping a genocide represents a sufficient just cause, then there are massive cases of systematic oppression, killing, and terror that, while not quite a genocide, also ground a sufficient just cause.[8] For example, if one could stop the ruthless ethnic cleansing of one hundred thousand people through a military intervention that would cost a few dozen lives, surely the prevention of that ethnic cleansing would represent a sufficient just cause.[9] In the case of Iraq, the gravity of atrocities (whether considered from a serial or ongoing perspective) was even greater than this. Therefore, *setting aside for now questions of proportionality*, there was a sufficient just cause. Furthermore, remember the crucial point made earlier, that when a people are severely oppressed, the sufficiency threshold is significantly lowered because the central moral concern that one would be interfering in and undermining a people's process of self-determination carries little, if any, weight.

Some may contend that despite the oppression, it is important that the people themselves be left to overthrow their oppressor, and therefore this oppression does not provide third parties with a sufficient just cause. This position, however, is morally untenable. First, there was no strong evidence that the Iraqi people themselves would have been able, in the foreseeable future, to overthrow the current regime and replace it with a more benevolent one, let alone a more democratic form of government and a just legal system.[10] Second, a similar contention made about a domestic case involving individuals would be morally absurd and even offensive. Imagine that a family is being ruthlessly oppressed by the father/husband under threats — often carried out — of grave beatings if they speak out against any of his commands or attempt to leave the house without him. The moral offensiveness of someone saying that it is not society's place to, if necessary, physically intervene is obvious.[11]

A critic might protest that, unlike the domestic case, it is important or even vital for a people themselves to overthrow the oppressor if they are to ultimately engage in a flourishing process of self-determination. Michael Walzer, in his discussion of self-determination, approvingly refers to Mill's 'stern doctrine of self-help' and quotes Mill's claim that '[i]t is during an arduous struggle to become free by their own efforts that these virtues [the virtues needed for maintaining freedom] have the best chance of springing up'. Walzer also goes on to say: 'revolutionary activity is an exercise in self-determination, while foreign interference denies to a people those political capacities that only such exercise can bring'.[12]

The correct response to Walzer and Mill is to simply observe that it is not true that the virtues or political capacities needed for maintaining freedom and exercising the right of self-determination can only arise through 'arduous struggle'. Surely people can learn to value freedom and develop the capacity to exercise it through, for example, education, learning of and empathizing with the positive and negative examples set by other peoples, and robustly engaging in a 'post-oppression' political environment. It may be true that people who have 'struggled' to exercise their right of self-determination will, for a period of time, have a heightened appreciation of the value of that right and of their freedom. But the heightened appreciation, even if it cannot be acquired except through an arduous struggle (a doubtful premise) is not an indispensable 'political capacity'. Even without such a heightened appreciation, people can grow to value and effectively exercise their right of self-determination and their freedom.

Another possible objection is that for humanitarian military intervention to be justified, it must have the support of those who are oppressed. For example, Jeff McMahan tells us that '[f]or humanitarian intervention to be justified, it must be consistent with the will of the supposed beneficiaries' and in the case of Iraq 'there was no indication that the people whom the US claimed to be saving actually welcomed American intervention'.[13] While I agree that the desires of the people sometimes do matter in determining whether there is a sufficient just cause, one must be careful in this regard.

First, the approval of the people is arguably not always necessary to justify humanitarian intervention. In particular, if systematic large-scale killing and torture is occurring, one may still be justified in interfering, even if the victimized people express a desire that others not interfere. While this last claim will be controversial, support for it can be found in an example of individual self-defence. Imagine that a group of armed attackers are torturing and killing a nearby family. You are part of an armed group (for example, you and your hunting buddies) who happen to pass the scene. You have no way of stopping the attackers other than using your guns, so you prepare to shoot. However, just at that moment the family yells at you to stop, explaining that they are committed pacifists and have chosen to suffer and die. Must you defer to their request and simply let the torture and killing proceed? Surely you need not. The act of torture and murder is a great evil — so great that you are permitted to stop the act even if the victims of the evil would rather you didn't do so. While the victims' personal convictions and autonomy rights do carry moral weight, they do not carry enough weight to make it wrong for you to intervene to stop such an immoral act. (This would be especially true if the family includes children on whose behalf the parents are making decisions.) Similarly, in a case of systematic large-scale government oppression, killing and torture, military intervention represents a sufficient just cause even if the vast majority of the victims are opposed to that intervention.

Second, even if expressed wishes carry some weight, when large-scale oppression and rights violations are occurring it is surely the wishes of the terrorized and oppressed populations that should be the central consideration, rather than the wishes of the entire population — many of whom may be beneficiaries of that oppression.

Third, there is reason to think that the people suffering under Saddam Hussein's rule did welcome the US action to remove his regime. In a Gallup Poll conducted in Baghdad between August 28 and September 4, 2003, 62 percent of citizens surveyed did 'think ousting Saddam Hussein was worth any hardships they have personally endured since the invasion' (*The Globe and Mail*, Thursday, September 25, 2003). And in a second country-wide Gallup Poll conducted for *USA Today* in March and April 2004, a clear majority of Iraqis (61 percent) answered 'Worth It' when asked: 'Thinking about any hardships you might have suffered since the US/British invasion, do you personally think that ousting Saddam Hussein was worth it or not?' Furthermore, and importantly given the observations in the last paragraph, in Shia and Kurdish areas the corresponding percentages were 74 and 97 percent respectively. (Poll results found on the *USA Today* website.)

In response, some people may contend that the current resentment regarding the ongoing occupation and the significant support for the actions of the insurgents both provide evidence that the invasion was unwelcome. Such a conclusion, however, would not be justified. First, it is doubtful that a majority of the Iraqi people support the acts of the insurgents. When asked in the *USA Today* poll: 'To what extent can you personally justify the following actions morally . . . Current attacks against US forces in Iraq', 25 percent said 'Cannot at all', 22 percent said 'Cannot somewhat', 22 percent said 'Sometime can/can't', 17 percent said 'Can somewhat', and 13 percent said 'Can completely'.

Second, even if a majority of Iraqis support the insurgents' actions, or support the immediate withdrawal of American troops from Iraqi territory, this does not demonstrate that the people of Iraq were, or are, opposed to the invasion and overthrow of Saddam Hussein's regime. There is nothing inconsistent in a people welcoming their liberators, but objecting to their ongoing occupation. Furthermore, support for the insurgents' acts may not even indicate opposition to short-term occupation. It rather could be grounded in: opposition to certain aspects of that occupation, or a desire to ensure that the occupation is only short-term, or anger based upon, for example, the perception (whether right or wrong) that America played a significant role in earlier injustices that the Iraqis and peoples of the Middle East experienced.

In summary, the humanitarian imperative provided a sufficient just cause. There were both collective and individual considerations that when combined, and probably even when considered separately, were of sufficient moral importance to justify third party military intervention.

## Right Intention

Even if there is a sufficient humanitarian just cause, many will contend that the war was immoral because the US and British governments' actual motivation for going to war was something other than the humanitarian cause. It has, for example, been contended that the 'true' intentions were one or more of the following: a concern for oil security, a (misguided) desire to rid Iraq of its WMD, a desire to establish a strong American base or hegemony in the Middle East, and even a desire on the part of George W. Bush to complete the war his father had begun.

In supporting this claim, however, some very difficult problems arise:

1. Whose intention is the relevant one? Is the relevant intention that of President Bush himself, that of the larger administration, or that of the relevant legislative bodies?
2. If the relevant intention is that of a group, how do you identify the group's intention?[14]
3. Should the right intention criterion require a *right* intention (for example, one appropriately connected to the sufficient just cause) or, instead, only require that certain bad intentions not be present?[15]

4. If there must be a *right* intention, is it sufficient that the intention simply be present or must it also carry motivational force? If the latter, must the motivational force meet some minimal threshold? And should that threshold be defined in some counterfactual way? For example, perhaps the right intention must be sufficient to motivate the relevant agent's actual decision even if there were no other motive. Or perhaps the counterfactual requirement is that the agent would not have gone to war in the absence of the belief that there was a just cause.[16]

Unless these questions are satisfactorily answered, the criticism based on wrong intention is problematic. But even if these questions can be satisfactorily answered, there is a deeper problem with the criticism. There are strong grounds for questioning the inclusion of the right intention criterion among the just war criteria.

Its inclusion suggests that an act of resorting to war should be judged not only on the basis of external features, but also on the basis of the internal motives, desires, and intentions of the agents. This suggestion, however, confuses two separate judgements. One judgement has to do with the moral character of the person or nation carrying out the act. The second judgement has to do with the morality of the act itself. The content of individuals' intentions, desires and motives are, for the most part, relevant to making judgements of character, but not to making judgements about the rightness or wrongness of an act. For example, stopping a murderer from assaulting and killing a victim is the right thing to do even if the person who intervenes does so solely in the hope that there will be a reward, and not out of any concern for the victim. Of course the motivation of the intervener is central to our judgement of the intervener's character, but it in no way influences the judgement about the correctness of the action. Similarly, it is sensible to talk about a person who, throughout her life, continuously does the right thing, but with the wrong motives. Such a person has a flawed moral character, and we would likely describe that person's life as morally flawed. Nonetheless, it still remains the case that the acts the person committed were the right acts.

The focus of just war theory is on the rightness or wrongness of *the act* of resorting to war, not the moral character of the interveners. Therefore, even untoward motives, desires, and intentions are permissible as long as the military declaration or intervention meets the other criteria — though such motives may be important when making judgements about the moral character of a nation or its leaders. Consider, for example, a case in which a junta is asked by another country to help it repel an unjust aggressor. That junta decides to assist that third party, not because there is a sufficient just cause (which there is) but because it will arouse a sense of patriotism in the people the junta rule — a sense of patriotism that the junta hopes will undermine any opposition to its rule. While such a cynical undertaking of a military campaign would comment heavily on the moral character of the junta's members, it would not undermine the justness of the military intervention itself.

A critic may suggest that while some immoral motives, desires and intentions are permissible, there are, nonetheless, a set of immoral motives, desires or intentions that go beyond the pale (for example, action done purely on the basis of hatred or racist sentiments[17]) and which make an action unjust. In response, consider the following modification to the earlier example of preventing a murder.

This time imagine that the individual's sole motivation for acting to prevent the assault and murder is something more heinous than a desire for the reward. Perhaps the individual takes pleasure in killing members of a certain race. Seeing that the attacker is of that race, he engages the attacker solely in the hope that the attacker will resist and need to be killed.

Of course there is a terribly offensive element in the intervener's motivation, and we are right to express revulsion regarding his character; nonetheless, surely we would not contend that he was wrong to intervene.[18] In short, there are no intentions, desires or motives that are 'beyond the pale' because such internal considerations are not determining factors in judging the rightness or wrongness of the act. One can do the right thing for horrifically wrong reasons.

In the international context then, what a nation must defend is not its intentions or motives, but rather the claim that its declaration of war or decision to use military force represents the undertaking of a sufficient just cause. That is to say, what needs satisfying is not the right intention criterion, but rather, the sufficient just cause criterion. What is of concern is not evidence per se of self-interested or even immoral motives or intentions, but rather evidence that a nation's military action is not systematically structured so as to achieve a sufficient just cause. Evidence of immoral intentions may well be a red flag to warn us that the military action is not so structured, but such intentions do not *in and of themselves* make the military action immoral.[19]

In summary, it is inappropriate to include the right intention criterion among the just war criteria. We should not give intentions and motives separate standing in the pantheon of just war criteria. The intentions of the leaders in the Iraq war might not have always been virtuous, but this, in itself, does not make the resort to war morally unjustified.

## Last Resort

Some may contend that in resorting to war to thwart Iraqi possession or development of WMD, the last resort criterion was not satisfied because there was another alternative that had a reasonable hope of succeeding, namely letting the UN inspectors, backed by international pressure, continue their work. Let us, for argument's sake, accept this criticism. This does not affect my argument, since I have claimed that the humanitarian imperative provided a sufficient just cause. Thus the question that needs answering is whether or not resorting to war to achieve the humanitarian aims met the last resort criterion.

The answer arguably hinges on whether or not there were other ways of substantially improving the humanitarian situation in the near term.[20] I see no reason to think that any 'other ways' could have been expected to succeed. It was not plausible to think (especially given the ineffectiveness of sanctions) that further economic and political pressure could be expected to substantially moderate the ruthless behaviour of the regime. Furthermore, there was little cooperation among members of the UN Security Council, and little reason to think that US and British diplomatic efforts would lead the Security Council to collectively act militarily, even if they had focused their appeal on the humanitarian injustices.[21] Finally, the chances of an internal uprising being successful in the near term were minimal given the regime's ability and willingness (as demonstrated, for example, by its actions against the Shiites and Kurds) to brutally crush any potential opposition and systematically terrorize and divide the population.

As a general rule, brutal ruthless dictatorships are not readily defeated by minimally armed populations.[22]

Perhaps some would contend that rather than a massive military action, a more selective targeting of force could have been used to remove Saddam Hussein and institute a more humanitarian government. The problem with this suggestion is that there is no evidence that such an approach was feasible. In fact, in the early days of the war the US did make attempts to target the high-ranking officials, including Saddam Hussein himself, but this proved to be in practice very difficult. And to the extent that such targeting did succeed, it did not seriously weaken the regime or its resolve. So there seems to be no basis for thinking that the alternative of more selective targeting prior to the war would have led to the institution of a more benevolent regime, let alone a democratic government. Also, if the US military and government thought such an alternative was available, surely they would have pursued it, rather than risk the lives of large numbers of civilians and US soldiers and incur the huge expense of fighting the war.

The war, combined with those early attempts to target and destabilize the regime, was the only approach that could reasonably be expected to, in the foreseeable future, overthrow the Iraqi regime. Therefore, the last resort criterion was satisfied.

## Legitimate Authority

There has been much discussion of legitimacy based on: 1) questions of international law, and 2) questions about the extent to which the Blair and Bush governments were not fully forthcoming regarding what they knew about Iraq's possession of WMD.[23]

With respect to international law, for argument's sake let us grant that the resort to war was illegal. Does this make the resort to war immoral? I contend that it does not. As a general rule, laws that are reasonably motivated and are not clearly unjust do carry moral weight. However, when that law demands that we not intervene to stop a wide-scale humanitarian catastrophe or moral injustice, it is not plausible, when the legal authorities will not take the needed action, to claim that the law carries sufficient moral force to make it morally wrong for others to intervene and prevent the catastrophe or injustice. Interestingly, I suspect that most of us recognize the truth of this claim in the domestic realm.

Imagine that your next-door neighbour was brutally beating his family and threatening to kill them. You have called the police, but they are unwilling to intervene — perhaps they claim no officers are available. If there were a law stating that only the police and not ordinary citizens could use lethal force against other citizens, surely the law would carry very little (or even no) moral force in deciding whether you are morally permitted to act. Despite the law, you would clearly be morally justified, if necessary, in killing the neighbour in order to save the family.

In contrast, in the international realm many have contended that due to international law it is not morally permissible for individual third party states to intervene in the affairs of fellow states, even when there are grave, systematic, and ongoing humanitarian catastrophes and injustices. However, this simply demonstrates an inconsistency in moral thinking rather than being grounded in some morally important difference between the domestic and international cases. It is true, as was indicated earlier, that there is value and even an associated right in a people engaging in a process of self-determination. However, it is important to recognize that the political state and the people are not one and the same. Furthermore, the moral rights of the state are ultimately grounded in the rights of the people. Thus when the state is engaged in grievous systematic activities that violate the individual and collective rights of the people, the oppressive political state may not, in objecting to possible military intervention, appeal to the people's collective right of self-determination since the state is not, as it stands, a plausible vehicle for exercising and protecting those collective rights. Such an appeal is no more plausible than the brutalizing family member claiming that outsiders may not intervene to stop him since the family has a collective right to privacy or non-interference.

It is sometimes suggested that if individual states violate international law, especially with respect to the third party use of military force, this will undermine the willingness of other states to respect the demands of international law. While there may be some truth here, we must remember that there are cases and there are cases.[24] When the violation of international law serves an important humanitarian purpose, it seems just as likely that this violation, rather than undermining international law, may well force the law makers to confront the moral failings in their laws and create new laws and structures which better reflect the moral imperatives. In the long-term this may actually increase respect for the law.

Furthermore, even if there is some risk that the violation of international law may undermine the respect others show for the law (and associated international organizations) this does not obviously undermine the morality of the act. Consider again the domestic example. If just prior to shooting your violent neighbour, someone pointed out that your doing so (given some strange scenario) would cause a degree of breakdown in general respect for law and authority, this does not entail that you should not act to save the family. It is unfortunate that others will use this opportunity to more generally disregard or undermine authority, but this does not make your action immoral. A similar line of reasoning applies in the international realm.[25]

In addition to concerns with international law, there have been post-war concerns raised regarding what undisclosed information the Blair and Bush governments had regarding Iraq's WMD program (or lack thereof) and to what extent those governments intentionally exaggerated the threat. Again, for argument's sake, let us assume that the Blair and Bush governments were deceptive in their presentation of the facts. Should we then conclude that the war to overthrow the Iraqi regime was immoral? The answer is, in an important sense, no.

It is certainly true that the act of deception, if it occurred, would be morally wrong, and those deceived would be right to express moral outrage. Also, it is possible that a moral or legal case could be made that because of this deception the culpable parties should resign or be impeached. Nonetheless, this does not make the resort to war immoral. Put very roughly, the deception is a moral matter internal to the deceiver and the deceived and can be separated from the question of the morality of the war. In slightly different terms, the deception provides no basis for Saddam Hussein (nor you or I) to claim that the resort to war was, *in itself*, immoral.

In hopes of making this point more compelling, I return once more to the violent neighbour case. This time, just as you head out the door to stop the neighbour, your spouse, out of concern for your safety and that of your family, demands that you not go. In response, and in order to get your spouse to concur with your decision, you lie, telling him or her that the neighbour has, in fact, explicitly told you that after killing his family, he is going to come next door and kill your family. Now your spouse agrees that despite the risk you should go next door and, if necessary, kill the neighbour.

If, after the fact, your spouse learns about your deception, she or he would be justified in taking offence. However, notice that the immorality of that deception did not make it immoral for you to proceed next door and stop the neighbour. There is an important moral line to be drawn between the act of deception and the act of stopping the neighbour. And a similar line exists between any deception carried out by the Blair and Bush governments and the moral judgement we make about the resort to war to overthrow Saddam Hussein's regime.

## Proportionality

Finally, we turn to the issue of whether the war in Iraq was a proportional war. That is, did the relevant good effects outweigh the relevant bad effects?[26] Admittedly, this is a difficult question to answer. In part, this is because it relies on empirical claims that are open to dispute. But it also reflects vagueness in the criterion. In particular, what precisely count as *relevant* good effects and *relevant* bad effects? I contend that the obvious relevant good effect consists in the achievement of the sufficient just cause. Furthermore, the achievement of that cause has these features: (a) preventing systematic oppression, killings, harms, and injustices that the Iraqi people would have incurred under current and future Iraqi regimes, and (b) providing the people with a chance to both engage in a process of political and cultural self-determination and live in a country that is respectful of fundamental individual and collective human rights. As for the relevant bad effects, these, I suggest, are the injuries, deaths, and injustices that were caused (or expected to be caused) by the war — including the risks of civil or a broader Middle East war.[27]

On the assumption that these are the relevant effects, the question remains whether the relevant good effects outweigh the relevant bad effects. An answer to this question may appear to require very difficult evaluations of the values that attach to goods and harms of very different kinds. For example, how does one weigh the value of providing a people an opportunity to be politically self-determining against the loss of civilian and military lives? Assuming there is some 'objective truth' about such values, I am unsure how to argue for particular evaluations. I suspect assigning values, even relative ones, will usually need to rely on considered judgements of individuals. And perhaps we can use some thought experiments to make progress on that count.

Imagine, for example, that you and your children are living under a ruthless regime similar to that of pre-war Iraq. You live in constant fear that you will be arrested and tortured, either for speaking out against the government or simply because someone reports you to the authorities. In the past, tens of thousands of your people have been killed in ruthless campaigns of oppression, and you do not know if or when another such campaign may be mounted. Finally, you fear for the future of your children. Not only will they likely experience the same oppression and systematic terror you face (including the risk of being forced to serve the military or oppressive apparatus of the state) they will also be subject to the harm of being indoctrinated by state propaganda.

If, under this scenario, a foreign power were considering an invasion to overthrow the current regime, with the promise to help the people institute more democratic institutions and a just rule-of-law, I suspect most people would agree that this opportunity would be worth the risks of war — even though those risks include death, horrible maiming and other severe hardships, and even if, as was surely true among Iraqis, there is some doubt about the intentions of the foreign powers.[28]

Even though some would be compelled by such thought experiments, especially if buttressed by further considerations that those oppressed in Iraq likely would share a similar view (see the earlier references to polls in Iraq in which a majority of Iraqis thought removing Saddam Hussein was worth the hardships they suffered), others would object that using such intuitive judgements as a criterion for deciding the (relative) value of certain goods and harms is at best doubtful. In particular, they would point to the possibility of divergence between individuals' 'considered' value judgements of moral worth (or the use of thought experiments to arrive at such judgements) and the 'truth' of those judgements. While I do not share such scepticism,[29] I do, fortunately, think there is another way of considering the proportionality of *this particular war* that does not rely on the sort of thought experiment and judgements employed so far.

This approach requires recognizing that applying the proportionality criterion involves comparing the relevant goods and harms that the war causes against those relevant goods and harms that would have occurred if the US (and others) had 'done nothing' to affect any reduction in the relevant harms and injustices that underlay the humanitarian sufficient just cause.

At first glance, the comparative use of the 'doing nothing' alternative may appear to be much too weak an interpretation of the proportionality test, as there are often many alternatives to war that involve more than doing nothing. This objection, however, misses the point of the proportionality test, which is precisely to test the war against such a base case. In contrast, it is in applying the last resort criterion, something I have already done, that one compares the particular 'war option' against the 'do something else' alternatives. Given this, one may be tempted to draw the conclusion that the proportionality criterion is redundant given the presence of the last resort criterion. This would be a mistake. To see the necessary role played by the proportionality test, one simply needs to recognize that the military option can have better relevant consequences than all the other alternatives that have some likelihood of achieving the sufficient just causes and yet still not satisfy the baseline test — i.e. still not be better than 'doing nothing'.[30]

Once we recognize that the proportionality test requires a comparison between the relevant goods and harms the war caused and those that could reasonably be expected to occur if nothing was done, we are able to show that the war was proportional without relying on comparisons of goods and harms of very different kinds. Instead, we can restrict ourselves to comparisons between similar kinds and show that each such comparison favours the war over doing nothing. This uniformity in results enables us to conclude that the proportionality criterion is satisfied.

Consider first the harm of civilian deaths, injuries and suffering. It is admittedly hard to be precise regarding the extent of suffering that would have occurred if the US had not led an invasion, but a credible argument can be made that the experience would have been much worse without the invasion. Under the roughly twenty years of Saddam Hussein's rule, it is widely agreed that the numbers killed, tortured and displaced was in the hundreds of thousands. Without military action it is very likely that Saddam Hussein and his successors would have continued to carry out large numbers of killings and continued an organized campaign of using torture, fear and displacement of peoples.[31] Even if the numbers only amounted to a fraction of those killed, tortured or terrorized in Saddam Hussein's first twenty years, this would eventually surpass all the civilian and military deaths that have occurred both in the war and in post-war attacks by insurgents and the invading forces. Furthermore, even if there was a chance that the people themselves (likely far in the future) could have overthrown the regime of Saddam Hussein and his successors, there is no reason to expect that such an event would not itself result in civilian deaths in numbers equal to or much greater than those that resulted, or could have been expected to result, from the invasion and its aftermath.

In response, some may contend that the pre- and post-war risk of the situation deteriorating into a civil war or long-term terrorist campaign by the insurgents must be considered, and that this makes the war, both prospectively and retrospectively (at the time of writing) disproportionate. While the risk of a civil war was and remains significant, I do not, *contra* the suggestion, think this negatively impacts the proportionality calculation. This is because the risk of civil war now or prior to the war was also present in the 'do nothing' alternative, in the eventuality that the Iraqi people would be able to overthrow the regime. In fact, it is arguable that if the people themselves overthrew the regime, there would be even less post-war structure and, therefore, even a greater risk that the situation would deteriorate into civil war or wars of succession. The 'do nothing' alternative must either, like the war, include the eventual risk of civil war or, on the assumption that the people would not be able to overthrow the regime, include a close to endless litany of acts of killing, torture, terror and oppression that, at some point, would amount to more harm than would likely occur in a civil war. Either way, the proportionality calculation is not negatively affected if we recognize the ongoing risk of civil war.

Consider next the major relevant good of enabling the people to both engage in a collective process of self-determination and establish a rule-of-law that respects human rights. The post-war US help in facilitating elections and in establishing a constitution gives more hope for realizing these goods than if the invasion had not taken place. If, without the US invasion, the people themselves had somehow managed to overthrow the regime, the chances of that regime being replaced with another totalitarian regime or repressive fundamentalist theocracy would be greater than they are under the US occupation. Furthermore, the war provided the opportunity to realize the above goods years and probably decades sooner than if nothing had been done — a benefit that carries substantial value for the people currently living in Iraq and which, therefore, significantly increases the value of relevant goods resulting from the war. In response, some may point to doubts they had (and continue to have) regarding the intentions of the Bush administration. Given, however, the pre- and post-war rhetoric of the Blair and Bush governments, and the scrutiny provided by the international community and the media, it is (and was) reasonable to conclude that the US and British would be 'forced' to move towards more democratic institutions and, ultimately, self-rule.

Thus whether considering harms to civilians and soldiers or the good of enabling the people to engage in a process of self-determination, the US led invasion is on balance substantially better than the alternative of doing nothing. Furthermore, arguably such a conclusion can be made not only post-war, but prospectively as well.[32] Therefore, both prospectively and retrospectively the war meets the proportionality criterion. In making this determination, I have attempted to reason in a way that sidesteps the need to undertake precise calculations of the costs and benefits of the war. However, some may remain unconvinced and still contend, at least retrospectively, that the proportionality issue cannot be decided without such calculations. In reply, I have three comments. First, at minimum my principled reasons for counting the war as proportional puts the onus on those who demand more precise numbers to explain why those numbers are required in the face of my arguments.

Second, the initial burden to provide the detailed calculations, if required, may also rest on the opponents of the war. Whether this is the case will depend on where one thinks the onus to demonstrate proportionality, or a lack thereof, lies. For example, if just war theory carries a presumption against war that extends to proportionality, then the onus will arguably lie on the supporter of the war to reasonably demonstrate the war's proportionality. However, if there is no such presumption against war, or if that presumption does not extend to the proportionality criterion, then the burden to determine the war's proportionality arguably lies at least as much on opponents of the war as the supporters. For example, in describing the proportionality requirement many contend that the war is unjust if the costs entailed are disproportionate to the expected benefits. In the face of the war meeting the other (*ad bellum*) just war criteria, this could be interpreted as requiring the war's opponent to demonstrate that it is disproportionate.[33]

Finally, for those who contend there is a need for detailed numbers, they must face the reality that there are a range of very complex factual and counterfactual issues in just war theory that have yet to be satisfactorily resolved. Until those issues are resolved, if they can be, any requirement to provide relevant hard numbers in most wars, including the war in Iraq, may well have to remain unanswered.

## Summary

In summary, I have argued that even if we accept the central claims of the opponents of the war, the resort to war in Iraq was morally justified, both prospectively and retrospectively. I have argued that it meets the sufficient just cause, last resort, and proportionality criteria, and that any failings in terms of legitimate authority and right intention do not undermine the morality of the act of resorting to war. In fact, we have discovered grounds for questioning the inclusion of the right intention criterion in the set of just war criteria.

At the same time it is important to acknowledge that horrific suffering, death and injustices occurred in the war and continue to occur post-war, and also to recognize that grave risks remain. The suffering and death is, of course, to be regretted; the perpetrators of the injustices should, to the extent possible, be punished; and as invaders and occupiers the Americans and the British are obligated to do much to improve the lives of the Iraqis and cooperate with them to help avoid or overcome the future perils they face. Nonetheless, even at this early post-war stage, the morality of resorting to war is clear.

**Postscript**

Since this article was published a number of reports have come out that underline the magnitude of death and violence that the Iraqis have incurred in the aftermath of the US led invasion of Iraq. For example, *The Lancet* recently published a study in which the authors estimate that as of July 2006 there were 654,965 excess deaths as a result of the war.[34] And the UN recently reported that over 34,000 Iraqis were killed in 2006.[35] Given these staggering numbers and the real possibility that large scale violence and killing will continue in the months and years ahead, one may reasonably ask if and how these figures, assuming their accuracy, impact on the morality of US led forces resorting to war.

In writing the original article, I strongly believed (for reasons spelled out in the article) that the most credible debate over the morality of resorting to war in Iraq lay in the debate over the war's proportionality. Given that I still believe this, I suggest the key question is as follows. Does the horrific extent of ongoing violence and killing give us reason to conclude that the resort to war was, retrospectively, not proportionate?

I still contend, for the reasons argued in the original article, that the answer to this question will crucially turn on whether the level of post-invasion violence is worse than the level of violence that one could reasonably expect to have occurred if the invasion had not taken place and, instead, Saddam's regime had, after some uncertain further period of repression, somehow been overthrown or transformed in some other way. On the assumption that this contention is right, I still — even in the face of the horrific violence in Iraq — see no compelling reason to believe that the 'other route' to transformation would have, after some further period of terrible oppression under Saddam and the Ba'ath Party, had a better likelihood of avoiding the level of violence we see today. (For more on why this counterfactual comparison is the appropriate one — and not, for example, a mere comparison of the state of affairs before the war with the state of affairs after the intervention — see my article 'Counterfactuals and the Proportionality Criterion', *Ethics and International Affairs*, 20, 4 (2006).)

However, in opposition to my contention others may assert that other paths would have led to the overthrow or transformation of the Iraqi government in ways that would likely have caused much less civil strife. It is hard to know how one can definitively settle such a debate — a debate that involves a variety of controversial empirical claims and counterfactual assertions. Given this difficulty, let me simply reiterate a point made in the original article, namely that a crucial factor in deciding the morality of the resort to war may well involve determining on whom, and to what extent, the onus lies to demonstrate whether or not the proportionality criterion is satisfied. Making the latter determination is not simply a problem in the current war in Iraq, but also more generally is a significant principled challenge facing just war theorists. Since I see no prospect for a resolution to this nettlesome problem in the near future, I must admit, upon further reflection and in light of the large scale violence, to being less certain about the extent to which, in the context of proportionality, *either side* can make a definitive case that, in retrospect, the proportionality criterion has or has not been adequately satisfied.

Finally, let me use this opportunity to finish with a few additional comments. Firstly, I see no reason to contend that the current magnitude of violence was anything near inevitable. The twists and turns of war, societies, and governments are notoriously difficult to predict. So just as it would have been a mistake, prior to the war, to contend that there would almost certainly be a straightforward transition to a flourishing and fairly liberal democracy in Iraq, it is equally implausible to contend post-invasion that the current level of strife was inevitable and that the coalition leaders should have realized this. The vast majority of the Iraqi people have always desired a better life with security, basic infrastructure, and self-rule. For one to claim that the desire for a better life was, in hindsight, *inevitably* to be thwarted post-invasion is simply not credible. Instead, I still contend that prospectively there was reason to expect, with some significant likelihood, an outcome better than has transpired. (One must also acknowledge that for many Iraqis things are better than under Saddam and that in certain areas of Iraq there are still reasonable expectations of improvement as we move forward.[36]) Based on these observations, it is worth emphasizing that even if, *for argument's sake*, one were to accept (contrary to my view) that the war retrospectively fails the proportionality criterion, it does not follow that those who made the original decision to go to war are, on that basis, morally culpable for making the (prospective) decision to resort to war. (However, any discussion of prospective proportionality must, like retrospective discussions, face the existence of the unresolved 'onus' problem highlighted in the previous paragraph.)

Secondly, even if the resort to war is morally justified, there may well still be substantial room for morally or strategically criticizing *in bello* or *post bellum* actions of the United States and other coalition members. With respect to moral criticisms, there may, of course, be certain *in bello* or *post bellum* actions that are in themselves immoral and for which those responsible deserve moral condemnation and punishment. This must be decided on a case-by-case basis. With respect to strategic criticisms one may also argue that certain *in bello* or *post bellum* actions or strategies have made the situation worse than it otherwise could have been. Such criticism or questioning represents crucial and appropriate follow-up to all the complexity that is inherent in undertaking a war and *post bellum* activities. However, even if such criticism highlights legitimate flaws, this need not entail that those responsible for the flawed strategies have acted in ways that make them deserving of moral condemnation. This would only be the case if there were further evidence of negligence. Again, the possibility of such negligence (or other immoral activities) would have to be explored on a case-by-case basis.

Finally, even if the resort to war was morally justified, this does not entail that the American and British peoples may not have cause to debate or question whether the resources used in war and post-intervention activities could not have been used more effectively elsewhere and without the terrible cost in terms of military lives. With the financial cost of the war being measured in the hundreds of billions of dollars, Americans should reflect upon and ask if that money (based on either prospective or retrospective estimates) would not have been better spent both domestically and internationally in ways that would have improved the plight of the world's poor and suffering, provided better schooling for America's youth, reduced the level of America's growing government debt, and so on. Such a debate is both appropriate and healthy for the simple reason that doing what is morally permissible or morally justifiable is not the same as doing what is best.

## Acknowledgements

My gratitude goes out to Dennis McKerlie, Thomas Hurka, Jeff McMahan, members of the Ethics and Political Philosophy Research Group at the University of Calgary, and readers for *the Journal of Applied Philosophy*, all of whom provided helpful comments on earlier drafts of this paper.

## NOTES

1 Consequently my argument will not speak directly to either those who take a principled pacifist position regarding the morality of war or those who adopt an act utilitarian view of morality — though the discussion will, tangentially, raise moral issues which both the pacifist and utilitarian need to address. The argument could speak to a rule utilitarian who adopts a set of rules regarding war that are sympathetic to those found in the just war tradition.

2 My list focuses on *ad bellum* criteria — those criteria that must be met for the resort to war to be fully justified. In this paper I will not consider *in bello* questions about whether particular acts in the war were morally justified.

3 As part of that process, I will raise questions about how the criteria should be defined and whether, in particular, the right intention criterion should be included in the list of criteria. This should not, however, be viewed as questioning my commitment to the just war tradition. Central to that tradition has been an ongoing debate both about which criteria must be met for a war to be justified and about how to define those criteria. Over time, and at any given time, the list of criteria proposed by just war theorists has varied in important ways. Admittedly, in questioning the relevance of the right intention criterion I am going against a long tradition, but this it is entirely in keeping with the spirit of just war theory. Furthermore, it was in large part my reflecting on the appropriateness of including the right intention criterion that led me to see the importance of writing a paper on the morality of the war in Iraq.

4 Elsewhere (D. Mellow, *A Critique of Just War Theory*, PhD dissertation, The University of Calgary, 2003) I argue that all sufficient just causes are grounded in these two general moral values.

5 Though both the United Nations' *International Covenant on Civil and Political Rights* and the United Nations' *International Covenant on Economic, Social and Cultural Rights* recognize that: 'All peoples have the right of self-determination'.

6 R. Norman, *Ethics, Killing and War* (Cambridge: Cambridge University Press, 1995), p. 153 (bracketed text added, italics in the original).

7 The quotes are found at: http://www.unhchr.ch/huricane/huricane.nsf/0/9792F0662148A0648025674B 00551A95?opendocument. Also see the Human Rights Watch Briefing Paper (January 2003) 'The Iraqi Government Assault on the Marsh Arabs' which also contains additional references to reports made by the Special Rapporteur. The Human Rights Watch Policy Paper (December 2002) 'Justice for Iraq' documents atrocities carried out by the Iraq regime in the 1980s and 1990s.

8 The implausibility, and even the offensiveness, of drawing a stark moral line, *for purposes of humanitarian interventions*, between genocides and something slightly less is highlighted by the recent *Report of the International Commission of Inquiry on Darfur to the United Nations Secretary General* (www.ohchr.org/ english/darfur.htm). The authors of that report conclude that 'no genocidal policy has been pursued and implemented in Darfur by the Government authorities, directly or through the militias under their control . . .'. Yet surely, regardless of the legal implications drawn on the basis of that conclusion, the slaughter and displacement of the people in Darfur is so widespread, grave and systematic that, assuming all the other just war conditions are met, military intervention to stop the slaughter would be permissible. (The authors go on to say that that their conclusion '. . . should not be taken in any way as detracting from the gravity of the crimes perpetrated in that region. International offences such as the crimes against humanity and war crimes that have been committed in Darfur may be no less serious and heinous than genocide'. In contrast with this claim, I contend that if there truly is not a genocide in Darfur, then what is taking place is, while morally less heinous than genocide, still so heinous that it represents a sufficient just cause.)

9 In the broader international community there is clearly growing recognition that humanitarian interventions are justified in cases other than genocides. For example, see the report by the International Commission on Intervention and State Sovereignty (December 2001) *The Responsibility to Protect* (Ottawa:

International Development Research Centre), p. 32, in which the commission contends a just cause exists when there is either or both: (a) *'large scale loss of life, actual or apprehended, with genocidal intent or not, which is the product either of deliberate state action, or state neglect or inability to act, or a failed state situation; or'* (b) *'large scale "ethnic cleansing", actual or apprehended, whether carried out by killing, forced expulsion, acts of terror or rape'.* See also A. Bellamy, 'Motives, outcomes, intent and the legitimacy of humanitarian intervention', *Journal of Military Ethics* 3,3 (2004).

10  The horrific consequences of the Shia uprising in 1991 provide evidence of just how unlikely it is that a domestic uprising could succeed.

11  It is worth noting that I will often make use of domestic analogies to test a claim or principle that I assert. I have found these examples helpful in testing out my own judgements about international issues, and I offer them in the hopes that they will help readers test their judgements. Some may be concerned that such domestic examples differ substantially from international examples. Elsewhere, I have discussed the ways in which those examples do and do not differ from the international cases (Mellow, 2003). For the purposes of this paper, let me simply point out that using examples quite different from the context under discussion to test a principle or claim is well established in the field of applied ethics. Of course once an example is presented, it becomes appropriate to question whether there are any morally relevant differences between the example and the case under consideration. I use the examples in this spirit, and often, after presenting the examples, I attempt to anticipate the differences that a critic may contend are morally relevant. At a minimum, I believe such examples are useful in making progress in thinking ethically, and once presented they shift the onus onto one's critics to explain why they think the example is not morally analogous — thereby entering into a dialogue that is very useful philosophically.

12  M. Walzer, *Just and Unjust Wars*, 2nd edn. (New York: Basic Books, 1992), pp. 87, 89 (bracketed text added).

13  J. McMahan, 'Unjust war in Iraq', Leiter Reports, 2004; http://leiterreports.typepad.com/blog/2004/09/the_moral_case_.html.

14  G. Kavka, 'Was the Gulf War a just war?' *Journal of Social Philosophy* 22,1 (1991).

15  The latter suggestion is found in Augustine's work — see D. Lackey, *The Ethics of War and Peace* (Englewood Cliffs, NJ: Prentice Hall, 1989), p. 32.

16  Mellow 2003, op. cit.

17  See footnote 15.

18  Furthermore, if a third party arrived on the scene — a party that had a good idea of our intervener's mental state — the third party should not prevent the intervener from acting. This is because stopping or preventing the act of rape is the right thing to do, *regardless* of the motivations of the intervener. While admittedly this last suggestion does not necessarily follow from the fact that the third party should not stop the intervener, it does seem to be the most compelling explanation of the fact. Furthermore, even if, in the face of my arguments, one continues to contend that while the intervener should not be stopped, by either the murderer or a third party, the intervener is still acting wrongly (a very odd position) notice that the much of the moral importance of the right intention criterion, and hence reason for its inclusion, has been lost. For surely most people, in pointing to violations of the right intention criterion are not merely making assertions about the wrongness of an act, but are contending, on the basis of that violation, that the act (e.g. the resort to war) should not be undertaken. Also see J. Thomson, 'Self-defense', *Philosophy and Public Affairs* 20,4 (1991) where she makes arguments parallel to mine against the '. . . very odd idea . . . that a person's intentions play a role in fixing what he may or may not do' (p. 293).

19  In an excellent article by Fernando Tesón, which was published after my first draft of this paper, he makes important points that support and echo some of what I have said about the right intention criterion (F. Tesón, 'Ending tyranny in Iraq', *Ethics & International Affairs* 19,2 (2005)). Ultimately, however, he contends, contrary to what I have proposed here, that intentions (when properly defined and distinguished from motives) still 'ought to be retained' when characterizing an action (e.g., of resorting to war). To support his position, he considers the example of the Falkland Islands war and, in particular, the role the defeat of Argentina played in replacing the country's illegitimate leaders with democratic institutions. Unlike Iraq, however, Tesón rightly observes we would not, as a result of the liberation of the Argentines, think it appropriate to describe the Falkland Islands war as a humanitarian intervention. According to Tesón, the reason for the difference is one which requires an appeal to intentions, namely that '[w]hile the restoration of democracy and human rights in Argentina was a humanitarian outcome, *neither the motive nor the intention* of Prime Minister Margaret Thatcher included freeing the Argentines. The liberation of Argentina was a relatively remote consequence of the war' (p. 8, italics in the original). I, however, don't

see why we need to appeal to intentions to explain why the Falkland Islands war does not count as a humanitarian intervention. The reason it does not count as a humanitarian intervention, either prospectively or retrospectively, is precisely and simply because the war was so structured that *the liberation of Argentina was a relatively remote consequence of the war.* Full stop. There is no need to invoke the intention of Prime Minister Thatcher. Expressed slightly differently, it is not Margaret Thatcher's intention that determines whether the war was humanitarian, but whether the military action was structured so as to plausibly or directly achieve a humanitarian just cause. In the case of the Falkland Islands war, there was no such structure.

20 I say arguably because some may question whether, in the face of ongoing grave systematic human suffering and injustices, the last resort test even applies (cf. J. McKenna, 'The just war' in J. Rachels (ed.) *Moral Problems*, 3rd edn. (New York: Harper and Row, 1979). Though I will not pursue the point here, I do think the last resort criterion, properly interpreted (Mellow 2003, op. cit.) still applies in such cases.

21 Even though it surely would not have been successful, it is legitimate to criticize the US and British governments for not, prior to the war, more forcefully emphasizing and considering the humanitarian injustices.

22 Interestingly, in the *USA Today* poll when the Iraqis were asked 'Would Saddam Hussein have been removed from power by Iraqis if US/British forces had not taken direct military action?' 89 percent said 'No' and only 4 percent said 'Yes'.

23 Some may also argue that the determination of legitimacy hinges on the issue of whether the Iraqi people supported the invasion. I have dealt with this issue in my discussion of the sufficient just cause criterion.

24 Echoing, in a different context, Judith Jarvis Thomson.

25 It is for reasons similar to these that when turning to the question of proportionality I will not entertain as a relevant harm the possibility that the war undermined respect for international law or international institutions.

26 J. McMahan and R. McKim, 'The just war and the Gulf War', *Canadian Journal of Philosophy* 23,4 (1993).

27 That not all good and bad effects count in the proportionality calculation is compellingly argued for by Thomas Hurka 'Proportionality in the morality of war' *Philosophy and Public Affairs* 33,1 (2005). To give one of his examples, imagine that our nation is in an economic recession and that fighting a war (for a just cause) will lift our nation and the world out of that recession. Hurka says: 'Although the economic benefits of war are real, they surely cannot count toward its proportionality or make an otherwise disproportionate war proportionate'. (p. 40). For discussion of which good and bad effects are relevant see also McMahan and McKim op. cit., and Mellow 2003, op. cit. By claiming that only relevant good and bad effects count in the proportionality calculation, I am not 'stacking the deck' in favour of the war in Iraq. My view of what count as relevant good and bad effects closely parallels that of McMahan who has written in opposition to the war.

28 For further discussion regarding why a people's capacity and right to be self-determining holds substantial value in proportionality calculations see Hurka op. cit., pp. 52–56. Though Hurka is considering the issue in the context of a military aggressor who is threatening a people's right to be self-determining, what he has to say also speaks to the question of what value legitimately attaches to an oppressed people's right and ability to be self-determining.

29 I do, however, recognize the difficulties that one faces in trying to provide a compelling response to the sceptic.

30 The idea of viewing the 'doing nothing' counterfactual as the appropriate baseline comes from Kavka op. cit., though he suggests there are difficulties with this suggestion — difficulties which I resolve elsewhere (Mellow 2003 op. cit.).

31 A point made earlier in the paper when discussing sufficient just cause, in part by demonstrating the ongoing nature of the large-scale human rights violations.

32 It may be important to have determined that the invasion is 'substantially better' than doing nothing, because it may be that the proportionality criterion requires more than mere 'on-balance better'. Though this possibility is not adequately addressed in the just war literature, it seems plausible that the relevant good effects could slightly outweigh the relevant bad effects and yet not satisfy the proportionality criterion. Imagine, for example, that you could militarily stop a mass killing of a million people, but in doing so would kill, as a side-effect, all but one thousand of those people. My intuition, which may be shared by others, is that such an intervention may not satisfy the proportionality criterion. This intuition may reflect the belief that when third party interveners do the killing, even as a side-effect, this is somehow worse than

a ruthless regime doing the killing, something I doubt, or it may reflect the thought that the proportionality criterion is more than an 'on-balance' test. If the latter, there remains the difficult question of the precise extent to which the relevant good effects must exceed the relevant bad effects. I am not sure what to say in this regard, and I suspect that an argument for any sort of precise ratio is not likely to be found. Instead, it is plausible that ultimately there will be a large grey area in which the proportionality of a military intervention is open to dispute and where the only arguments available will involve appeals to (intuitive) considered judgements.

33 I am indebted to David Rodin for the points made in this paragraph.

34 G. Burnham, R. Lafta, S. Doocy and L. Roberts, 'Mortality after the 2003 invasion of Iraq: a cross-sectional cluster sample survey', *The Lancet*, 368 (2006). This article is a follow up to an earlier article: L. Roberts, R. Lafta, R. Garfield, J. Khudhairi and G. Burnham, 'Mortality before and after the 2003 invasion of Iraq: cluster sample survey', *The Lancet*, 364 (2004).

35 *The New York Times*, January 17, 2007.

36 Obviously conditions are shifting fairly quickly in Iraq, but I refer the reader to the following poll carried out by a number of media organizations: http://news.bbc.co.uk/1/hi/world/middle_east/4514414.stm

# 6 Moral Tragedies, Supreme Emergencies and National-Defence

DANIEL STATMAN

## I. Introduction

Consider the following situation: Some group, A, is under a serious, unjustified threat from some other group, B. The only way group A can defend itself is by using lethal force against group B. Alas, the standard conditions for using force in self-defence are not met here, either because this use of force involves the intentional killing of the innocent, or because the harm and death it will cause would far exceed the harm and death which its use would prevent, thereby violating the proportionality condition. What should group A do? Ought it to avoid the use of force even if this means yielding to an aggressive, evil power? I think most people would resist this conclusion, yet given the violation of essential conditions for self-defence, this resistance is hard to justify.

The aim of this paper is to point to an interesting yet unnoticed move made by some philosophers to find a way out of this problem, a move which relies on construing the situation at hand as a *tragic dilemma*. Accordingly, I shall call the solution they offer to the above predicament, the 'Tragedy Solution'. It is utilized to help solve two disturbing problems, that of supreme emergencies, and that of national-defence wars. I am not suggesting that the philosophers in question explicitly make this argument, but that it is the argument that they would have made had their arguments been cast in the most plausible light given their broader philosophical commitments. This is close to saying that the Tragedy Solution is the most charitable reading of a certain argument made by these philosophers.[1]

I begin with a discussion of supreme emergencies, which I use as my primary illustration of the Tragedy Solution. I then turn to discuss its application to the problem of national-defence wars. In both contexts, I show that the proposed solution does not work.

## II. The Tragedy of Supreme Emergencies

Almost everybody agrees that there are moral limits to what might be done in the waging of war. In particular, there is general consensus that a distinction between combatants and noncombatants must be maintained. Yet, many also agree that if the threat from the enemy is grave enough, then most, if not all, rules of war can be broken. Even some moral philosophers hold this view, notably Michael Walzer, who, in *Just and Unjust Wars*, refers to such cases as cases of 'supreme emergency'.[2] Walzer's well-known example of such an emergency is the situation of the UK in the days of the *Blitz* during World War II, when the bombing of German cities seemed to be the only available way to stop, or at least to slow down, the Nazi aggression. On Walzer's view, because in those days (though not later in the war) the situation was one of supreme emergency, Churchill was justified in ordering such bombing in spite of the fact that it involved a direct and intentional attack on the innocent. Let us call the assumed permission to carry out such attacks, or, more generally, to use measures that would be forbidden in non-emergency situations, 'Special Permissions'.

In another paper, I discuss at length possible justifications for such permissions, and show how problematic they are.[3] I argue there that the best route to take in order to establish a moral justification for Special Permissions is based on a collectivist ethics, but that this ethics has serious flaws that make it quite unattractive. It is, thus, not surprising to find philosophers trying an altogether different route, namely, an attempt to justify the use of Special Permissions *without presuming to show that such use is in itself morally justified*. The Tragedy Solution is part of this attempt.

To get an initial grasp of the kind of solution under discussion, let me start with the way it is formulated by Brian Orend.[4] According to Orend, Walzer's doctrine of supreme emergencies is either a form of consequentialism ('only a matter of arithmetic'),[5] or a form of moral paradox ('In supreme emergencies, our moral judgments are doubled . . . we say yes *and* no, right *and* wrong')[6] neither of which is consistent with other doctrines held by Walzer. A different way of understanding such situations is needed, and here is what Orend proposes:

> Supreme emergencies, I believe, are not instances of genuine paradox. They are, rather, cases of moral tragedy. A moral tragedy occurs when, all things considered, every viable option one is confronted with involves a serious moral violation. In a supreme emergency, this is clear: if one violates *jus in bello*, one commits murder and perhaps other crimes. On the other hand, if one does not violate *jus in bello*, one's omissions may contribute causally to the death and devastation of one's people at the hands of a brutal, rights-violating aggressor.[7]

Perceiving supreme emergencies as cases of moral tragedy implies that, in such cases, one faces a 'moral blind alley' (ibid.), with nowhere to turn, and no way to stay morally clean. But precisely because the alley is blind, i.e. all options are morally unacceptable, one cannot be blamed for choosing one option (committing murder or other crimes) over the other (negatively contributing to the death of one's own people and the devastation of one's own land), because such choice does not amount to neglecting the right course of action. The Tragedy Solution, then, offers the following argument: (1) In moral tragedies, the agent cannot be blamed for any course of action she chooses, because no respectable course of action is available; (2) Supreme emergencies are cases of moral tragedy; (3) Hence, in supreme emergencies, the political and military agents cannot be blamed for killing the innocent, or for committing other problematic actions against the enemy (given that such actions are necessary for victory). On Orend's view, then, Walzer might have been right in assuming that Churchill's bombing of German cities was immune to moral reproach, but for reasons different to those he mentioned. The immunity is not the result of some kind of utilitarian calculus, but an implication from the tragic nature of the situation.

The attraction of the Tragedy Solution can easily be appreciated. It allows you to have your cake and eat it too: On the one hand, you can fully maintain the conviction that innocent human beings ought never to be directly targeted. On the other, you are allowed to kill many innocent people, if necessary, to prevent the nightmare of 'entire peoples being enslaved and massacred'.[8]

In reconstructing Orend's argument, I have ascribed to him the view that killing the innocent in supreme emergencies is *permissible*. But, in fact, Orend does not use this language, but rather says that such killing is *excusable*. In supreme emergencies, he says, a just state will commit actions which are morally wrong in order to save itself: 'While wrong, such actions may nevertheless be excused on grounds of extreme duress'.[9] But if all Orend had in mind was an *excuse*, his argument would offer no solution to the problem at hand. As Hare emphasizes throughout his moral writings, a moral question arises when one must choose between two or more options, because if a person is forced to do something, no such question arises. The situation of politicians and generals in supreme emergencies is definitely not one in which they can be said to be *forced* to choose the option of killing the innocent, in such a way that a moral question does not arise at all for them. As they can choose, they ought to prefer the morally better option, and to do that, they need some kind of justification, not excuse. To say that an excuse is granted to some action concedes that the action is wrong, but if it is wrong, it cannot be approved of prospectively. Thus, even if Orend is right in arguing that supreme emergencies provide an excuse for killing the innocent, if they provide no justification, he should speak unequivocally against such killing. But he doesn't.

Moreover, as pointed out by Rodin, duress is not generally thought to provide a legal or moral excuse for wrongful *killing*. When threatened with death, the moral and legal expectation is that one would die rather than commit a wrongful act of killing.[10] Finally, the idea of duress in supreme emergencies is, in any case, distinct from and independent of the idea of tragedy. Orend might be right in suggesting that a state would be excused for the use of immoral measures to save itself, but that doesn't presuppose that all of the options faced by the state were wrong. Immoral behaviour, such as killing somebody in order to harvest his heart, might be excused as 'extreme duress' even when, in the circumstances, a perfectly acceptable moral option is available (not killing that somebody and dying of heart problems).[11]

This ambiguity between justification (or permission) and excuse can be found in all the writers discussed here. On my reinterpretation of their views, they want the Tragedy Solution to provide more than a mere excuse to do otherwise wrongful actions, such as killing the innocent. They want it to ground an *ex ante* permission for doing so. If some politician came to them and asked whether it was morally okay to kill the innocent in supreme emergencies, or go to a national-defence war, their answer wouldn't be, 'No, overall this is morally not permissible, hence *don't do it* (though *post factum* you might be excused, under duress, from reproach or punishment)', but rather something like, 'It is indeed awful to do such and such. Nevertheless, in the circumstances, it is morally okay for you to do so'.

However, the Tragedy Solution cannot provide the goods expected from it. To see its main defect, let me start with a general point about moral tragedies. Such tragedies occur, assumes Orend, when an agent has no acceptable moral route to take, when all available options are wrong. But according to a central position in the philosophical debate about moral dilemmas, dilemmas might be real and tragic, even when one option is morally preferable to the other.[12] Raz, for instance, who agrees that moral dilemmas are cases of 'choice between evils',[13] contends that, nonetheless, in many dilemmas, the choice is 'between a lesser and a greater evil'.[14] The point of saying that such a situation represents a real dilemma is to emphasize that the intrinsically evil character of the lesser evil option is not erased by the overall judgment that, in the circumstances, it should be preferred over the other (the greater evil) option. An action may be both justified and intrinsically bad.[15] But if that is so, then the claim that some choice represents a moral dilemma, or a moral tragedy, says nothing about how it should be solved, hence in itself it can provide no excuse, and definitely no justification, for preferring one option above the other. This means that premise (1) of the Tragedy Solution argument is false. The fact that all available options are morally wrong does not mean that they are *equally* wrong, and when they are not, then the agent *is* culpable for failing to choose the one that is less wrong.

Elsewhere I have shown that it is quite rare to find a dilemma where the options are morally equal in a way that blocks in advance criticism of the agent for failing to take the morally preferred (=less unacceptable) path.[16] At any rate, the claim that two options are *equally* wrong requires additional evidence beyond the evidence required to claim that they are both *wrong*. To assume that if A and B are wrong they are necessarily equally so is to assume that wrongness is an all-or-nothing notion, which allows for no degrees. But that is a misconception. An action might be more or less wrong, and more or less right, depending on the nature and significance of the values violated or promoted.

The upshot of these considerations is that the fact that a situation is a moral tragedy does not mean that the agent cannot be advised to take one course of action rather than the other, or that he cannot be criticized *post factum* for failing to do so. The implications for the problem of supreme emergencies are clear. Even if supreme emergencies are moral tragedies, in the sense of offering no morally acceptable option, one option, e.g. killing the innocent might still be morally worse than the other, with the implication that such killing would be overall *forbidden* in the circumstances — contrary to what Orend wanted to establish.

Furthermore, Orend assumes a non-consequentialist ethics, which means that he accepts the existence of deontological constraints. Once such constraints are assumed, they imply that the onus is on the shoulders of those who wish to violate them, and if the onus cannot be met, then the default position is to regard these constraints as binding. Because of its agent-relative nature, a deontological position is essentially biased towards the avoidance of wrongful acts, particularly acts involving killing the innocent, over the prevention of unwanted results stemming from the acts of others, or from nature. Hence, granted that both options in supreme emergencies are evil, i.e. the situation is tragic, a non-consequentialist would be expected to stick to his or her principles and refrain from killing the innocent, unless overwhelming reasons could justify defying them, reasons that Orend fails to produce.

Orend probably sensed that the idea of tragedy is insufficient to do the required work in the argument, hence he briefly points to another direction.[17] He says that we should understand supreme emergencies 'as a case where we exit the moral realm and enter the harsh Hobbesian realm of pure survival'. But that is far too permissive, and could easily be applied to ordinary wars too. In fact, it comes very close to the moral realist view on wars, according to which wars lie outside the realm of morality. Moreover, if supreme emergencies mark an 'exit' from the moral realm, then in this new (or old) territory, neither justification nor excuse are in place, because moral distinctions do not hold 'out there' (see chapter 14 of the *Leviathan*), and certainly there is no possibility of moral *tragedy*.

Having explained the structure and motivation of the Tragedy Solution, we can now realize that it is endorsed by other writers too. A rather surprising instance is Nagel's by now classic article, 'War and massacre', first published in 1972.[18] It is surprising because Nagel's main purpose in this paper is to establish the validity of moral constraints, and show that 'there is a moral basis for the rules of war',[19] and, indeed, the article earned a reputation as a powerful defence of such constraints. Against what Nagel saw as the apathetic reaction to the atrocities committed in Vietnam by the USA, he seeks to put down a clear argument for the morality of warfare, based neither on pragmatic considerations nor on utilitarian calculations. Problematic acts, such as murder and torture, says Nagel:

> . . . are not just supposed to require unusually strong justification. They are supposed *never* to be done, because no quantity of resulting benefit is thought capable of justifying such treatment of a person.[20]

Defending oneself by targeting the wives or children of one's enemy is no less than 'Hiroshima on a smaller scale',[21] and is therefore strictly forbidden.

However, in the last two pages of the paper, Nagel makes a rather unexpected move. He refers to situations of 'deadly threat, particularly where a weaker party is threatened with annihilation or enslavement by a stronger one'. In such situations, which are precisely those that Walzer has in mind when talking about supreme emergencies, Nagel argues that the dilemma between the duty not to kill the innocent and the duty to protect a collective from enslavement or annihilation is irresolvable:

> We must face the pessimistic alternative that these two forms of moral intuition are not capable of being brought together into a single, coherent moral system, and that the world can present us with situations in which there is no honorable or moral course for a man to take, no course free of guilt and responsibility for evil.[22]

The reality of tragic moral dilemmas, then, shows how it might be acceptable to violate binding deontological constraints in supreme emergencies. As the dilemma under discussion is irresolvable, it makes no (moral) difference which horn is taken by the political and military leaders, that of committing atrocities, or that of refraining from them. If they choose to keep their hands clean, that's okay. If they choose to dirty them by the slaughter of thousands, that's okay too.

Nagel is more explicit than Orend about the irresolvability of the dilemma, yet, he, too, makes no serious effort to establish it. At one point he seems to argue that what constitutes the irresolvability is the fact that the conflicting intuitions are so different that they 'are not capable of being brought together into a single, coherent moral system'.[23] That would fit Nagel's well-known view about the 'fragmentation of value', according to which the sources of value are plural, hence conflicts between fundamentally different values are not resolvable.[24] But Nagel surely doesn't subscribe to the view that incommensurability implies complete incomparability, because had he done so, he wouldn't have restricted the discussion to conflicts between the prohibition against acts like murder and torture and a 'very high' utilitarian cost. He would have said that *any* conflict between utilitarian gain and deontological commitments is irresolvable. But, of course, he doesn't, hence the doctrine at hand must be far more sensitive to the particularities of each situation in order to determine whether it is solvable or not. As Dworkin often reminds us, the claim that a dilemma is irresolvable is a positive claim that needs evidence to support it, no less than saying that it has such and such a solution.

Furthermore, given that such situations tend to be vague and ambiguous with respect to both their factual and their moral elements, one would have thought that the safest moral advice is: Do no harm. As I said earlier, to take seriously the agent-relative perspective means giving priority to the avoidance of evil actions over carrying out good ones, such as acts of rescue.

To this Nagel might reply by saying that though refraining from murder and torture are almost always mandatory, when the 'utilitarian cost' of such a restraint is too high, it overrides the former obligation. But, first, if that's the case, then the idea of a moral blind alley plays no role in establishing the permission to murder and torture. If the existence of the entire human race depended on the killing of one innocent person, then the dilemma *would* be solvable, i.e. to kill the innocent person. Second, though Nagel does at times depict the relevant conflict as one between deontological constraints and utilitarian gain, when he illustrates his general point he refers to a case in which 'a weaker party is threatened with annihilation or enslavement by a stronger one'.[25] I take it for granted that on his view (as on Walzer's), the right of the weaker party to defend itself from 'annihilation or enslavement' does not depend on such defence passing the utilitarian test. Moreover, Nagel might allow the weaker party to defend itself even if the deaths and damage it would be forced to bring about would be *greater* than those it would suffer if it refused to violate deontological constraints. As I show elsewhere,[26] the framework assumed here is not that of the lesser evil, but that of self-defence. But the right of self-defence is of course limited, particularly insofar as it concerns innocent bystanders. In the present context, the question is how it could be permissible for some collective to save itself by killing thousands of human beings who are neither materially nor morally responsible for the grave threat against it, and, in that sense, are just like innocent bystanders. Nagel's ideas about tragic conflict and about the fragmentation of value fall short of providing any satisfactory answer to this question.

To sum up: In supreme emergencies, when collectives stand with their backs to the wall, many are inclined to accept Walzer's advice 'to do whatever is military necessary to avoid the disaster',[27] including the taking of many innocent lives. This permission is very hard to square with our fundamental moral doctrines; hence the following line of argument suggests itself:

'True, ultimately such killing cannot be morally justified. But this is a tragic situation, in which *whatever* one does, one would be doing wrong. Hence, it makes no moral difference whether one chooses one option or the other, and one cannot be *condemned* for choosing the option of killing the innocent over that of refraining from doing so and letting the bad guys triumph'.

I tried to show that this line of argument fails. First, that a choice is (morally) tragic, in the sense that all the options it confronts are wrong, does not entail that all options are *equally* wrong, hence does not in itself license the option of murder and torture.

Second, given a situation in which a weak collective is threatened by a stronger one, the appropriate normative framework to analyze it is that of self-defence, and within this framework it is even less likely that the dilemma can be presented as one in which all options are equally wrong. Abstaining from killing an innocent person, at the price of losing my own life, is no doubt a tragedy, but not a *moral* one. That's how a decent person is expected to behave.[28] Why should things be different when it is not myself I'm willing to sacrifice (or not to save), but my group?

## III. The Tragedy Solution and Wars of National Defence

On common-sense morality, as well as on international law, nations have a right to use force in order to defend themselves from threats to their territorial integrity and political sovereignty. They may go to war even if it is not the lives of their individual members that they are defending (there is no threat of genocide), but rather, in some analogical way, the life of the nation. Yet this widespread view has been challenged in the last decade by several writers, notably Richard Norman and, more recently, David Rodin.[29] Their main argument is that the right to wage war in order to protect national sovereignty violates one of the central conditions for the legitimacy of self-defence, i.e. the condition of *proportionality*. Just as, in individual self-defence, the evil brought about by the defensive act must be proportional to the evil prevented, in national-defence too, the evil brought about by the act of war must be proportional to the values defended. However, these writers argue, this is simply not the case. As valuable as territorial integrity and political sovereignty are, they are not valuable enough to justify the large scale killing and the vast destruction involved in waging war. Traditional just war theory, concludes Norman, 'does not succeed in its primary aim. It does not provide a way of rebutting the initial moral presumption against war in any form', and Rodin reaches the same conclusion, asserting 'that the conception of a moral right of national-defence cannot, in the final analysis, be substantiated'.[30]

The logical conclusion from these last statements seems inevitable. They imply that while nations are allowed to take up arms and go to war if the very existence of their members is in danger, namely to defend themselves from some kind of genocide (or a threat of a similar scale), they are not allowed to go to war to defend political sovereignty, a common way of life, or the right to self-determination, the values for which ordinary wars are fought. In other words, the bottom line of the analyses offered by Norman and Rodin should be an endorsement of pacifism.[31]

But it is not. At the very last minute, each of these writers steps back and ratifies, so to say, the just war theory permission to use force in national-defence. And the way they do so is by relying on versions of the Tragedy Solution. Or so I shall argue.

Let us start with Norman. After concluding that just war theory fails to justify ordinary wars, in the last chapter of his book, he then introduces the notion of a moral tragedy, which, following Nagel, he defines as 'a situation where whatever one does, though one may feel morally compelled to do it, it is also wrong'.[32] Like Nagel, Norman believes that our fundamental moral values are incommensurable; hence their relative weight cannot be measured on a single scale of value.[33] Moral tragedies, then, are irresolvable, and this is precisely the category to which the dilemma of whether or not to go to war belongs:

> There will be cases where the only way to resist aggression or oppression will
> be to engage in the wholesale destruction of human lives, but the refusal to
> fight and to kill will be a failure to resist intolerable evil.[34]

In such cases, no right answer exists:

> Some will plausibly say that there is no choice but to fight, as the only alter-
> native is to submit, and that is morally unthinkable. Because the pacifist can
> equally say that the wholesale slaughter which war involves is morally unthink-
> able, we are faced with a tragic conflict of values. The conflict is irresolvable
> in the sense that neither side can be convicted of error.[35]

One cannot fail to see the Tragedy Solution structure here: The dubious moral action,
i.e. going to war, is perceived as morally wrong, but so is the other option. Opting for
the former does not involve any *error*, and does not involve a failure to take the morally
better (or less unacceptable) course of action. It is, as Norman puts it, a 'personal
decision'.

Before I turn to Rodin, let me register two critical comments which apply specifically
to Norman. First, a word on incommensurability. According to Norman, the reason
that the dilemma under discussion is irresolvable is that the options are incommensurable. But, again, I wonder how seriously the notion of incommensurability is taken
here. If incommensurability is taken to imply total incomparability, then Norman
would be committed to the position that regardless of the stakes at both sides, one can
never make a rational decision in a dilemma between fighting or not fighting, because
any such options would be incommensurable. That would imply that however we play
with the stakes — raising them higher on the one side and lowering them on the other
— the same answer would be given. But that is unreasonable. Surely the worse the
expected evil from the aggressor, the stronger the reason to prefer the path of war. If
the expected evil is massacre and enslavement, then the justification for war is far
stronger than if the expected evil is mere loss of territory. Similarly, such justification
depends on the expected losses incurred by war: The fewer the human beings expected
to be killed, the more tolerable the option of war seems. If Norman really believed
that incommensurable options could not be compared, that would lead to permissive
implications of a kind he would never accept. If there were no way of comparing killing
human beings and yielding to evil, then even if the evil is minor, and the killing massive,
the killing might still be all right, which runs against the spirit of his entire book.

It seems that Norman implicitly acknowledges this point, because when he describes
the dilemma at hand, he assigns to one side of the scales 'the wholesale destruction of
human lives', while to the other 'a failure to resist *intolerable evil*' (italics added). The
problem is that the detailed argument Norman develops in chapter four of his book
strongly undermines this last assumption by showing that the life of a political community is not, in its own right, so valuable as to justify killing in its defence. The loss
of political sovereignty, so he argued, is no doubt an evil, but not an *intolerable* one that
could compete successfully with the *really* intolerable evil of the wholesale killing
involved in war.

A different argument suggested by Norman to justify going to war despite the
assumed defects of just war theory is based on the idea that one is allowed not to take
the morally preferred course of action if such an action constitutes an attack on one's

*integrity*. Norman makes this point rather briefly saying that for some people to submit 'would be to abandon one's deepest moral convictions, those convictions which are a precondition for making any moral choices at all'.[36] In a footnote, he refers to Williams's famous discussion of integrity in his criticism of utilitarianism, where Williams argues that to avoid an attack on one's integrity, one is allowed not to carry out the preferred moral action (not to kill the one Indian in order to save the nineteen). But even if this view is granted, I doubt whether it can help Norman in the present context. A central point in Williams's account of integrity is the distinction between what one *does* and what one merely *lets happen*. Norman, too, emphasizes this point, arguing that actions play a much stronger role than omissions in our sense of what we are, and that there is 'a deep connection between agency and identity'.[37] This means that integrity is typically violated when an agent is required to *act* contrary to his basic convictions, like Jim killing the innocent person, not when he is required to let some evil happen, like Jim standing by while Pedro kills the twenty. The problem is that in the present context, namely, going to war, what Norman presents as 'abandoning one's deepest moral convictions' is not an action like killing innocent people, but rather an omission, namely, *not* fighting against an aggressive country, thereby letting the enemy win the day. The analogue to Williams's Jim in the international arena would be someone who refuses to dirty his hands by participating in the wholesale destruction of human life, in spite of his assumed negative responsibility to prevent evil. Therefore, in Norman's own terms, the value of integrity seems to support, rather than limit, the pacifist conclusion of the argument.

I turn now to Rodin. As mentioned above, Rodin's main thesis is the repudiation of the category of national defence as a legitimate moral category. And the basic lesson he draws from this thesis is that our traditional conceptions of international law and international ethics need to be fundamentally re-thought. As Rodin himself notes, that may sound like a messianic expectation. What are we to do in the meantime? Must we refrain from using military force in the face of aggressions threatening our collectives? Rodin refuses to answer in the affirmative to this last question as the reader would expect, and, instead, in the last two pages of his book, he argues that the situation presents us with a 'terrible dilemma'. On the one hand, fighting a war of national defence is 'deeply problematic'. On the other, failing to resist aggression is 'morally unacceptable', probably because of a 'consequentialist concern for the costs of not resisting aggression'.[38] The costs are so appallingly high, especially in case of aggressors like Nazi Germany or Stalinist Russia, that one may come to the conclusion that one simply *must* fight, that there is 'no choice'.

But focusing on leaders like Hitler and Stalin is misleading in the present context, as the threat they posed was a threat to the life, dignity and freedom of many *individuals*, hence self-defence against Hitler and Stalin could have been justified on the basis of *individual* self-defence. The whole point of Rodin's project is to show that national defence cannot be reduced to a collective application of personal rights of self-defence, but rather seeks to defend the existence of a *nation* — its way of life, sovereignty, and autonomy. And the conclusion he arrives at is that these values are not as important as they are thought to be. Hence, to conclude the discussion by saying that the cost of not defending them by force is 'appallingly high' is inconsistent.

This brings me to the last point I would like to raise against the Tragedy Solution to the problem of national defence. Both Norman and Rodin draw an analogy between the idea of a right to national defence and that of individual self-defence. With respect to the latter right, it is obvious that if the conditions for its application are not met, then the potential victim is simply forbidden to use force in order to defend him- or herself, even if that means suffering great harm or death. Thus, if the only way to save my life is to kill an innocent bystander, I should die and not kill the person.[39] Similarly with the condition of proportionality: Taking this condition seriously means that even if my attacker is morally culpable, if the threat is not that severe, and if the only way to defend myself from it is by killing the aggressor, I am not allowed to do so, even if that means suffering painful harm or offence. This distribution of harm looks unfair — why should *I* suffer rather than the aggressor? — and indeed it has led some thinkers to cast doubt on the very validity of the proportionality condition.[40] But as both Norman and Rodin accept it,[41] these doubts can be put aside in the present context. My point is that once they accept this condition *and* believe that it is not fulfilled in the case of wars of national defence, then, just as with individual self-defence, they should conclude that the attacked nation has no choice but to suffer the harm incurred by the aggressive country.

What does such suffering have to do with *moral tragedy*? That an individual suffers because the proportionality condition prevents her from killing the aggressor is unjust and distressing, though to describe it as a tragedy would probably be an exaggeration (if it were a tragedy, then the proportionality condition probably would be met). In any case, there is no *moral* tragedy here because the victim violated no moral principle by not killing the aggressor.[42] The same holds true for the defence of nations. *If* the price of defending the nation from an aggressive attack exceeds the worth of the values under threat, as both Norman and Rodin argue, then the attacked nation has no choice but to give up the use of military force, which, in reality, almost necessarily means surrender to the aggressive side. As such surrender will have a negative effect on the lives of millions, the term 'tragedy' seems more appropriate here than it did in the context of individuals. Still, there is no *moral* tragedy, for exactly the same reason: Collectives are not at moral fault for refusing to go to war in cases where doing so is incompatible with the conditions of self-defence. In such cases, they have no other moral choice than to surrender (or, at any rate, to avoid *violent* resistance). If just war theory fails in justifying wars of national defence, pacifism is inevitable. The Tragedy Solution is, then, no solution to the problem of national-defence, just as it is not a solution to the problem of supreme emergencies. Whether or not there is some other escape route from pacifism, or from passivity in the face of genocide, is a question that is beyond the scope of the present paper.[43]

### Acknowledgements

I am very grateful to Colleen Murphy, David Rodin and Saul Smilansky for helpful comments on earlier drafts of this paper.

### NOTES

1  I'm indebted to David Rodin for his insistence and assistance in clarifying this methodological point.

2  M. Walzer, *Just and Unjust Wars* (New York: Basic Books, 1977), chapter 16, and, more recently, his chapter on 'Emergency ethics' in M. Walzer, *Arguing About War* (New Haven, CT: Yale University Press,

2004). See also John Rawls, *The Law of Peoples* (Cambridge, MA: Harvard University Press, 1999), pp. 98–99.

3 D. Statman, 'Supreme emergencies revisited', *Ethics* 117 (2006): 58–79.

4 B. Orend, 'Just and lawful conduct in war: Reflections on Michael Walzer', *Law and Philosophy* 20 (2000): 1–30. See also his 'Is there a supreme emergency exemption?' in M. Evans (ed.) *Just War Theory: A Reappraisal* (Edinburgh: Edinburgh University Press, 2005).

5 Walzer op. cit., p. 254.

6 Op. cit., p. 326.

7 Orend op. cit. p. 20.

8 Walzer op. cit., p. 257.

9 *Ibid.*

10 D. Rodin, *War and Self-Defense* (Oxford: Oxford University Press, 2002), p. 171.

11 I am assuming that by refraining from killing an innocent person in order to save my life (e.g. by using his heart), I am not making even a minimal *moral* concession, neglecting, as it were, the moral obligation I have to save my *own* life.

12 I'm assuming there are only two options, in accordance with the etymology of 'dilemma', though this, of course, is not necessarily so.

13 J. Raz, *The Morality of Freedom* (Oxford: Clarendon Press, 1986), p. 359.

14 Op. cit., p. 365.

15 Op. cit., p. 405.

16 See chapter 3 of my *Moral Dilemmas* (Amsterdam: Rodopi, 1995). The problem of irresolvable dilemmas in moral philosophy is analogous to that of hard cases (or 'ties' in Ronald Dworkin's terminology) in legal philosophy. For a systematic comparison of these two problems, see D. Statman, 'Hard cases and moral dilemmas', *Law and Philosophy* 15 (1996): 117–148.

17 Orend op. cit., p. 29.

18 T. Nagel, 'War and massacre', *Philosophy & Public Affairs*, 1 (1972); reprinted in T. Nagel, *Mortal Questions* (New York: Cambridge University Press, 1979), ch. 5. All references are to this latter source.

19 Op. cit., p. 53.

20 Op. cit., p. 73.

21 Op. cit., p. 69.

22 Op. cit., pp. 73–74.

23 Op. cit., p. 73.

24 T. Nagel, 'The fragmentation of value', in *Mortal Questions*, ch. 9, esp. p. 134.

25 Op. cit., p. 73.

26 'Supreme emergencies revisited', op. cit., section II.

27 Walzer (2004) op. cit., p. 40.

28 It should come as no surprise to find that some version of the Tragedy Solution would become attractive within the context of individual self-defence too, as a way of accounting for the assumed permission to kill an innocent attacker. See Y. Benbaji, 'Culpable bystanders, innocent threats and the ethics of self defense', *Canadian Journal of Philosophy* 35 (2005): 582–622.

29 R. Norman, *Ethics, Killing and War* (Cambridge: Cambridge University Press, 1995); Rodin op. cit.

30 Norman op. cit., p. 206; Rodin op. cit., p. 196.

31 See Norman op. cit., p. 207 ('The failure both of utilitarian arguments and of "just war" arguments seems to be pushing us in the direction of a pacifist conclusion') and Rodin op. cit., p. 163 ('It might be supposed that the only conclusion we can draw from this result will be a form of pacifism').

32 Norman op. cit., p. 223.

33 Op. cit., p. 226.

34 Op. cit., p. 223.

35 Op. cit., p. 230.

36 Op. cit., p. 219.

37 Op. cit., p. 91.

38 Rodin op. cit., pp. 198–9.

39 For those philosophers who believe that innocent attackers (always, or in some cases) have the same moral status as innocent bystanders (e.g. McMahan, Otsuka and Rodin), this requirement would apply to them too, namely: If the only way to save my life is by killing an innocent attacker, I have no (moral) choice but to let the innocent attacker kill me.

40  See esp. L. Alexander, 'The doomsday machine: punishment, proportionality and prevention', *Monist*, 63 (1980): 199–227, and idem. 'Self-defense, punishment, and proportionality', *Law and Philosophy*, 10 (1991): 323–328.

41  Norman op. cit., pp. 118–119, 30–131; Rodin op. cit., pp. 40–48 and 124 ('defensive rights are governed by an intrinsic limitation of proportionality').

42  The victim's situation here is different from that of a third party, who might be said to have a *moral* duty to intervene in order to prevent an immoral attack. This raises a problematic self-other asymmetry which I cannot discuss here. See M. Slote, *From Morality to Virtue* (New York: Oxford University Press, 1992), pp. 39–44.

43  For a recent potential solution, see S. Smilansky, 'Some thoughts on terrorism, moral complaint, and the self-reflexive and relational nature of morality', *Philosophia* 34 (2006): 65–74, who explores the idea that those who use terror cannot complain when terror is used against them, hence nations that use (or are about to use) terror against some other nation or collective cannot complain when this other group (or a third party) utilizes Special Permissions in self-defence. While this idea might help with supreme emergencies, it doesn't seem to offer any rescue with regard to national-defensive wars. A state that violated the political sovereignty of another state might be said to have thereby 'invited' a similar violation of its own sovereignty, but it cannot be said to have 'invited' the wholesale killing of war, hence it has not lost its right to complain about such killing.

# 7 Assassination and Targeted Killing: Law Enforcement, Execution or Self-Defence?

MICHAEL L. GROSS

Since the resumption of fighting between Israel and the Palestinians in 2000, Israel's policy of targeted killings has met with considerable controversy. At first blush this is odd, as targeted killings seem to reflect nothing more than the inevitable death of combatants during armed conflict. Why then all the fuss, particularly as the targets are terrorists?

Paradoxically, targeting terrorists, that is, those who egregiously violate humanitarian law and wantonly murder civilians, complicates the conceptual framework that justifies killing during war and distinguishes it from murder. As observers evaluate the merits of targeted killing and assassination, they find it difficult to categorize the actors and their actions clearly. Are targets of assassination ordinary soldiers, war criminals or illegal combatants? Do perpetrators of assassination seek retribution, deterrence, interdiction or pre-emption? Are targeted killings acts of self-defence or extra-judicial execution?

Answering these questions depends upon which of the two paradigms that justify lethal force — war or law enforcement — we choose to analyze targeted killing. The conventions of war permit combatants to use lethal force against enemy soldiers with relatively few restrictions. Law enforcement, on the other hand, permits police officers to employ lethal force against suspected criminals but remains tightly circumscribed. Police officers may kill in self-defence in unusually threatening and dangerous circumstances, but they may not otherwise harm a criminal in the absence of due process. Once we focus upon the criminal dimension of terrorism, the paradigm shifts from war to law enforcement and with it to the restriction that the latter places upon using lethal force. Which paradigm, if either, applies? The very fact that we ask this and other questions suggests that targeted killings pose special problems that set the practice apart from 'ordinary' killing during wartime.

What, exactly, is a targeted killing or assassination? By most accounts, targeted killings consist of, first, compiling lists of certain individuals who comprise specific threats and second, killing them when the opportunity presents itself during armed conflict. I will therefore refer to assassination and targeted killings as 'named killing'. The targets are usually terrorists, that is, those who operate at the behest of known terrorist organizations. Few suggest targeting or naming ordinary combatants. Nevertheless, named killings do not occur in any context other than war. Most often, these are non-conventional wars that do not necessarily signify an armed conflict between two or more nation states but, instead, comprise hostilities between state and sub-state actors. Are named killings justified?

Answering this question largely depends upon how one views the status of terrorists, the nature of the reigning paradigm, and the conditions that belligerents must meet before undertaking a named killing. At one extreme, many human rights groups maintain that terrorists do not enjoy combatant status. 'Armed Palestinians are not combatants according to any known legal definition', writes Yael Stein, of B'tselem, The Israeli Information Center for Human Rights in the Occupied Territories: 'They are civilians — which is the only legal alternative — and can only be attacked for as long as they actively participate in hostilities'.[1] Stein's remarks highlight the problem of shifting identity that plagues the definition of combatant. It seems that terrorists maintain two statuses. On the battlefield, they are something like combatants; off the battlefield and at the time they are targeted they are something like civilians or some other form of noncombatant. I will return to this issue later. For now, it is important to see where the noncombatant paradigm leads. Noncombatants are, generally, innocent of any wrongdoing. The conventions of war and the laws of armed conflict protect them from unnecessary harm or murder, and prohibit belligerents from killing or otherwise harming noncombatants unless necessary and unavoidable to achieve important military goals. These conditions are inherent in the idea of collateral damage and the double effect.[2] However, collateral damage only pertains to harm that befalls *innocent* noncombatants. Terrorists, however ambiguous their status, assume something like combatant status when they take up arms and fight. It stands to reason that they remain non-innocent once they have left the battlefield. From any informed perspective, they are not, as some human rights advocates seem to suggest, civilians who occasionally and only marginally contribute to armed struggle. On the contrary, they maintain their hostile status off the battlefield as they prepare for battle, lay plans, tend to their weapons and maintain their fighting capability. At the same time, there is good cause to suspect that terrorists are guilty of war crimes and criminal activity.

The criminal behaviour of terrorists may then lead officials to invoke the law enforcement paradigm. This demands that states treat terrorists just as they would any heinous criminal, whether an ordinary lawbreaker or war criminal. Law enforcement entails arrest, trial and sentencing, and only permits law enforcement officers to use lethal force when either their lives or the lives of bystanders are in immediate danger.[3] Noncombatant status, however, does not preclude the death penalty in those nations that permit execution, but does demand due process in spite of the difficulties this may entail. Without due process, named killings are nothing but extra-judicial execution and murder. This has led some observers, myself included, to suggest that any party practicing named killing must preserve due process either by maintaining judicial review or by conducting trials *in absentia*.[4] However, as Tamar Meisels points out, neither process is easy to implement with any degree of judicial consistency.[5]

In contrast, the war paradigm carries none of these difficulties or conditions. Combatants are vulnerable regardless of the threat they pose. While they may be shot on sight, combatants nevertheless retain certain rights once they have laid down their arms. Because soldiers are morally innocent, that is, permitted to kill under carefully defined conditions but not guilty of any crime, they may suffer capture and incarceration but only as long as hostilities endure. Once armed conflict ends, prisoners of war no longer pose a material threat and, having committed no crime, are free to return home. Execution or continued imprisonment is not appropriate for combatants unless they have violated the conditions under which they are permitted to harm others either by torturing other combatants, killing them by forbidden means or wantonly taking the lives of noncombatants. In all other cases, solders may kill during armed conflict when it is necessary, proportionate and consistent with the demands of utility. These are the common principles of just war and the conventional laws of armed conflict. Necessity allows nations to exercise armed force only when no other means are feasible to stave off armed aggression. Utility demands that belligerents do not cause more harm that the good they hope to achieve while proportionality limits *excessive* harm so that even important or necessary goals may not be secured at any cost. In most cases, the cost is measured by harm to noncombatants; proportionality rarely pertains to soldiers. Unless nations face a 'supreme emergency' that is, an otherwise unavoidable genocidal threat, there are no grounds for violating the laws of armed conflict.[6] In spite of what human rights activists and indeed, some advocates of named killing maintain, it may make sense to view terrorists as combatants *cum* war criminals. This compels one, however, to extend them the rights and protections both combatants and war criminals enjoy, including protection from named killing.

## The Prohibition of Named Killings

International law does not ban assassination unequivocally, but instead prohibits 'perfidy' or those acts that abuse the protections that the laws of armed conflict guarantee. Common examples of perfidy include attacking from under the protection of a while flag or harming combatants who lay down their arms. These protections are integral to modern warfare and underlie the conventions of surrender. Without them, war would end only in extermination or the proverbial fight to the death. Assassination is perfidious only insofar as it abuses these or similar protections. This may happen when one adversary assassinates another under the guise of safe passage or kills another by employing traitors. While it remains difficult to target terrorists without assistance from local collaborators and traitors, few commentators see this as a serious impediment to named killings and remain convinced, it seems, that armed forces may use informers to track down terrorists just as police do to apprehend criminals. Convincing or not, it is important to see how this argument reverts to the logic of law enforcement, for only the target's suspected *criminal* behaviour justifies recourse to informers and collaborators. The paradigm of conventional war, on the other hand, forbids an appeal to criminal behaviour to justify collaboration. Ascriptions of criminality violate the fundamental assumption that soldiers are innocent, while collaboration can undermine the war convention with treachery.

The utter absence of criminal culpability among combatants led early commentators to forbid named killings during armed conflict in the strongest terms:

> The law of war does not allow proclaiming either an individual belonging to the hostile army, or a citizen, or a subject of the hostile government an outlaw, who may be slain without trial by any captor, any more than the modern law of peace allows such international outlawry; on the contrary, it abhors such outrage. The sternest retaliation should follow the murder committed in consequence of such proclamation, made by whatever authority (Lieber Code, paragraph 148).

While Lieber's prohibition did not make its way into the Geneva Conventions, its spirit lingers on in many military manuals.[7] As written, it is an odd prohibition. The objection to named killing cannot be that enemy soldiers are simply slain without trial, for that is the way of war. Rather, it is the presumption that underlies assassination, namely that specific enemy soldiers are, in some way, guilty of outlawry that rankles Lieber. Named killing places certain soldiers outside the laws regulating human behaviour and armed conflict. Lieber reserves his wrath for the proclamation and the murder that follow. There are no grounds for tagging specific soldiers for murder.

The logic behind Lieber's consternation turns on the innocence of enemy soldiers. Killing only in self-defence, all combatants enjoy the presumption of innocence. Soldiers are not criminals; they do not commit murder in the course of ordinary warfare nor can they be tried or incarcerated for their activities. At best, they are agents of the states whose interests they fight to defend. Even in the worst of cases, when these states are blatant aggressors, soldiers retain a measure of innocence on the assumption that many may have been conscripted or, however misguided, believe in the justice of their cause. Innocence, in this case, is not material. No one is suggesting that soldiers do not represent material threats to others. On the contrary, any uniformed soldier is vulnerable. Their innocence, however, is moral. Soldiers may kill in the service of their state and are therefore innocent of any wrongdoing, a sweeping authorization that international law and all nations endorse.[8] Once we name soldiers for killing, however, we upset this innocence with precisely the argument that Lieber presents. Naming names assigns guilt and, as Lieber suggests, proclaims soldiers outlaws. In doing so, named killing places war itself beyond convention. If one side can declare another's soldiers outside the law, then others are free to follow suit. The war convention disintegrates, and armed conflict is no longer amenable to Lieber's effort to regulate war by the force of enlightened principles of reason. Named killings, in other words, attack the Enlightenment project at its base. Does modern day terror alter this conclusion?

## Permitting Named Killings in Times of Terror

Agreeing that the conventions of war prohibit named killing in principle, Daniel Statman argues that the prohibition no longer matters when one side employs terror:

> With targeted killings, human beings are killed not simply because they are 'the enemy', but because they bear special responsibility or play a special role in the enemy's aggression. This is particularly true in wars against terrorism, where those targeted are usually personally responsible for atrocities committed against the lives of innocent civilians.[9]

Statman defeats Lieber's argument but only at the price of imputing criminal responsibility. Lieber forbids combatants from naming other soldiers as outlaws solely because they are enemy soldiers, a presumption that is central to the laws of armed conflict. Statman circumvents Lieber's concerns when he declares that certain combatants are 'personally responsible for atrocities' and therefore subject to special denunciation. This claim is not controversial. Parties to an armed conflict (and, indeed, any nation) may always charge specific combatants with war crimes if they egregiously violate the conventions of war. In doing so, however, the reigning paradigm returns to law enforcement and, with it, the requirement of due process that governs the prosecution of any war criminal.[10] Inevitably, the desire to contain terrorists by targeted killings poses an intractable dilemma for international law. As ordinary combatants, terrorists are as vulnerable as any other is; as criminals, however, they gain special protections that make it *more* difficult to harm or kill them. Finding a solution will require us to abandon one paradigm or the other.

Interestingly, Israel went through a paradigm shift of its own since the beginning of the current round of fighting. Initially, officials appealed to law enforcement as they considered terrorists on par with suspected, dangerous criminals. While they preferred to arrest and try terrorists, operational difficulties often made arrest difficult and dangerous. With their lives threatened, law enforcement officers (in this case, special forces soldiers) were free to open fire and kill those they ostensibly came to arrest. In this vein, Israel made it clear that its armed forces would only employ lethal force when terrorists either threatened the lives of arresting soldiers or were caught planting a 'ticking bomb' thereby compelling troops to use lethal force to prevent harm to others. The law enforcement paradigm permits lethal force in both cases. However, when it became clear that this *modus operandi* did not match the facts on the ground, officials abandoned this line of thinking and invoked self-defence.[11]

An appeal to self-defence is potentially more promising than law enforcement and both Statman and Tamar Meisels turn in this direction to justify named killings. Inasmuch as the Israeli-Palestinian conflict is an armed conflict, considerations of self-defence are obvious. Self-defence does not require that combatants be 'caught in the act' or present a material threat before they can kill one another. Self-defence also allows states to consider pre-emptive actions and weigh the merits of inflicting harm to achieve a credible deterrent. Some observers broaden the war paradigm to permit retribution or punishment, a throwback to Roman theories of just war.[12] Each of these motives for killing or causing harm is foreign to law enforcement but consistent with the laws of armed conflict. For this reason, it seems more reasonable to abandon the paradigm of law enforcement and consider named killings solely from the perspective of war and self-defence.

## Named Killings, War and Self-Defence

The first casualty of any attempt to link named killings with self-defence and war must be the assumption of guilt or criminal responsibility. Guilt invokes the law enforcement paradigm and therefore any attempt to justify named killings without running afoul of due process must succeed without imputing criminal responsibility. Terrorists, for the purposes of naming and killing them, must be on par with ordinary soldiers. The argument will be symmetrical. If it is permissible to target and kill terrorists, it is equally permissible to attack ordinary combatants in the same manner. There is no room, as Meisels hopes, for a policy that eschews 'positively endorsing assassination in written law' but approves of 'silent acquiescence' in the face of named killings. Why acquiesce silently if it is possible to outline a cogent argument for named killing? To do so, however, one must look beyond the criminality of terror.

Lieber assumed it was impossible to make the argument for targeted killings without giving way to the charge of outlawry. Given the conditions of warfare in his day and, indeed, in most of the modern period he was probably right. Soldiers wore uniforms and insignia, and were easy to identify. Naming names added nothing to their vulnerability nor did it render any person a more legitimate target. On the contrary, it only presupposed an element of moral culpability that Lieber found loathsome. Naming names would also have profound implications for the everyday conduct of war, placing political leaders and other traditional non-combatants at risk while threatening the hierarchy necessary to wage war without anarchy. Beyond obscuring the distinction between combatant and noncombatant, named killing also undermines the relative peace characterizing civilian centers of population by threatening to bring the battlefield home and upsetting the equanimity that civilians (usually those on the stronger side) attempt to preserve as their nations wage war.[13]

Warfare, however, has changed considerably since World War II, and now blurs the line between combatants and noncombatants in a way that many theorists and jurists hoped to avoid. These changes were the inevitable outcome of post-WWII guerrilla wars of liberation and the fight many emerging nations waged against 'colonial, alien and racist' regimes. These 'CAR' conflicts dominated warfare in the post-war period and threatened to overwhelm the Geneva conventions. In response, the international community amended the existing laws of armed conflict by ratifying Protocol I and II in 1977. Although neither Israel nor the US accepted these changes, some observers now claim that the Protocols carry the force of customary international law.[14] Extending the safeguards of the 1949 conventions to the myriad of new actors emerging in the post-war period, the Protocols also provide additional protection to residents of occupied nations who were hitherto unprotected victims of non-international armed conflict.

The Protocols also offer protection to insurgents. Recognizing that guerrillas do not always wear uniforms or identifying insignia, Protocol I dramatically relaxes the requirements necessary to maintain combatant status:

> . . . combatants are obliged to distinguish themselves from the civilian population while they are engaged in an attack or in a military operation preparatory to an attack. Recognizing, however, that there are situations in armed conflicts where, owing to the nature of the hostilities an armed combatant cannot so distinguish himself, he shall retain his status as a combatant, provided that, in such situations, he carries his arms openly:
> (a) during each military engagement, and
> (b) during such time as he is visible to the adversary while he is engaged in a military deployment preceding the launching of an attack . . . (Protocol 1, Article 44).

These regulations tend to obscure rather than sharpen combatant status. On one hand, combatants must serve in a hierarchically structured armed force that supervises compliance with international and humanitarian law (Article 43). The sponsoring authorities may be conventional nation-states, guerrilla organizations or militias. On the other hand, combatants need not wear uniforms nor carry their arms openly at all times. Protocol I extends combatant status to militants, insurgents and guerrillas. What, then, of terrorists?

Terrorists, and the organizations they serve in, do not observe humanitarian law. While this alone might be sufficient to deny them combatant status, it is not always easy to identify terrorists solely based on organizational affiliation. Some groups practice nothing but terror; others are mixed. Among the latter, some militants participate in terror while others do not. Those that do not, retain the protection of combatants and enjoy POW status if captured. There is no consensus, however, about the status of those who belong to an organization that does not meet the minimal standards set by Protocol I. Characterizing terrorists as 'unprivileged' or 'illegal' combatants, some observers argue that they do not enjoy the rights of ordinary combatants (such as POW status or repatriation following the cessation of hostilities).[15] But the idea of 'illegal' combatant remains murky. Neither the Geneva Conventions nor the Protocols recognize the term 'illegal combatant'. One is either a legal combatant or a civilian. War criminals are a subset of the former, ordinary criminals a subset of the latter. As either type of criminal, terrorists are subject to arrest, trial and punishment for the crimes they commit.[16] Terrorism should not warrant named killing but demand, instead, due process. Nevertheless, the danger of shifting status and the inability to identify combatants in the absence of clear insignia may overwhelm the law enforcement paradigm and justify named killing in self-defence.

## Justifying Named Killings

Soldiers are vulnerable solely because they are members of their nation's armed services. Their vulnerability has nothing to do with the threat the pose personally. Instead, they are part of a collective, organizational threat that waxes and wanes during warfare. As adversaries judge the threat their enemies pose, they formulate their military strategy and tactics accordingly. The war convention assumes a clear, consistent and fixed definition of combatant. Ordinarily, a uniform or insignia is the sole indication of organizational affiliation. Without one or the other, it is impossible to determine an actor's status, his or her degree of vulnerability, or the rights and protections individuals enjoy as either combatants or noncombatants. Un-uniformed combatants, however, can change status almost at will and, as a result, enjoy a unique advantage during a guerrilla war or insurgency. On the battlefield and bearing their arms openly, they are combatants. Off the battlefield, they hide their arms and seemingly revert to noncombatant status. Without uniforms or insignia, it is impossible to identify un-uniformed militants as combatants. They not only melt in with those around them but suddenly seem to acquire their status as well. In practice and in principle, these fighters become civilians. Their fluid and amorphous status lies at the heart of the argument that Stein and other fierce opponents of named killings make: lacking firm status as combatants, guerrillas, militants, terrorists and others without uniforms must be civilians.

While the framers of Protocol I do not address this problem directly, they are often acutely aware of the severe difficulties that allowing combatants to eschew uniforms presents. The subject of spies, for example, is particularly vexing. By definition, uniformed soldiers cannot be spies. Without uniforms, however, anyone might be a spy thereby making it difficult to protect a bona fide but un-uniformed combatant from charges of spying or sabotage.[17] Lack of uniforms therefore, makes it difficult to determine affiliation and jeopardizes the rights of both combatants and noncombatants, most often the latter. As the distinction between combatants and noncombatants blurs, belligerents must assume either that many un-uniformed combatants are actually noncombatants and avoid harming them, or as more likely will be the case, assume that most noncombatants are, in fact, un-uniformed combatants, and, as they do so, inflict excessive harm. Either option undermines the laws of armed conflict.

In spite of the ease in which un-uniformed guerrillas seemingly shed and shift their status, it cannot be that they are no longer combatants simply because they leave the scene of a battle and discard, as it were, the only earmarks of combatant status. Once a combatant, by whatever criteria and including the lax conditions of Protocol I, guerrillas, militants and insurgents remain combatants whether on the battlefield or off. They never leave the armed forces that are party to the conflict. As such, the problem is primarily one of properly identifying combatants in the absence of uniforms or other markings. Here is where 'naming' is useful: if one cannot determine organizational affiliation by uniforms or insignia, it is reasonable, indeed imperative, to turn to alternative methods. Naming does not imply guilt or impute 'special responsibility' as Statman claims, but establishes affiliation in the same way that uniforms do. Naming combatants is considerably more difficult than recognizing them by uniform and so demands careful intelligence to allow an adversary to assemble a list of individuals affiliated with their enemy's armed forces. Armed with this list and a reasonable method of ascertaining a person's identity, it is then possible to establish combatant status. At that point, a named, un-uniformed combatant is as vulnerable as one in uniform; both may suffer harm as adversaries defend themselves.

## Named Killings and Moral Responsibility

Although the logic of named killing does not preclude the prosecution of terrorists on charges of war crimes, the requirement to 'cleanse' terrorists of moral and criminal responsibility in order to kill them outright and by name during armed conflict remains odd, a vestige of those theories of just war and military practice that assume the moral equality and shared innocence of all soldiers. Perhaps it is more reasonable to think that some combatants are unjust, and that those espousing an unjust cause and/or fighting by unjust means merit a response *more* severe than do those combatants who are just. Rather than ignore the moral responsibility of terrorists and their supporters, their moral non-innocence justifies stronger and harsher measures than one would normally inflict on an adversary. Perhaps targeted killings are an appropriate response to terrorism precisely because terrorists deserve to suffer harm in a way that just combatants do not.

Jeff McMahan, who does not discuss targeted killings, sets the stage for this argument as he discusses the limits of permissible harm that one may cause when facing a threat. In the context of traditional just war theory, a just and proportionate response hinges upon the magnitude of an emerging threat and the costs and benefits of responding in one way or another. An acceptable response is necessary, cost-effective and one that avoids excessive non-combatant casualties; it does not vary relative to an adversary's moral responsibility. Echoing Statman and Meisels' concern for the 'special responsibility' or 'culpability' that terrorists bear, McMahan suggests, however, that we carefully weigh a belligerent's moral responsibility and respond more harshly to those combatants who are unjust.[18] Unfortunately, assessments of moral responsibility often lead in conflicting directions.

Agents incur moral responsibility insofar as they knowingly support an unjust war and/or wage war by means they know to be unjust. This places moral responsibility along a continuum. At the weak end are those who lend little support to an unjust war and/or grasp little in the way of its injustice. At the strong end are those who actively support an unjust war fully aware (or, at least, capable of becoming fully aware) that it defies the demands of justice. In between, might be common soldiers who fight what they honestly, although mistakenly, believe is the good fight. Different levels of moral responsibility demand different responses so, to use McMahan's example from the first Gulf War, the Iraqi Republican Guards, an elite, volunteer force loyal to a regime waging an unjust war of aggression, merit the full brunt of a harsh military response while uneducated and poorly armed conscripts deserve some of the same care and consideration just combatants sometimes offer civilians to minimize the harm they suffer.[19]

In which category do terrorists belong? Placing them in company of the Republican Guards, that is, at the strong end of moral responsibility, suggests that terrorists and those who support them are vulnerable to *greater* harm — from collateral damage or assassination, for example — than one may otherwise inflict on an enemy. Targeted killings are then a proportionate rather than excessive response to terror, a conclusion that Statman and Meisels support. Yet moral responsibility may also cut in the opposite direction. Coerced and indoctrinated, poor and uneducated, some suicide bombers may only reach relatively low levels of moral responsibility, certainly lower than many other combatants may reach.[20] At the same time, there are good reasons to conclude that some terrorists, particularly Palestinians and other parties to CAR conflicts, pursue a just cause (in spite of their unjust means) as they fight an occupying power. If moral responsibility considers just cause (and it is at the centre of McMahan's argument) then these terrorists are less unjust in some important ways than other kinds of unjust combatants (such as those waging a relentless war of aggression). These two factors — diminished moral responsibility and a just cause — then place some terrorists and those who support them at the weaker end of the responsibility scale and among those whose actions warrant *lesser* harms than are otherwise allowed.

Although the idea of moral responsibility is intuitively appealing, it can, in this case, lead to conflicting conclusions that reinforce Lieber's insistence that it be left aside. Rather than fall back on the presumption of guilt or responsibility to justify named killings or, alternatively, to dismiss its importance altogether, it is perhaps more accurate to say that we must 'bracket' rather than ignore moral non-innocence during war. In response, some might argue that ignoring the heinousness of terror inures us to the threat that terrorism poses. Terrorists, one might claim, present a special kind of threat the severity of which might be lost if we bracket their non-innocence. But this is not so. Independent of whatever moral responsibility we may ascribe to them (and which makes them culpable as war criminals), terrorists pose grave material threats to civilian populations. But, then again, so do bomber pilots. For the purpose of assessing a threat and targeting it accordingly, it is not necessary to consider that terrorists are acting unlawfully or immorally while bomber pilots fight within the bounds of conventional war. In either case, a belligerent sizes up the threat it faces and then considers how best to defend itself. In spite of the very great temptation to attribute criminal behaviour or moral responsibility to some belligerents, neither innocence nor non-innocence adds to or detracts from the magnitude of the threat a nation faces. Setting aside moral responsibility, however, still leaves us to assess named killings as an expedient response to an armed threat. As such, named killing can be a legitimate form of self-defence if it can meet the demands of necessity, utility and proportionality.

### Named Killing: An Effective and Proportionate Response?

Accepting named killing as a legitimate form of warfare does not preclude a careful assessment of necessity, civilian costs and military benefits. Are named killings necessary to forestall the threat a nation faces from armed insurgents? Are they effective? Do they limit or exacerbate harm to civilians? There is no easy way to answer these questions because criteria are so elusive. Both Statman and Meisels argue that a 'reasonable hope of success' is sufficient to justify named killings.[21] Certainly this is true, but what does it mean? More importantly, what of the cost? Given sufficient firepower, one can always find a tactic that offers a 'reasonable hope of success'.

I have argued at length that named killings carry costs not typically associated with ordinary killing during wartime.[22] The legitimacy of naming to determine affiliation does not allay these costs, many of which are inseparable from the process of identification. Un-uniformed militants are difficult to identify without extensive intelligence that comes largely from a well-watered network of collaborators and traitors. Unlike police informers, collaborators are neither of the same ilk as those they inform on, nor concerned citizens anxious to rid their neighbourhood of criminal elements. Instead, many collaborators are ordinary citizens responding to threats of imprisonment and torture, or offers of money, medical care or travel permits from occupation authorities. Others turn to collaboration to exact revenge and settle scores. It is not a healthy situation for any society, and while Palestinians struggle to come to grips with the collaborators among them and the relative ease in which outsiders infiltrate their community, Israel has proved adept at exploiting this social malady to compile lists of un-uniformed combatants. These costs are far from trivial and may explain, at least in part, the vicious response that often follows named killings fuelled by collaboration.

Other costs arise as troops carry out named killings and bystanders are killed as un-uniformed combatants are 'liquidated'. Between September 29, 2000 and January 15, 2006 Israeli troops successfully targeted 204 named combatants while killing 115 civilians.[23] Are these casualties excessive or reasonable? For some, these numbers may represent reasonable levels of collateral damage, particularly as Israel makes considerable efforts to limit civilian casualties. Moreover, it may only be that isolated missions, rather than Israel's policy in general, cause disproportionate casualties.[24] Nevertheless, claims of proportionality are pointless if strikes are ineffective and bring additional costs and casualties.

Are named killings effective? Do they enhance security, disable the enemy and improve the prospects for eventually ending armed conflict? Critics charge that assassinations only incite further attacks and often slide from interdiction to retaliation, retribution and revenge. Proponents argue that the situation has improved. Here, too, firm criteria are lacking. Statman, for example, describes how in January 2004, 'the situation is much better . . . than it was in March 2002, when Israel was facing two to three terrorist attacks a day, resulting in the deaths of more than a hundred Israelis in one month'.[25] While March 2002 was, indeed, a watershed that prompted sweeping military action in the West Bank to root out terrorists, it is not obvious that the situation two years later was much better. Named killings were a fixture of the fighting since November 2000 and it is not clear if and how they reduced the threat of terror.[26] In the 18 months following Israel's reinvasion of the West Bank in the summer of

2002, the number of Israelis killed by terrorists within the Green Line has held steady at about fifty in each six-month period.[27] Subsequently, however, the situation improved (as measured by casualties), a fact some attribute to the separation fence. I do not intend to settle the issue here, but only point out that assessments of efficacy require some criteria beyond a 'reasonable hope'. These include civilian security, economic well-being, international standing, and progress toward peace. By these measures, some may find it difficult to see how the situation in Israel improved during the period prior to Arafat's death in November 2004. There is also growing evidence that named killings only *increase* the incidence of terror bombings. Although preventive arrests can dramatically decrease the number of suicide bombings, named killings draw significant numbers of new recruits that replenish the 'terror stock', that is, the cadre of men and women willing to undertake suicide bombings. The result is a greater number of terror attacks.[28] While one may appeal to the long-term hope that named killings will forestall terror in spite of its high short-term costs, there are no clear indications that they were or will be effective in this way.

**The Future of Named Killing**

While the consequences of named killings should mitigate against the practice, it is conceivable that some belligerents — perhaps those on the battlefields of Iraq and Pakistan — may overcome its high cost. Should named killings become an established norm of armed conflict, however, one major consequence may be that uniforms will continue to lose their significance. They certainly would not protect anyone deemed a sufficiently serious threat from a named killing. While it is difficult, in other words, to depart from the war convention and justify named killings without raising the otherwise insurmountable difficulty that non-uniformed combatants pose, it is quite likely that this link will soon be forgotten. Named killings will simply offer another avenue for waging war. The costs might be high, but this will only tend to limit naming to those extreme situations and overwhelming threats that cannot be met by other means. This is acceptable if nations manage to resist the temptation to impute guilt to their adversaries. Otherwise, Lieber is right, the war convention will disintegrate amidst charges of mutual outlawry, and the modest protection it affords to combatants will vanish. With this caveat in mind, named killings will form part of conventional war but must have little to do with the war on terror, *per se*, or with international law enforcement.

   If this is the correct way of looking at named killings, one cannot preclude any side form adopting similar tactics when the benefits justify the costs. No one should be surprised, then, if Palestinians or similarly situated parties to a CAR conflict decide to pursue named killing and, for example, target young pilots whether in the field or at home on leave. Based solely on the threat they pose to civilians, bomber pilots are not necessarily any less menacing than terrorists are. Should Palestinian militants or other insurgents ever achieve the means to respond in kind, Israel and other conventional powers might then find cause to desist and restore the convention that forbids named killing. Bomber pilots, after all, are considerably more expensive to train than suicide bombers. Unfortunately, once this particular genie is out of the bottle, it might not be that easy to get it back inside again.

## NOTES

1 Yael Stein, 'By any name illegal and immoral: Response to 'Israel's policy of targeted killing' by Steven David', *Ethics & International Affairs* 17, 1 (2003): 127–140.

2 Michael L. Gross, 'Killing civilians intentionally: Double effect, reprisal and necessity in the Middle East', *Political Science Quarterly* 120, 4 (2005): 555–579.

3 See *Basic Principles on the Use of Force and Firearms by Law Enforcement Officials*, adopted by the Eighth United Nations Congress on the Prevention of Crime and Treatment of Offenders, Havana Cuba, 27 August to 7 September 1990, reprinted in Nigel S. Rodley, *The Treatment of Prisoner's Under International Law* (Oxford: Clarendon Press, 1999), pp. 440–444.

4 Michael L. Gross, 'Fighting by other means in the Mideast: A critical analysis of Israel's assassination policy', *Political Studies* 51 (2003): 350–68; Gad Barzilai, 'Islands of silence: democracies kill?', *Annual Meeting of the Law and Society Association*, Budapest, 2001, p. 10, cited in Tamar Meisels, 'Targeting terror', *Social Theory and Practice* 30, 3 (2004): 297–396.

5 The difficulties of maintaining due process are not insignificant and would affect the ability to preserve due process whether the suspect was a terrorist or war criminal (See Meisels, pp. 305–6). Nevertheless, every effort is made to maintain due process in the latter case insofar as the nature of military tribunals allow. See, Jennifer Elsea, *Terrorism and the Law of War: Trying Terrorists as War Criminals before Military Commissions* (Washington: Congressional Research Service, The Library of Congress, 2001).

6 The grounds for supreme emergency remain contentious. See A. J. Coates, *The Ethics of War* (Manchester University Press: Manchester, 1997), pp. 234–272; Brian Orend, 'Just and lawful conduct in war: reflections on Michael Walzer', *Law and Philosophy* 20 (2000).

7 See Leslie C. Green, *The Contemporary Law of Armed Conflict, Second Edition* (Manchester: Manchester University Press, 2000), p. 144, n. 148.

8 The moral equality of soldiers, long a lynchpin of just war theory and the law of armed conflict, has recently been questioned. See Jeff McMahan, 'The ethics of killing in war', *Ethics* 114 (2004): 693–733; David Rodin, *War and Self-Defense* (Oxford: Oxford University Press, 2002), pp. 165–173.

9 Daniel Statman, 'Targeted killing', *Theoretical Inquiries in Law* 5 (2004): 191. Meisels writes, 'I assume here further that there is little disagreement among Western liberals concerning the immorality of terrorists and their abhorrent deeds. Nor is there usually any doubt as to the culpability of the pursued targets (Meisels op. cit., p. 298).

10 Green op. cit., pp. 286–316.

11 Gross, 'Fighting by other means' op. cit., pp. 352–4.

12 Steven R. David, 'Israel's policy of targeted killing', *Journal of Ethics and International Affairs* 17, 1 (2003): 111–118.

13 Statman op. cit., p. 196.

14 Gregory M. Travalio, 'Terrorism, international law and the use of military force', *Wisconsin International Law Journal* 18, 1 (1999): 145–191.

15 See, Human Rights Watch. *Background Paper on the Geneva Conventions and Persons Held by US Forces*, January 29, http://www.hrw.org/backgrounder/usa/pow_bck.htm#P49_10180; Elsea op. cit., p. 2.

16 If the logic of named killing requires that we classify terrorists as combatants, any crimes attributable to their actions are war crimes. This includes terror no less than any other grave breach of humanitarian law. Terror, as a recent UN report defines it, is 'any action intended to cause death or serious bodily harm to civilians or noncombatants, when the purpose of such an act, by its nature or context, is to intimidate a population or to compel a government or international organization to do or abstain from doing any act (see, *A More Secure World: Our Shared Responsibility*, Report of the High-level Panel on Threats, Challenges and Change (December 1, 2004): 49. (http://www.unis.unvienna.org/documents/unis/A59565.pdf).

   Putting aside the political context, terrorism is certainly consistent with crimes against humanity as the London Charter defines them, namely, 'murder, extermination, deportation and other inhumane acts committed against any civilian population'.

17 *Commentary*, Article 46, Protocol Additional to the Geneva Conventions of 12 August 1949, and relating to the Protection of Victims of International Armed Conflicts (Protocol I), 8 June 1977, paragraph 1776.

18 McMahan op. cit., p. 727.

19 McMahan op. cit., p. 725.

20 Observers disagree about the profile of suicide bombers. Rubin describes bombers as often unmarried, religious and unemployed. Pedahzur, Perliger and Weinberg conclude that suicide bombers draw from 'a

society with excessive regulation and where the socioeconomic development of people is impeded and aspirations are stifled by an oppressive discipline'. Pape, on the other hand, suggests that suicide bombers are 'not mainly poor, uneducated, immature religious zealots or social losers. Instead . . . they resemble the kind of politically conscious individual who might join a grass roots movement more than they do wayward adolescents or religious fanatics'. Clearly, moral responsibility will vary subject to these conflicting profiles. (See, Elizabeth Rubin, 'The most wanted Palestinian'. *The New York Times Magazine* (June 30 (2002): 26–31, 42, 51–5; Ami Pedahzur, Arie Perliger and Leonard Weinberg, 'Altruism and fatalism: The characteristics of Palestinian suicide terrorists', *Deviant Behaviour* 24 (2003): 421; Robert Pape, *Dying to Win: The Strategic Logic of Suicide Terrorism* (New York: Random House, 2005), p. 216.

21  Statman op. cit., p. 193.
22  Gross, 'Fighting by other means' op. cit.; Michael L. Gross, 'Assassination: killing in the shadow of self-defense' in J. Irwin (ed.) *War and Virtual War: The Challenges to Communities* (Amsterdam: Rodopi, 2004), pp. 99–116.
23  Figures are compiled from B'tselem, Israeli Information Center for Human Rights in the Occupied Territories, (http://www.btselem.org/english/statistics/Palestinians_killed_during_the_course_of_an_assasination.asp).
24  For example, one of the most widely condemned missions took place on July 23, 2002 as 15 civilians died in a strike killing Salah Shehadeh, the head of the Hamas military wing (See, International Policy Institute for Counter-Terrorism, *Casualties & Incidents Database — Targeted Killing* (www.ict.org.il/).
25  Statman, op. cit., p. 192.
26  Yael Stein, *Position Paper: Israel's Assassination Policy: Extra-judicial Executions*, B'tselem, Israeli Information Center for Human Rights in the Occupied Territories, 2001, http://www.btselem.org/Download/200101_Extrajudicial_Killings_Eng.doc
27  B'tselem, *Israeli Civilians killed by Palestinians within the Green line*, www.btselem.org.il.
28  Edward Kaplan *et al.*, 'What happened to suicide bombings in Israel? Insights from a terror stock model', *Studies in Conflict and Terrorism* 28, 3 (2005): 225–235.

# 8  Torture — The Case for Dirty Harry and against Alan Dershowitz

UWE STEINHOFF

What is so bad about torturing people, anyway? People also kill people. Soldiers kill people, policemen kill people, doctors kill people, executioners kill people and ordinary people kill people. Some of these killings are justified. So why shouldn't it be justified in some cases to torture people? After all, being killed seems to be worse than being tortured. Even most of the tortured people seem to see it this way; otherwise they would kill themselves in order to escape further torture (yes, some do, but they are only few). So, if killing is sometimes justified, torture too must sometimes be justified.

Henry Shue thinks that this is a weak argument. Referring in particular to the legitimate killing of people in war, he states:

> Even if one grants that killing someone in combat is doing him or her a greater harm than torturing him or her . . . , it by no means follows that there could not be a justification for the greater harm that was not applicable to the lesser harm. Specifically, it would matter if some killing could satisfy other moral constraints (besides the constraint of minimizing harm) which no torture could satisfy.[1]

The moral constraint he has in mind is the prohibition of assaults upon the defenceless. However, it can be doubted whether this is a valid constraint at all. Shue's idea that it is valid is based on the fact that one 'of the most basic principles for the conduct of war ( *jus in bello* ) rests on the distinction between combatants and noncombatants and requires that insofar as possible, violence not be directed at noncombatants'.[2] One fundamental function of this distinction, according to Shue, is to try to make a terrible combat fair. No doubt, the opportunities may not have been anywhere near equal — it would be impossible to restrict wars to equally matched opponents. But at least none of the parties to the combat were defenceless.[3]

To be sure, Shue admits that this 'invokes a simplified, if not romanticized, portrait of warfare', but he explains that

> . . . the point now is not to attack or defend the efficacy of the principle of warfare that combat is more acceptable morally if restricted to official combatants, but to notice one of its moral bases, which, I am suggesting, is that it allows for a 'fair fight' by means of protecting the utterly defenceless from assault.[4]

It is true that the fact that the prohibition of assaults upon the defenceless is not always obeyed in war does not pose any problem for Shue's argument. What does pose a problem, however, is that this principle is no *jus in bello* principle at all, and it does not, *pace*

Shue, underlie the principled distinction between combatants and non-combatants.[5] This can be seen quite easily. Suppose an army that possesses superior artillery advances upon the enemy trenches. It has two options. It can shell the enemy trenches from a safe distance with artillery fire. The enemy would be entirely defenceless against such an attack; his weapons do not have the range for fighting back.[6] (This was pretty much the situation in the first and the second Iraq wars.) Or it can advance without shelling the enemy first. Here the enemy would be able to fire upon the advancing troops and to inflict heavy casualties. The point now is that there is simply no article in the laws of war (and no constraint in just war theory, for that matter) that would rule out the first option as such. Of course, if the objectives of the war could be achieved without shelling the enemy in its death-trap trenches *and* without inflicting higher casualties on one's own forces, this alternative course of action would have to be adopted. But the reason for this is the principle of proportionality.[7] An alleged principle of the immunity of the defenceless plays no role here.

To be sure, I do not deny that there is something fishy about attacking the defenceless. What is fishy about it might be captured very well in this passage:

> The pilot of a fighter-bomber or the crew of a man-of-war from which the Tomahawk rockets are launched are beyond the reach of the enemy's weapons. War has lost all features of the classical duel situation here and has approached, to put it cynically, certain forms of pest control.[8]

Judged from a traditional warrior's code of honour, a code that emphasises, among other things, courage, there is nothing honourable in killing off defenceless enemies (whether it is therefore already *dis*honourable is yet another question). But honour and morality are not the same, and honour and the laws of war are not either. In short, the prohibition of assaults upon the defenceless is neither an explicit nor an implicit principle of the laws of war or of just war theory.

Moreover, it is not even clear what should be unfair about killing the defenceless in war in the first place. If the rules of war allowed both sides to kill, for example, defenceless prisoners of war, where is the unfairness? Both sides are in the same situation. And if the laws of war allowed the torture of POWs, the same would be true. Invoking principles of fairness does not deliver an argument against either of the two practices.

David Sussman has recently attempted to give another explanation of why torture, allegedly, 'bears an especially high burden of justification, greater in degree and different in kind from even that of killing'.[9] However, he also cautions that this 'is not to say that when torture is wrong, it is worse that [sic] wrongful acts of maiming and killing' or that 'it is more important for us to prevent torture than it is to prevent murder, or that torturers should be condemned or punished more severely than murderers. The moral differences between torture, killing, and maiming may not always make a difference in such third-personal contexts'.[10] But why, then, should torture bear an 'especially high burden of justification'? Does it bear such a higher burden only in second-person or first-person contexts? But what is that supposed to mean? That whereas one does not need a better justification for allowing others to torture or for not condemning torturers than for allowing others to kill or for not condemning killers, one does need a better justification for torturing (and perhaps also for risking being tortured) than for killing? Sussman argues that:

. . . torture forces its victim into the position of colluding against himself through his own affects and emotions, so that he experiences himself as simultaneously powerless and yet actively complicit in his own violation. So construed, torture turns out to be not just an extreme form of cruelty, but the pre-eminent instance of a kind of forced self-betrayal, more akin to rape than other kinds of violence characteristic of warfare or police action.[11]

He elaborates:

> What the torturer does is to take his victim's pain, and through it his victim's body, and make it begin to express the torturer's will.[12]
> . . . Torture does not merely insult or damage its victim's agency, but rather turns such agency against itself, forcing the victim to experience herself as helpless yet complicit in her own violation. This is not just an assault on or violation of the victim's autonomy but also a perversion of it, a kind of systematic mockery of the basic moral relations that an individual bears both to others and to herself. Perhaps this is why torture seems qualitatively worse than other forms of brutality or cruelty.[13]

But all this can hardly explain the alleged difference between 'third-personal' and other contexts. In fact, it would seem rather natural to assume that, if torture isn't worse than killing from a third-person perspective, it isn't so from a second- or first-person perspective either. If Sussman sees this differently, the high burden of justification, it appears, would be on him.

Conversely, assume a dictator confronts prisoner A with the following choice — to either kill one of ten prisoners or to torture one of them for two hours (all these prisoners are innocent and have no special relation to the first prisoner).[14] If A refuses to choose and to act on his choice, all ten prisoners will be killed. If he decided to choose (and it seems plain to me that he is justified in choosing even though he may not be obliged to do so), should the prisoner facing the choice rather kill one prisoner than torture one of them for two hours? This is to be strongly doubted. On the other hand, there can hardly be any doubt that the ten prisoners would prefer him to opt for torture if he asked them what to do — to refuse to choose, to choose to kill or to choose to torture. He is not permitted to ask them (if he did, all ten prisoners would be killed). However, in light of the fact that it is reasonable to assume that they would prefer two hours of torture to being killed for good, he should honour that preference if he decides to choose. It seems, then, that torture is easier to justify than killing even from a first-person perspective.

Moreover, the feature that in Sussman's eyes makes torture so bad is by no means unique to torture. We find it, in fact, even in armed robbery. If a robber points a gun at a victim and threatens to kill him if the victim does not give his money to the robber, the robber, if successful, also turns the victim's agency against the victim himself. He makes the victim's fear express his, the robber's, will; and the victim, in handing over the money for fear of death, is 'complicit' in his own violation.

It is important to note here that the victim will also normally not react to the threat with a utility/risk-calculation, i.e. with rational deliberation. If, especially at night in a dark alley, one has a gun pointed at one's head and hears: 'Give me your f . . . money or I'll f . . . kill you', one will hardly engage in deliberations of this kind: 'The probability that his threat is meant seriously lies around $x$; my options to defend myself or to escape are this and that, with this and that probability of success; if, on the other hand, I give him the money, this will cost me certainly $y$ money units, which in turn leads with probability $z$ to my not being able to pay in time for this and that thing, which in turn . . . and therefore I will . . .'. Rather, many people threatened with deadly violence will think: 'Oh my God, he wants to shoot me, he wants to shoot me . . . I'll give him the money!': thus, the sudden death threat and the perceived time pressure will in many if not most cases severely disturb the ability to deliberate rationally if they do not completely undermine it. In short, fear may overwhelm one as pain overwhelms the victim of torture. There may be differences of degree but no qualitative ones. Besides, at least some forms of torture will undermine the ability of some torture victims to think rationally less than some forms of death threat would of some threatened people.

Thus, Sussman is not able to show that there is a higher burden of justification on torture than on killing. Conversely, thought experiments like those of the ten prisoners strongly suggest that it is the other way around.

Of course, it is true that *emotional reactions* to displays of torture, for example in movies, are much stronger than those to displays of killing. And I suspect that much of the conviction that torture is somehow more terrible than death is sustained by these immediate emotional reactions. In fact, however, little of moral relevance follows from them. After all, the emotional reactions to scenes involving large amounts of faeces or cockroaches, for example, are mostly also stronger than to scenes involving killing, at least when it is a quick killing. When the killing is prolonged the reactions are stronger, but they are then prompted by the displayed suffering — sometimes simply in the form of fear — not by the impending death itself. The point is that *we simply cannot empathise with the dead*. There is nothing we can empathise *with*. We do not know how it is to be dead, and there is certainly no possibility to *feel* dead (in any non-metaphorical sense). We do know, however, what it is to feel *pain*. Therefore, if we see how pain is inflicted on another person, we can feel quite literally *com-passion*. There is no such compassion possible with the dead (we can only feel sorry for them, but that is a completely different and far less intense feeling). In other words, our emotional re-actions to displays of torture or killing respectively are distorted by certain limits of empathy. What are not distorted are our emotional reactions to the prospect of our *own* death. Most of us fear it more than torture (that is limited in time). Whether killing is worse than torturing, then, should be measured against the preferences of people facing the alternatives of torture (over a certain limited time) and death — most prefer torture. To measure it against emotional reactions to displays of torture would by way of extension also mean that it is better to shoot someone dead than to push him into a bathtub filled with cockroaches. But such an implication obviously reduces the premise to absurdity.

Thus, it seems the argument in defence of torture given at the beginning is not such a weak one after all. We can now slightly rephrase it in the light of our findings: If it is permissible to kill a defenceless enemy combatant in order to avoid own casualties, why should it not be permissible to torture a defenceless terrorist in order to avoid own casualties?

One might try to answer this by saying that the enemy soldiers in my example may be defenceless in the situation in which they are shelled or attacked with missiles, but that they *still pose a threat* — they threaten our advancing troops, which is precisely the reason why we take them out by artillery or rockets. The detained terrorist, on the other hand, does not pose a threat any more. For what can he do?

Sanford Levinson states that 'the defender of torture would dispute the premise that the captured prisoner is no longer a threat, at least if the prisoner possesses important information about the future conduct of his fellow terrorists'.[15] The case of the defender of torture can be made much stronger, however, if we take the infamous ticking bomb case. The terrorist has somewhere hidden a bomb that will, if it goes off, kill a high number of innocents (maybe it is even a nuclear bomb that would destroy one of the ten biggest cities in the world). He does not want to say where it is. Would it not be justified to torture him in order to make him disclose the vital information and find the bomb in time to disable it?

Some might be inclined to argue that *withholding* vital information (i.e. an omission) couldn't reasonably be described as a threat. Perhaps, perhaps not. However, people culpably posing a threat and aggressors are not the only persons that can be legitimately killed. For it seems, as Phillip Montague has pointed out, that, in cases in which one cannot save oneself from the negative consequences of another person's acts in any other way than by diverting or inflicting them on this person, one is justified in doing so. Montague states the following conditions for this:

> (i) individuals $X_1 \ldots X_n$ are situated so that harm will unavoidably befall some but not all of them; (ii) that they are so situated is the fault of some but not all members of the group; (iii) the nature of the harm is independent of the individuals who are harmed; (iv) Y, who is not necessarily included in $X_1 \ldots X_n$ is in a position to determine who will be harmed.[16]

The inflicting of harm (for example in the form of an attack or in the form of torture) on a certain person, thus, is not legitimised here by a *present* aggression but by the person's culpably causing the threat of harm. This cause can lie in the past. Montague adduces the example of a doctor who wishes for the death of a cardiac patient and therefore swallows the pacemaker the patient needs. The only chance to get the pacemaker quickly enough to save the patient's life is to perform a hasty operation on the doctor, which, however, would be fatal to him. Hence, one faces here a situation in which either the innocent patient or the malicious doctor has to die. However, if one of the two has to die anyway and one has to decide who it is going to be, then one clearly should, says Montague, decide against the person who has culpably brought about this situation. That seems to be a pretty reasonable stance, and I agree with him. The application to the case of the terrorist who has hidden a bomb to kill innocents is obvious.

It even suffices when the bomb would kill only *one* innocent. We do not have to assume a ticking nuclear bomb, killing thousands or even millions. Consider the Dirty Harry case. In the Don Siegel movie *Dirty Harry* someone kidnaps a female child and puts her in a place where she will suffocate if not rescued in time. There is not much time left, according to the very claims of the kidnapper. The police officer Harry (Clint Eastwood) is to deliver the ransom to the kidnapper. When they finally meet at night in a park, the kidnapper knocks Harry down with his gun and tells him that he will let the girl die anyway. He also tells Harry that he wants him to know that before he kills him too. In the moment he is about to shoot Harry, who lies defenceless and badly beaten to his feet, Harry's partner interferes (and is shot). The kidnapper can escape, wounded. Harry pursues him. Finally he corners him, and the kidnapper raises his arms to surrender. Harry shoots him in the leg. The kidnapper is frightened to death, tells Harry not to kill him and that he has rights. Harry asks him where the girl is. The kidnapper talks only about his rights. Harry sees the kidnapper's leg wound and puts his foot on it, torturing the kidnapper. The camera retreats. In the next scene, the girl is saved.

The Dirty Harry case, it seems to me, is a case of morally justified torture. But isn't the kidnapper right? Does not even he have rights? Yes, he has, but in these circumstances he does not have the right not to be tortured. Again, the situation is analogous to self-defence. The aggressor does not lose all of his rights, but his right to life weighs less than the innocent defender's right to life. The aggressor culpably brings about a situation where one of the two — he or the defender — will die. It is only just and fair that the harm that will befall in this situation upon one of the two is diverted to the person who is responsible for the harm — the aggressor. In the Dirty Harry case, the kidnapper brings about a situation where a person is tortured or will continue to be tortured until death (being slowly suffocated in a small hole *is* torture). It is only just and fair that this harm befalls the person responsible for the situation — the kidnapper. Moreover, the choice is made even easier by the fact that being tortured for a small period of time is better than being tortured until death. Harry made the right decision.

Two replies might be made at this point. The first one — repeated like a litany by certain opponents of torture — is that interrogative torture simply does not work. That, however, is simply wrong. Sometimes interrogative torture does work, and the torturer gets the information he was looking for.[17]

Well, one might say, but at least interrogative torture is not very reliable. Apart from the fact that even that is not so clear, it would not even help. Consider the following case: An innocent person is being attacked by an aggressor, who fires a deadly weapon at him (and misses him at first but keeps firing). The attacked person's only possibility to save his life is by using the One-Million-Pains-To-One-Kill-Gun that he happens to have with him. On average, you have to pull the trigger of this gun one million times in order to have one immediately incapacitating projectile come out of it (it incapacitates through the infliction of unbearable pain). All the other times it fires projectiles that only ten seconds after hitting a human target cause the target unbearable pain. Thus, firing this gun at the aggressor will certainly cause the aggressor unbearable pain, but the probability that it will save the life of the defender is only 1:1,000,000. I must admit that I cannot even begin to make sense of the suggestion that, given these odds, the defender should not use the gun against the aggressor. Yes, the pain inflicted by the weapon on the aggressor is extremely unlikely to secure the survival of the defender, but there still *is* a chance that it will, so why should the *defender* forgo this chance for the benefit of the *aggressor*? Obviously, there is no reason (at least none that I could see). Again, the application to the torture of ticking bomb terrorists and Dirty Harry kidnappers is obvious.

What is the second reply? Richard H. Weisberg takes issue with the example of the ticking bomb case:

> . . . the hypothetical itself lacks the virtues of intelligence, appropriateness, and especially sophistication. Here, as in *The Brothers Karamazov* — *pace* Sandy Levinson — it is the complex rationalizers who wind up being more naive

than those who speak strictly, directly, and simply against injustice. 'You can't know whether a person knows where the bomb is', explains Cole in a recent piece in the *Nation*, 'or even if they're telling the truth. Because of this, you wind up sanctioning torture in general'.[18]

To begin with, by allowing torture in the ticking bomb case one does *not* necessarily wind up sanctioning it in general. Killing (of certain people) is sanctioned in war but not in general. The actual second reply I was referring to, however, is *that you do not know whether you have the right person*. (That you do not know whether the person speaks the truth is simply the first reply. We have already dealt with it.) But what does it mean: 'You don't know'? Does it mean you do not know for certain? If not knowing for certain whether you have the right person would be sufficient reason not to harm that person, we would not only have to abstain from self-defence but also from punishment. You *never* know for certain!

Take the example of a man who draws a gun in front of a head of state and aims at him. The bodyguards simply cannot know (for certain) whether this person wants to shoot, they cannot even know whether it is a real gun. Maybe the 'attacker' is only a retard with a water pistol. So the bodyguards of the head of state (whom we want to assume innocent) should not shoot at such a person who, for all they *can* know, seems to be attacking the person they are to protect? Actually, if shooting (and probably killing) him is the only way to make sure that he is not able to pull the trigger, they *should* shoot him.

One might say that this person, even if he does not really want to shoot and has no real gun, at least *feigns* an attack, and this makes him liable to counter-attack. Whoever credibly feigns an attack on another person cannot later, after having suffered from severe countermeasures, complain that he 'only' feigned it. He shouldn't have feigned it at all. We can, however, have a comparable situation with a terrorist. If a person says to other persons that he is going to build a powerful bomb to blow up a kindergarten and has the necessary skills and buys the necessary chemicals, he had better not, when the security service storms his hideout where he is surrounded by his bomb-making equipment, sneeringly say: 'You are too late. I have already planted the bomb. It will go off in 12 hours and kill hundreds of children'. If he then is tortured by the security service, which wants to find out where the bomb is, he is not, it seems, in a particularly good position to complain about that *even if he has not planted a bomb*.[19] Moreover, even if a real or supposed terrorist has not made that particularly threatening statement, hanging around with the wrong people in the wrong situations can also make you liable to attack. Suppose an innocent woman is hunted by a mob. Maybe they do not like her skin colour, her ethnic group, her religion or whatever. The mob has already killed other people for the same reason. She hides with the hand grenade she fortunately has, behind a bush. Suddenly one of the group sees her, points his finger at her, shouts 'There she is', and the armed members of the group raise their guns to shoot at her. Not all members of the group have guns. Some are unarmed and shout: 'Kill her, kill her!' Others do not even shout but sneer, foaming at the mouth (I am not talking about completely innocent people, who just 'happen' to be there for no fault of their own). The only way she can save herself is to throw the grenade at the mob, which will kill all of them, including the unarmed ones. Is she justified in doing so? I would think so. Being a member of certain groups that collectively undertake aggressive acts or intentionally pose a threat to innocent people makes one liable to severe counter-measures. Consequently, a member of a terrorist group might be liable to torture in the ticking bomb case, even if he does not know were the bomb is.

It helps, by the way, very little to aver at this point that torture is simply not compatible with liberalism. David Luban, for example, claims that torture aims 'to strip away from its victim all the qualities of human dignity that liberalism prizes' and that 'torture is a microcosm, raised to the highest level of intensity, of the tyrannical political relationships that liberalism hates the most'.[20] However, prisons are also 'microcosms' of tyranny; yet, most liberals do not find them incompatible with liberalism. Where is the difference? Maybe it lies in the fact that in torture tyranny is 'raised to the highest level'. But, first, it is far from clear that one hour of torture is more tyrannical than 15 years of prison. Second, even if torture were more tyrannical than prison, and liberalism abhorred tyranny, there remained still the fact that liberalism can accommodate quite intense forms of tyranny, such as incarceration for life (or for a decade and more). Why should it not also be able to accommodate the most extreme form of tyranny? 'Because it is the most extreme form' is in itself no answer to this question.

More importantly, liberalism is not so much about 'dignity' — which is a quite elusive concept, anyway (in particular, I deny that the dignity of the culpable aggressor is violated by Dirty Harry's action any more than it would be violated by Dirty Harry's killing him in self-defence) — but about liberty. It is called liberalism, not 'dignism'. It is also not about just anybody's liberty. It is about the liberty of the innocent. This is why there is no particular problem in liberalism to kill aggressors or to deprive them of their liberty if this is the only way to protect innocent people from these aggressors. The core value of the liberal state is the protection of the liberty and the rights of *innocent* individuals against *aggressors*. The state can be such an aggressor, but the state can and must also protect against other aggressors. To keep Dirty Harry in the situation described from torturing the kidnapper, therefore, would run against the liberal state's own *raison d'être*. The state would help the aggressor, not the victim; it would help the aggressor's tyranny over the innocent and therefore actually abet the relationship it hates the most.

Since my description of the core value of liberalism, as I submit, is at least as plausible as Luban's (and I think it is historically much more plausible), the appeal to liberalism cannot help absolute opponents of torture. To claim that liberalism 'correctly understood' absolutely prohibits torture simply engages in an attempt of persuasive definition and begs the question. Besides, why could liberalism, 'correctly understood', not be wrong?

But — speaking about the innocent — what about the risk of torturing a completely *innocent* person, a person that made itself *not* liable? Yes, that risk exists, as it does in the case of punishment. In the latter case, the risk of punishing innocent persons has to be weighed against the risk of not at all punishing the non-innocent and of not at all deterring potential criminals. In the case of interrogative torture in the context of a ticking bomb situation, the risk of torturing an innocent person has to be weighed against the risk of letting other innocent persons die in an explosion. If the weighing process in the former case can justify punishment, it is unclear why the weighing process in the latter case could not sometimes justify torture. If the odds are high enough, it does. In fact, the justification in the latter case might even be easier — easier at least than justifying capital punishment, for death, as already noted, is worse than torture (at least for most people who are confronted with a decision between their death and being tortured for a limited time). It might even be easier than justifying incarceration for one or two decades, for it is not clear that many persons would not prefer some hours or even days of torture to that alternative.

To sum up the discussion so far: A compelling argument for an absolute *moral* prohibition of torture cannot be made. Under certain circumstances torture can be justified. *Justified*, not only excused. I emphasise this because some philosophers claim that situations of so-called necessity or emergency can only *excuse* torture (and some other extreme measures). But there is nothing in the meaning of the terms 'necessity' or 'emergency' themselves that could warrant that view. For example, the German penal code distinguishes between 'justifying emergency' and 'excusing emergency'. § 34 reads:

> Whosoever, in order to avert a not otherwise avoidable present danger to life, body, freedom, honour, property, or another legally protected interest, acts so as to avert the danger to himself or others, does not act illegally if, upon consideration of the conflicting interests, namely of the threatened legally protected interests and of the degree of the threatened danger, the protected interest substantially outweighs the infringed interest. This, however, is true only if the act is an adequate [in the sense of means-end rationality ('angemessen')] means to avert the danger.[21]

He does not act illegally, and that means his act is legally justified. If the protected interests do not substantially outweigh the infringed interest, however, he can at best be excused (§ 35). The moral case is not different. There can be situations where torture is an instrumentally adequate and the only means to avert a certain danger from certain morally protected interests and where the protected interests substantially outweigh the infringed ones. Therefore, if the odds are high enough, torture can be not only excused but morally justified.

No doubt, an absolutist opponent of torture will not be particularly impressed by the argument offered so far. In fact, absolutists normally (although perhaps not always) do not even try to refute the arguments adduced against their absolutist positions; they tend to just persistently and dramatically reaffirm their positions. The writer and poet Ariel Dorfman is a good example:

> I can only pray that humanity will have the courage to say no, no to torture, no to torture under any circumstance whatsoever, no to torture, no matter who the enemy, what the accusation, what sort of fear we harbor; no to torture no matter what kind of threat is posed to our safety; no to torture anytime, anywhere; no to torture anyone; no to torture.[22]

Moral absolutism is a dangerous and mistaken view. If, for example, humanity would face the choice (maybe posed by some maniac with the ultimate weapon or by an alien race, or what have you) between being exterminated or torturing one particularly bad man (let us say Idi Amin) for an hour or a day, it is far from clear why any person in his right mind — both intellectually *and* morally — should pray that humanity said 'no to torture'.[23] And what, by the way, if the choice is between all human beings (that includes children) being *tortured* by the alien race or only one particularly bad man being tortured by some humans? Consequences count; they cannot simply be ignored for the benefit of some allegedly absolute rule, especially if they might be catastrophic. *Fiat justitia, pereat mundus* is an irrational and immoral maxim.

To say it again: A compelling argument for an absolute *moral* prohibition of torture cannot be made. But what about the legal prohibition of torture? If torture can be morally justified under certain circumstances, should it also be legalised?

It could seem that torture is already legal under the German penal code. For if, as I claimed, the interests which are protected by torturing a terrorist can substantially outweigh the infringed interests (most notably of the terrorist), then torture must be legal. However, the fact that this outweighing can occur from a moral perspective does not yet mean that it can also occur from the legal perspective of a certain penal code. Each system of laws is in principle free to stipulate an *absolute* prohibition of torture. The German law does this in so far as it accepts certain international absolute prohibitions of torture as binding. That is, according to German law *nothing* can (legally) outweigh the interest of not being tortured (or at least of not being tortured by state officials or agents acting on behalf of a state). That torture is illegal under all circumstances in a given system of law, however, does not exclude the possibility that the practice might under some circumstances be excused by the law. It seems to me that it would be reasonable to excuse it under some circumstances.[24] I shall, however, say nothing further on this topic here.

Instead, I shall say something about the proposal to *justify torture before the act* (rather than excusing it *ex post*). The lawyer Alan Dershowitz made the infamous suggestion to introduce legal 'torture warrants', issued by judges.

> ... it is important to ask the following question: if torture is being or will be practiced, is it worse to close our eyes to it and tolerate its use by low-level law enforcement officials without accountability, or instead to bring it to the surface by requiring that a warrant of some kind be required as a precondition to the infliction of any type of torture under any circumstances?[25]

And he states:

> My own belief is that a warrant requirement, if properly enforced, would probably reduce the frequency, severity, and duration of torture. I cannot see how it could possibly increase it, since a warrant requirement simply imposes an additional level of prior review. . . . here are two examples to demonstrate why I think there would be less torture with a warrant requirement than without one. Recall the case of the alleged national security wiretap being placed on the phones of Martin Luther King by the Kennedy administration in the early 1960s. This was in the days when the attorney general could authorize a national security wiretap without a warrant. Today no judge would issue a warrant in a case as flimsy as that one. When Zaccarias Moussaui was detained after trying to learn how to fly an airplane, without wanting to know much about landing it, the government did not even seek a national security wiretap because its lawyers believed that a judge would not have granted one.[26]

A few things must be said concerning this argument. First, closing one's eyes to the practice of torture is not the only alternative to the introduction of torture warrants. Unfortunately, Dershowitz seems to have difficulties grasping the difference between closing one's eyes on the one hand and exposing and condemning on the other. To wit, he criticises William Schulz, the executive director of Amnesty International USA, who asks whether Dershowitz would also favour brutality warrants and prisoner rape warrants. (Dershowitz answers with a 'heuristic yes', whatever that is supposed to be.)[27] And he quotes himself saying: 'My question back to Schulz is do you prefer the current situation in which brutality, testilying and prisoner rape are rampant, but we close our eyes to these evils?'[28] Who is 'we'? Certainly not Schulz or Amnesty International.[29]

Second, Dershowitz admits that he 'certainly cannot prove . . . that a formal requirement of a judicial warrant as prerequisite to nonlethal torture would decrease the amount of physical violence directed against suspects'.[30] It seems, however, that Dershowitz should offer something more than his personal 'belief' and two examples to back the quite grave proposal to legalise torture. That he does not displays a lightness about the matter which is out of place. To be sure, he also adduces John H. Langbein's historical study of torture,[31] and although he concedes that it 'does not definitely answer' 'whether there would be less torture if it were done as part of the legal system', he thinks that it 'does provide some suggestive insights'.[32] Yet, before drawing 'suggestive insights' from Langbein's study and from history, one should get both straight. Dershowitz does not.[33] In fact, Langbein leaves no doubt that torture was *not* part of the judicial system in England. Not only 'law enforcement officers' but also the courts (and judges) could not warrant torture. Langbein even states:

> The legal basis, such as it was, for the use of torture in the eighty-one known cases appears to have been the notion of sovereign immunity, a defensive doctrine that spared the authorities from having to supply justification for what they were doing.[34]

The facts, then, are that torture was never part of the English judicial system (if it was ever legal in England at all) whereas it *was* part of the Continental legal system. Extensive (not to say epidemic) use was made of torture on the Continent but not in England. Obviously, these facts suggest insights quite different from the ones Dershowitz comes up with.

Moreover, it is also funny that Dershowitz thinks that his two examples *support* his case. What his examples show (if they show anything) is that an attorney general who is *authorised* to put a wiretap without judicial warrant is more likely to put a wiretap than an attorney general who does need a warrant. However, the question to be answered is whether torture would be less likely under a requirement of a judicial warrant than *under a total ban*. To suggest a positive answer to this question by way of an analogy, Dershowitz would have to compare a legal arrangement in which the attorney general is *prohibited* from putting a wiretap with a legal arrangement where he is authorised to do so if he has a warrant. Dershowitz does not do that. It is he who engages in 'tortured reasoning', to use his term,[35] not his critics.

Finally, why shouldn't state agents who do not get a warrant torture anyway? They do not get a warrant today, and some of them torture anyway. Dershowitz answers that:

> . . . the current excuse being offered — we had to do what we did to get information — would no longer be available, since there would be an authorized method of securing information in extraordinary cases by the use of extraordinary means.[36]

First, people who escape detection are not in need of excuses to wriggle out of punishment in the first place. Besides, the excuse *would* be available. It would be: 'Since the judge didn't give us the warrant — he did not realise the seriousness of the situation (or there wasn't enough time) — we just had to torture under these circumstances without a warrant in order to get the information and to avoid a great evil'.

In short, Dershowitz has not offered the slightest bit of evidence — not even anecdotal — for his bold claim that the introduction of torture warrants would reduce torture or as much as increase accountability. Yet there is very good evidence to the contrary. Since Dershowitz invited us to draw suggestive insights from history, especially on the basis of Langbein's study, it might be worthwhile to note what Langbein himself has to say:

> Another insight from history is the danger that, once legitimated, torture could develop a constituency with a vested interest in perpetuating it.[37]

And that, to draw the conclusion Dershowitz isn't able to draw, would hardly help to reduce torture or to increase accountability.

But why *should* we try to reduce torture? After all, in the first part of this paper I have argued that no compelling argument for an absolute moral prohibition of torture can be made; yes, not even for a prohibition in the Dirty Harry cases. I have also argued that torture is not worse than death and probably not worse than a decade of incarceration. So since we have legal incarceration, why shouldn't we have legal torture too?

One very straightforward answer is: because we don't need it. The ticking bomb case or the Dirty Harry case is a very rare case. In fact, it is safe to assume that all the torture that happened or happens in Abu Ghraib, Afghanistan and Guantanamo simply has nothing to do with ticking bombs or hostages who are about to die. The same holds for the overwhelming majority of all other cases of torture. Ticking bomb and Dirty Harry cases are *exceptions*. An emergency or necessity paragraph along the lines of § 35 of the German penal code can deal with such exceptions, and perhaps not even that is needed. If the stakes are high enough and no other option is available, police officers or other state agents will probably use torture even if they face prosecution if caught (that is, incidentally, what Dershowitz himself claims). Besides, if punished, they might still be allowed the benefit of mitigating circumstances.

Second, that being tortured (or torturing someone) is not necessarily worse than being killed or incarcerated for a long time (or than killing someone or incarcerating him for a long time) does not imply that introducing a *wider practice* of torture is not worse than introducing or maintaining a wider practice of incarceration or killing. Dershowitz, for example, acknowledges:

> Experience has shown that if torture, which has been deemed illegitimate by the civilized world for more than a century, were now to be legitimated — even for limited use in one extraordinary type of situation — such legitimation would constitute an important symbolic setback in the worldwide campaign against human rights abuses.[38]

However, he thinks:

> It does not necessarily follow from this understandable fear of the slippery slope that we can never consider the use of nonlethal infliction of pain, if its

use were to be limited by acceptable principles of morality. After all, imprison-
ing a witness who refuses to testify after being given immunity is designed to
be punitive — that is painful. Such imprisonment can, on occasion, produce
more pain and greater risk of death than nonlethal torture.[39]

It does indeed not follow that we can never consider the use of non-lethal infliction of
pain, but it does follow that *institutionalising* torture — for example with torture warrants — is a bad idea. In particular, the analogy with the practice of coercing witnesses
through imprisonment into testifying is misleading. The practice is designed to be
punitive, yes, but that is not the same as being designed to be *painful*. Not every
aversive treatment causes pain. It is important not to blur the distinctions. Further, the
very fact that imprisonment produces only *on occasion* more pain and greater risk of
death than non-lethal torture (although I suppose that non-lethal imprisonment would
carry no risk of death) shows that it is not designed to produce pain and death. After
all, being released can, on occasion, also produce more pain and greater risk of death
than non-lethal torture. But how is that supposed to support the case for torture or for
torture warrants? Thus, by using imprisonment as a method of punishment we are *not*
already on the slippery slope.

Even if legalising torture puts us on a slippery slope, couldn't we stop the slide
downwards? Dershowitz proposes a 'principled break':

> For example, if nonlethal torture were legally limited to convicted terrorists
> who had knowledge of future massive terrorist acts, were given immunity,
> and still refused to provide the information, there might still be objections to
> the use of torture, but they would have to go beyond the slippery slope
> argument.[40]

Actually, one argument that could be made here is that a *convicted* terrorist will
hardly be a ticking bomb terrorist, unless, of course, he has set the time fuse on a few
months or even years in the future *or* his conviction was made without due process.
Giving up due process, however, does not look very much like a 'principled break', at
least if the principle is supposed to be compatible with the rule of law. That notwithstanding, it has to be admitted that 'massive terrorist acts' will have to be planned long
enough in advance so that a convicted terrorist might have knowledge of them. Consequently, torturing him might be a means to thwart the attacks.

However, Dershowitz's talk about a 'principled break' does, in fact, not address the
problem of an 'important symbolic setback in the world-wide campaign against human
rights abuses' at all. The symbolic setback consists precisely in undermining the *absolute* prohibition on torture and cannot be compensated, probably not even mitigated,
by recourse to alleged 'principled breaks'. Moreover, the whole idea of a 'principled
break' in connection with 'security laws' that cut down on civil liberties and individual
rights is rather naïve. (I put 'security laws' in quotation marks because cutting down on
civil liberties and individual rights hardly increases an individual's security from the
state — the political entity, it should be remembered, that has slaughtered more people
than any other political entity in history and is certainly more dangerous than any sub-
national terrorist organisation.) Experience shows that measures introduced against
putative terrorists in alleged conditions of emergency tend to be doubly extended,
namely, beyond the emergency and to crimes or offences of lesser seriousness. In the

UK, for example, emergency anti-terrorist measures, such as limitations on the right to silence, admissibility of confession evidence and extended periods of pre-judicial detention, have infiltrated ordinary criminal law and procedure.[41] Once advertised as being targeted only against terrorists, they can now befall any citizen who gets involved in criminal procedure.

It is to be expected, then, that the legalisation of torture for certain specific circumstances will, just like other so-called security laws, come with an inherent 'metastatic tendency'[42] that in time extends it beyond those circumstances. Apart from this dangerous tendency of 'security laws' in general there is, in addition, something very *special* about torture. Jeremy Waldron has argued that the prohibition of torture is archetypical of the idea:

> ... that even where law has to operate forcefully, there will not be the connection that has existed in other times or places between law and *brutality*. People may fear and be deterred by legal sanctions ... they may even on occasion be forced ... to do things or go places against their will. But even when this happens, they will not be herded like cattle or broken like horses; they will not be beaten like dumb animals or treated as bodies to be manipulated. Instead, there will be an enduring connection between the spirit of law and respect for human dignity — respect for human dignity even *in extremis*, where law is at its most forceful and its subjects at their most vulnerable.[43]

That the prohibition of torture is a legal *archetype* means that it has 'a significance stemming from the fact that it sums up or makes vivid to us the point, purpose, principle, or policy of a whole area of law'.[44] For example, Waldron shows that decisive court rulings against lesser forms of police brutality — lesser, that is, than torture — were made with reference to torture. The similarities with torture were invoked to reject those other brutalities. This, of course, would not be possible if torture itself became regularised and justified by law, for the similarity with a regular legal practice could hardly count against some other practice. As Waldron puts it:

> The idea is that our confidence that what lies at the bottom of the slope (torture) is wrong informs and supports our confidence that the lesser evils that lie above torture are wrong too.[45]

Thus, by undermining the archetype of the prohibition of torture one also undermines the prohibition of lesser forms of brutality. The whole set of injunctions against brutality would unravel and the character of the legal system would be corrupted.[46]

What is so frightening about such a brutalisation of the legal system is that it is also the brutalisation of its *enforcer* — which, in modern societies, is ultimately the *state*. It is one thing to grant to an individual in a certain situation the moral justification to torture another individual; it is a completely different thing to allow the state to legally institutionalise torture in certain circumstances. Dirty Harry has to justify himself not only morally but also legally. He might face legal charges, and that might make him think twice before he tortures someone. This, in fact, ensures that the slope of the moral permission of torture in certain cases does not become too slippery to be acceptable. Dirty Harry takes his decision as an individual, not as an agent of the state. The state is not behind him. But if law enforcers can resort to torture knowing in advance that the state is behind them, the worst has to be expected — on a large and inevitably growing scale. Here it is worth noting that the argument that the prohibition of torture is an archetype and the argument that the legal introduction of torture would have a metastatic tendency reinforce each other. The further the practice of torture extends, the more it will undermine the archetypical character of the prohibition; the more that happens, the further the practice will extend. It is not only a slippery slope but also a slope that on its way down gets exponentially steeper. One of the functions of the rule of law is to keep the power of the state under control. But this doesn't work with *any* law. It doesn't work with a brutal or brutalised one. Torture warrants are indeed a 'stunningly bad idea'.[47]

## NOTES

1  H. Shue, 'Torture' in S. Levinson (ed.) *Torture: A Collection* (Oxford: Oxford University Press, 2004), pp. 49–60, at p. 49.

2  *Ibid.*

3  *Ibid.*, pp. 50f.

4  *Ibid.*, p. 51.

5  Henry Shue has meanwhile in conversation distanced himself somewhat from drawing a parallel between the prohibition of torture and *jus in bello* requirements.

6  David Rodin claims that, contrary to torture victims, soldiers in trenches are not entirely defenceless, for they could surrender, retreat or dig into deeper trenches; and, had they been better prepared, they would have found more protective shelter or been equipped with longer-range guns (personal communication). However, had the torture victim been better prepared she might have escaped or killed herself in order not to become a torture victim in the first place. But if she indeed has become a torture victim, she is defenceless under the torture, as are the soldiers in the trenches who are not lucky (or good) enough to have suitable weapons. As to the first point, the torture victim can surrender too and disclose the information. Such surrender might not always be accepted, but likewise the surrender of soldiers in trenches is not always seen by artillerists miles away or hidden behind a cloud of smoke. Finally, to suggest that trench soldiers subjected to heavy artillery fire should in that situation be able to dig into deeper trenches seems to be as unrealistic as to suggest that a torture victim should protect herself by yoga or meditation techniques.

7  Jeff McMahan thinks that the relevant principle here is not proportionality but minimal force. (Personal communication) I disagree, but the disagreement may simply be a semantic one, namely one about what 'proportionality' *means* within the context of *jus in bello*. Be that as it may, the important point for the purposes of the present discussion is that an alleged principle of the immunity of the defenceless plays no role here.

8  H. Münkler, *Die neuen Kriege* (Reinbek bei Hamburg: Rowohlt, 2003), p. 234, my translation.

9  D. Sussman, 'What's wrong with torture?', *Philosophy and Public Affairs* 33, 1 (2005): 4.

10  *Ibid.*, n. 10.

11  *Ibid.*, p. 4.

12  *Ibid.*, p. 21.

13  *Ibid.*, p. 30.

14  The example is a variant of Bernard Williams's famous example of Jim and the twenty Indians.

15  S. Levinson, 'The debate on torture: war on virtual states', *Dissent* (Summer) (2003): 79–90, at pp. 83f.

16  P. Montague, 'The morality of self-defense: a reply to Wasserman', *Philosophy and Public Affairs* 18 (1989): 81–89, at pp. 81f. Ryan advocates a similar position to Montague's. See C. C. Ryan, 'Self-defense, pacifism, and the possibility of killing', *Ethics* 93 (1984): 508–524, at pp. 515ff.

17  See S. Levinson, 'Contemplating torture: an introduction' in Levinson (2004) op. cit. (see n. 1), pp. 23–43, at pp. 33ff., and the further references there.

18  R. H. Weisberg, 'Loose professionalism' in Levinson (2004) op. cit., pp. 299–305, at p. 304.

19  Jeff McMahan agrees that this person cannot complain under the circumstances but thinks that this still does not make him liable to be tortured, the reason being that 'torturing him serves no purpose under the circumstances'. (Personal communication) However, if he cannot complain, he cannot be being wronged

(for then he obviously could complain); and I think that the only possible reason why someone is not wronged by an attack (for example in the form of torture) is that he is liable to the attack. In fact, this seems to be pretty much the meaning of 'liable to attack'. Besides, if someone unjustly shoots at me and I shoot back, hitting him in the shoulder, and he continues shooting and kills me, then my counterattack has served no purpose under the circumstances (if it had, I would not be dead). That makes my counterattack hardly unjust or the attacker not liable to be shot at (otherwise every unsuccessful defender would also be an unjust defender, which is absurd).

20  D. Luban, (2005) 'Liberalism and the unpleasant question of torture', http://ethics.stanford.edu/ newsletter/_old/december/Liberalism%20and%20the%20Unpleasant%20Question%20Question%20of% 20Torture.doc, accessed on 2 October 2005, electronic resource. A comparable argument is put forward by K. Seth, 'Too close to the rack and the screw: constitutional constraints on torture in the war on terror', *University of Pennsylvania Journal of Constitutional Law* 6 (2003–2004): 278–325.

21  The translation is mine.

22  A. Dorfman, 'The tyranny of terror: is torture inevitable in our century and beyond?' in Levinson (2004) op. cit., pp. 3–18, at p. 17.

23  Torturing this person would, of course, be a case of self-preservation and not of self- or other-defence (or something close to it) as in the Dirty Harry case.

24  That seems to be the position of Shue op. cit., pp. 58f., and R. A. Posner, R. A. 'Torture, terrorism, and interrogation' in Levinson (2004) op. cit., pp. 291–298, at pp. 297f.; and it is the position of O. Gross, O. 'The prohibition on torture and the limits of the law' in Levinson (2004) op. cit., pp. 229–253, esp. at pp. 231 and 239–250.

25  A. Dershowitz, 'Tortured reasoning' in Levinson (2004) op. cit., pp. 257–280, at p. 257. He emphasises that *that* was his question and not the 'old, abstract' one 'over whether torture can ever be justified', and he complains about 'misleading' descriptions of his proposals. *Ibid.*, p. 266. Maybe the next time he addresses the former question instead of the latter he could help to avoid 'misleading' descriptions of his intentions by not using titles like 'Should the Ticking Bomb Terrorist Be Tortured?' See A. Dershowitz, *Why Terrorism Works: Understanding the Threats, Responding to the Challenge* (New Haven, CT: Yale University Press, 2002) p. 131.

26  Dershowitz (2004) op. cit., pp. 270f.

27  *Ibid.*, pp. 266f.

28  *Ibid.*, p. 267. '"Testilying" is a term coined by New York City police to describe systematic perjury regarding the circumstances that led to a search, seizure, or interrogation'. *Ibid.*, p. 278, n. 13.

29  Compare E. Scarry, 'Five errors in the reasoning of Alan Dershowitz' in Levinson (2004) op. cit., pp. 281–290, at p. 288.

30  Dershowitz (2002) op. cit., p. 158.

31  J. H. Langbein, *Torture and the Law of Proof: Europe and England in the Ancien Régime* (Chicago, IL: University of Chicago Press, 1977).

32  Dershowitz (2002) op. cit., p. 158.

33  On Dershowitz's misreading of Langbein see also J. Waldron, 'Torture and positive law: jurisprudence for the White House', *Columbia Law Review* 105 (2005): 1739, n. 250.

34  J. H. Langbein, 'The legal history of torture' in Levinson (2004) op. cit., pp. 93–103, at p. 100.

35  Dershowitz (2004) op. cit., p. 257.

36  *Ibid.*, p. 276.

37  Langbein (2004) op. cit., p. 101.

38  Dershowitz (2002) op. cit., p. 145.

39  *Ibid.*, p. 147.

40  *Ibid.*

41  P. Hillyard, 'The normalization of special powers from Northern Ireland to Britain' in N. Lacey (ed.) *A Reader on Criminal Justice* (Oxford: Oxford University Press, 1994); O. Gross, 'Cutting down trees: law-making under the shadow of great calamities' in R. J. Daniels, P. Macklem and K. Roach (eds.) *The Security of Freedom: Essays on Canada's Anti-Terrorism Bill* (Toronto: Toronto University Press, 2001), pp. 39–61, esp. at 47ff. I owe the references to these articles to L. Zedner, 'Securing liberty in the face of terror: reflections from criminal justice', pp. 7 and 15, and to C. Warbrick, 'Terrorism, counter-terrorism, international law', p. 9, unpublished papers held at the colloquium *Moral and Legal Aspects of Terrorism*, Corpus Christi College, Oxford, 5 March 2005.

42  Shue op. cit., p. 58.

43 Waldron op. cit., pp. 1726f.

44 *Ibid.*, p. 1723.

45 *Ibid.*, p. 1735.

46 *Ibid.*, p. 1728–1739.

47 J. B. Elshtain, 'Reflections on the problem of "dirty hands"' in Levinson (2004) op. cit., pp. 77–89, at p. 83. I owe thanks to Patrick Lenta, Jeff McMahan and David Rodin for helpful comments on an earlier draft of this paper.

# 9 Torture, Terrorism and the State: a Refutation of the Ticking-Bomb Argument

VITTORIO BUFACCHI AND JEAN MARIA ARRIGO

It should not come as a surprise that human rights are among the first casualties in the War on Terrorism.[1] Yet recent policy proposals in the fight against terrorism are threatening to take human rights violations to a level until recently unimaginable. In the corridors of the White House, and perhaps behind the doors in Downing Street, arguments have begun to surface that in certain extreme cases the use of torture may be justified, and therefore ought to be legalized.

This paper argues for the unconditional refutation of any attempt to justify torture, under any circumstances.[2] After giving a brief account of the concept of torture in Part I, and the standard deontological arguments against torture in Part II, in Part III the best-known argument in favour of the legitimate use of state-sponsored torture on terrorists will be put forward — the ticking-bomb argument. This will be followed in Part IV by a classification of different types of torture. Parts V, and VI will expose two major fallacies in the ticking-bomb argument: the Deductive Fallacy highlights the problems with the premises used by the ticking-bomb argument to infer its conclusion regarding the justified use of torture interrogations; the Consequentialist Fallacy points to the empirical evidence suggesting that the negative consequences of implementing a policy of torture interrogation outweigh any possible positive consequences; therefore arguments for torture interrogation of terrorists can be refuted on consequentialist grounds. Part VII will reject the moral calculus of torture endorsed by the ticking-bomb argument.

## I. Definition of Torture

Torture is universally condemned in international law. The English Declaration of Rights barred cruel and unusual punishments 300 years ago, while in the United States the prohibition of cruel and unusual punishment was incorporated into the US Constitution more than 200 years ago. In the 20th century, torture was outlawed by the Universal Declaration of Human Rights in 1948, and the United Nations passed the Declaration against Torture in 1975. In 1984 the UN General Assembly adopted the Convention Against Torture and Other Cruel, Inhuman or Degrading Treatment or Punishment (hereafter Torture Convention), which was ratified in 1987.[3]

The Torture Convention gives the following definition of torture (Article 1):

> Any act by which severe pain or suffering, whether physical or mental, is intentionally inflicted on a person for such purposes as obtaining from him or a third person information or a confession, punishing him for an act he or a

third person has committed or is suspected of having committed, or intimidating or coercing him or a third person, or for any reason based on discrimination of any kind, when such pain or suffering is inflicted by or at the instigation of or with the consent or acquiescence of a public official or other person acting in an official capacity.

There are a few aspects of this definition worth accentuating. First of all, torture can be both physical and/or psychological, and it need not result in death. That is to say, torture is still torture even if its victims are not on the brink of death. Secondly, torture is a form of political violence, being administered by people acting in an official capacity. Finally, Article 2.2 states that there can be no exceptions to the ban on torture ('No exceptional circumstances whatever, whether a state of war or a threat of war, internal political instability or any other public emergency, may be invoked as a justification of torture'), and Article 3.1 states that outsourcing torture is illegal ('No State shall expel, return or extradite a person to another State where there are grounds for believing that he would be in danger of being subjected to torture').

The United States, Britain, and all other liberal democracies are signatories to this Convention; indeed the international legal definition of torture is universally recognized and accepted. Yet, in 2002 Amnesty International reported state-sponsored torture or severe abuse in over 100 countries.[4] Furthermore not all of the countries that practice torture are totalitarian regimes, or enemies of liberal democracies. It is a well known fact that in the past, and most probably the present too, the United States used torture, but in a sinister way, by sending suspects they wanted to interrogate to other countries where torture is practiced.[5]

Although methods of torture are so varied as to defy easy definitions,[6] there seem to be certain commonalities in the stratagems and techniques used by torturers.[7] In contemporary, politically motivated torture, it appears that the essence of the practice is degradation of the subject. Standard methods are sexual violations and humiliations; exposure to filth, especially excrement;[8] desecration of religious objects and rituals; and corruption of relationships with family members, compatriots, or military comrades.

## II. A Deontological Refutation of Torture

From a deontological perspective, there are two ways of explaining why torture is wrong. First, if we assume a moral duty to treat each and every human being with due concern and respect, torture is wrong to the extent that it is cruel and degrading, and it constitutes a violation of fundamental rights. Secondly, as David Sussman (2005)[9] argues in a recent article, the wrongness of torture cannot be fully grasped by understanding torture as just an extreme instance of other kinds of violence, cruelty, or degrading treatment. Instead, Sussman believes that there is a core concept of what constitutes torture that corresponds to a distinctive, special kind of wrong. What makes torture more morally offensive that other ways of inflicting great physical or psychological harm is the element of self-betrayal, to the extent that torture forces its victims into a position of colluding against themselves, making the victim an active participant in his or her own abuse.

Whichever line one takes on the nature of the wrongness of torture, there are some aspects of torture that any adversary of this practice agrees on, for example, the moral prohibition to humiliate another human being. The literature of testimonial evidence from different parts of the world, including Algeria, Latin America, Iraq, Ireland, Korea, Vietnam, Tibet, Soviet Union and South Africa, suggests that the essence of torture is humiliation. This would in part explain why some male prisoners are sodomized, and as Deborah Blatt (1992)[10] points out, it also explains why torturers often rape women. Many women endure further degrading and humiliating treatment that accompanies rape, for example being stripped naked in front of their community prior to being raped, or being raped in the presence of their family.[11] Rape as torture reflects everything that is wrong with torture: no-one has a right to undermine the dignity of another person,[12] nor to violate their integrity, diminishing their sense of personhood, depriving them of their self-respect and self-esteem.[13]

We suspect many would be convinced by the deontological argument, yet consequentialist defences of state-sponsored torture interrogation practices could object that this argument is valid for the vast majority of cases, but it does not extend as far as to cover exceptional circumstances. In other words, one can be in agreement with the deontological argument, and still argue that extraordinary behaviour is necessary under extraordinary circumstances; there are times when torture is the only option, a lesser evil compared to the greater evil of innocent people being killed.

## III. The Ticking-bomb Argument

Much of the literature on torture in recent years takes the position of denouncing torture as a basic rule, while allowing for exceptions to the rule in extreme circumstances.[14] In what follows we will refer to this as the Rule-and-Exception Argument. Following in the footsteps of Jeremy Bentham,[15] this type of argument has been embraced by both moral philosophers and legal experts in recent years.

Amongst the philosophers, two notable examples stand out. Although it would appear that he has since revised his views on the question, in a famous article published almost thirty years ago, after doing a very thorough job of discrediting the standard arguments behind the justification of torture, Henry Shue (1977–78, p. 57)[16] allows for the possibility that, at least in theory, in certain extreme scenarios interrogational torture can be permitted: 'Nevertheless, it cannot be denied that there are imaginable cases in which the harm that could be prevented by a rare instance of . . . torture would be so enormous as to outweigh the cruelty of the torture itself'.[17] Similarly Bernard Gert (1969, p. 623)[18] is prepared to argue that while all killing and torturing for pleasure or profit is clearly immoral, 'killing and torturing to prevent greater killing and torturing may sometimes be allowed by public reason'.

One finds the same line of reasoning in the works of legal theorists. In postulating a situation where killing an innocent person may save a whole nation, Charles Fried (1978, p. 10)[19] is adamant in his view that 'it seems fanatical to maintain the absoluteness of the judgment, to do right even if the heavens will in fact fall'. Similarly Richard Posner (2004, p. 294)[20] argues that 'there is such a thing as a lesser wrong committed to avoid a greater one. There is such a thing as fighting fire with fire, and it is an apt metaphor for the use of torture and other extreme measures when nothing else will avert catastrophe'.

Here we are confronted with justifications, initially of a legal nature but ultimately also moral, for torturing terrorists in extreme circumstances. We believe this is the correct interpretative key not only in the case of Posner and Fried, but also of two other influential legal experts, namely John Parry and Alan Dershowitz.[21] Thus, after denouncing torture as a violation of international and domestic law, legal theorist John Parry (2004, p. 160)[22] says, 'Torture may be a legitimate option — the lesser of two evils — in rare circumstances. In theory, we can admit an exception to an otherwise universal prohibition'. Similarly after declaring that he is opposed to torture on normative grounds, Alan Dershowitz (2004)[23] argues that in a ticking-bomb argument it may be permissible to allow terrorists to be tortured, a radical solution offered on pragmatic grounds as a way of reducing or eliminating the widespread but illicit use of torture in the United States today.

The positions advocated by Parry and Dershowitz are radically different, and should not be amalgamated. Parry argues that while torture should not be legitimate, if torture provides the last remaining chance to save innocent lives in imminent peril, after the event the 'necessity defence' should be available to justify the interrogators' conduct in a court of law.[24] On the other hand Dershowitz famously puts forward the idea of a 'torture warrant', which legalizes the use of torture prior to its use. Parry and Dershowitz present different reasons for justifying torture interrogations of terrorists, indeed Parry is very critical of Dershowitz' proposal, yet both authors have no qualms about using the ticking-bomb argument in order to justify their conclusions.

Descriptions of the ticking-bomb argument vary,[25] yet all the different accounts of this hypothetical scenario have three common elements: (1) the lives of a large number of innocent civilians are in danger; (2) the catastrophe is imminent, therefore time is of the essence; (3) a terrorist has been captured who holds information that could prevent the catastrophe from occurring. Under these extreme circumstances, Parry and Dershowitz argue that torturing the terrorist who has the information needed to save the lives of the innocent civilians can be justified, either because the torturer can appeal to a necessary defence argument (Parry), or because the interrogators were issued with a valid torture warrant (Dershowitz).

Drawing conclusions from thought-experiments is not as easy at it may seem. The ticking-bomb argument is so hyperbolical to have more affinities with science fiction than political science. As Shue (2003) rightly says, justifications for torture thrive in fantasy, and as every moral philosopher knows only too well, fantasy makes for bad ethical theory. Utilitarian philosopher Russell Hardin (1988, pp. 22–23)[26] also reminds us that the use of hypothetical examples in consequentialist moral reasoning, especially peculiar examples, may be subject to various distortions, overburdening our limited reasoning capacities: 'once the value of entertainment enters discussion, it too often drives out other values, especially reasonableness, relevance, and even understanding'.

In the hypothetical ticking-bomb argument, it is simply assumed that torture is the only way of extracting information from a terrorist, not merely an accompanying condition. But in the real world, torture may not be the cause of success. The following case history, provided by a former US interrogator in the Middle East, illustrates this point.[27]

> Five foreign terrorists were captured by the local [counterterrorist police team]. All were found under arms with explosives and maps of targets. . . . The question of how many [terrorist] cells were to be sent to the country to other targets

was of interest. The first three terrorists were not even questioned, only shot. The next two were asked the question separately. One shot was heard. The officer said to the last terrorist, 'Do you also want to remain silent?' The guy began to lay out the entire operation, the training the cells had received, where they were to meet, where the weapons depots were located, and the route that the terrorists were to take to exfiltrate the country. . . . The other cells were picked up along with in-country support personnel.

A hypothetical case admits no probes. But in this actual case, we were able to ask how the fifth man was chosen.

The group was searched and then fed and given tea as per the *Shariat* law of the Koran. Those who refused to eat or drink and made intense hostile eye contact were selected as the first three. The body posture decided who went fourth. The youngest, who ate the bread, drank tea, and thanked his captors was determined to be the least experienced. His AK rifle was not even clean . . . and he did not appear committed to the *jihad*.[28]

From the elaboration of the scenario arise other possible explanations for the co-operation of the fifth terrorist, such as his liberation from the coercion by the elder terrorists or his susceptibility to bribery or good care. The narrative certainly does not support the interpretation that shooting any four of the terrorists was a necessary or sufficient condition for the fifth terrorist to reveal the terrorist operation. As for most ticking-bomb success stories, the efficacy of torture interrogation is demonstrated only if the case is framed on that premise.

Notwithstanding its extreme hypothetical nature and often circular reasoning, the ticking-bomb argument is being taken very seriously, not only by legal theorists and experts, but also (more worryingly) in the corridors of power.

## IV. A Classification of Torture

In the rest of this paper we are going to argue that torture cannot be justified, not even in theory, or under the most exceptional circumstances of the ticking-bomb scenario. But before we put forward reasons why the ticking-bomb argument cannot justify the use of torture, in an effort to make the strongest case for torture interrogation of terrorists, it is necessary to be clear on the type of torture being discussed in this paper. First of all, it is important to distinguish between Terroristic Torture and Interrogational Torture.[29] Terroristic Torture refers to torture used as a deterrent, a statement of intent by the State. Terroristic Torture is meant as a signal to those who defy the legitimacy of State authorities. During the civil war in Guatemala (1960–1996), for example, the Guatemalan army made extensive use of Terroristic Torture, leaving the bodies of torture victims on the side of the roads for everyone to see.[30] Interrogational Torture on the other hand is used exclusively with the intent of extracting information from the terrorists. It is Interrogational Torture rather than Terroristic Torture that will be the topic of our analysis in this paper.

It is also important to distinguish between Backward-Looking and Forward-Looking Interrogational Torture. Backward-Looking Interrogational Torture occurs when torture is used to extract confessions from terrorists regarding past terrorist actions; Forward-Looking Interrogational Torture occurs when torture is used to extract information regarding future terrorist plots. In what follows, by torture we mean exclusively Forward-Looking Interrogational Torture. It is this type of torture that Parry and Dershowitz believe can be justified. Contrary to the views of Parry and Dershowitz, in what follows we are going to argue that not even Forward-Looking Interrogational Torture presents an exception to the unconditional veto on torture by a democratic state. In particular we are going to argue that the ticking-bomb argument falls prey to two fallacies: the Deductive Fallacy and the Consequentialist Fallacy.

## V. The Deductive Fallacy

The Deductive Fallacy occurs when a certain argument infers invalid conclusions from certain premises, either because the conclusions rest on a different set of premises, and/or because the premises don't support the conclusions. The ticking-bomb argument follows a deductive line of reasoning concerning the efficacy of torture interrogation.

> (P1): Terrorist is captured.
> (P2): If the terrorist is tortured, he/she will reveal information regarding the location of the primed bomb before the bomb detonates.
> Therefore (C1): Terrorist ought to be tortured.
> Therefore (C2): The information regarding the location of the primed bomb is retrieved.
> Therefore (C3): The bomb is found and disconnected before it explodes, saving the lives of many innocent people.

There are two sets of problems with this argument. The first problem is that the Conclusions C1, C2 and C3 do not follow from Premises P1 and P2. In order to draw these conclusions, other 'invisible' premises must be in place. The second problem is that the premises (both visible and invisible) from which the ticking-bomb argument deduces its conclusions are illegitimate, being questionable from an empirical point of view.

In order to deduce Conclusions C1, C2 and C3, all the above premises are required:

> (P1): Terrorist is captured.
> (P1*): It is almost certain that this is the terrorist holding information regarding a primed bomb.
> (P2): If the terrorist is tortured, he/she will reveal information regarding the location of the primed bomb before the bomb detonates.
> Therefore (C1): Terrorist ought to be tortured.
> Therefore (C2): The information regarding the location of the primed bomb is retrieved.
> (P3): It is almost certain that the terrorist will reveal the correct information.
> Therefore (C3): The bomb is found and disconnected before it explodes, saving the lives of many innocent people.

All the premises in the argument are contentious from an empirical point of view. First, 'intelligence' is never infallible, as the fiasco regarding the weapons of mass destruction in Iraq clearly demonstrates; therefore the assumption that the terrorist captured is 'almost certainly' the terrorist holding the information is problematic. There is no guarantee that the suspects being interrogated are in fact terrorists, or, even if they are involved with a terrorist group, that they in fact have the information that we seek.

Second, torture is not guaranteed to work, and the assumption that torture will make terrorists collaborate is both over-simplistic and over-optimistic. The French General Paul Aussaresses (2002),[31] chief intelligence officer in the Battle for Algiers (1955–1957), in his memoir, described terrorists dying under torture with their secrets or exasperating him to the point of murdering them himself. Between 1987 and 1994, the Israeli General Security Service officially interrogated 23,000 Palestinians, torturing the great majority, yet terrorism flourished.[32]

Third, there is very little evidence suggesting that torture obtains the results within a short time period. Indeed counterinterrogation training of operators may prescribe resistance for 24 hours, so as to allow colleagues to alter plans before exposure.[33] The extreme urgency of the ticking-bomb argument also works against the strength of torture interrogation, which is not quick coercion but degradation of the subject's resistance over months rather than minutes. Al Qaeda suspect Mohamed al-Kahtani, reputedly the missing twentieth hijacker, was turned away by a customs agent at Orlando International Airport on August 4, 2001. He returned to Afghanistan and was captured in December, fighting for Osama bin Laden. It was only after months of imprisonment, under harsh interrogation assisted by military doctors, that he divulged information on his meetings with Osama bin Laden.[34]

Fourth, even if an interrogator can torture some information out of a suspected terrorist, there is no guarantee that the information given under duress is in fact the correct information. Therefore, the assumption that the terrorist will 'almost certainly' reveal the correct information is questionable. Torture increases physiological and psychological variability in subjects and hence unpredictability. Empirical evidence indicates that more times than not the information gathered under torture is the wrong information, being the result of a false confession.[35] Terrorists may say anything for the sake of temporarily stopping the torture, but the information they reveal may be the wrong information, as has been found common in criminal confessions under coercive interrogation. Interrogation further creates opportunities for deception by savvy captives. In a famous World War II incident, American fighter pilot Marcus McDilda, captured by the Japanese on August 8, 1945, 'revealed' under rough interrogation that the US would drop atomic bombs on Kyoto and Tokyo within a few days.[36] Commander James Stockdale (2001, p. 328)[37] ordered his fellow American POWs in Vietnam to 'resist to the point of permanent injury or loss of mental faculty, and then fall back on deceit and distortion'.

Finally, captives may reveal what they wrongly believe is the correct information, for handlers may feed false information to 'expendable agents' and send them into situations of certain capture to reveal the lies under torture. The Chinese military theorist Sun Tzu recommended this strategy in the 6th century BC.[38]

Apart from the fact that the ticking-bomb argument draws its conclusions from a set of empirically questionable premises, there is also another problem, of a different nature, with the logic of the ticking-bomb argument. In (P2) we seem to be presented with a very simple factual premise, namely, that if the terrorist is tortured, he/she will reveal information regarding the location of the primed bomb. This premise is then used as the main grounds for a deductive argument. In what follows we will show that this premise is standing-in for a more complex thesis, one about the best method for maximizing welfare. In other words, a consequentialist argument is being made without its being presented as such. Yet, once spelled out, the consequentialist nature of this premise can be seen to be false.

## VI. The Consequentialist Fallacy[39]

From a moral point of view the appeal of the ticking-bomb argument depends on a consequentialist intuition, whereby the costs of allowing the practice of torture interrogation are counterbalanced and outweighed by the gains of the practice. In what follows, we are going to adopt a consequentialist argument to undermine the consequentialist reasoning used to justify torture interrogations. We believe the ticking-bomb argument ultimately fails as a consequentialist argument because it ignores the intensive preparation and larger social consequences of state-sponsored torture. The validity of any consequentialist argument rests on a costs and benefit analysis. We argue that empirical evidence clearly suggests that institutionalizing torture interrogation of terrorists has detrimental consequences on civil, military and legal institutions, making the costs higher than the benefits. As an indication of the devastation to key social institutions, we examine potential consequences of making torture interrogations legitimate on the medical establishment, the scientific establishment, the police, the military establishment, and the legal establishment.

### *The Medical Establishment*

If the terrorist dies under torture, crucial information may be lost. Merely hooding a suspect who has asthma, for example, can cause death. In Afghanistan, US military police accidentally killed two detainees in 2002 by beating their legs. The beatings unexpectedly complicated pre-existing coronary artery disease in one detainee and created a pulmonary embolism in the other.[40] To prevent such losses of information, state sponsors of torture routinely employ medical professionals to determine the types of torture the subject can endure, monitor the subject for endurance under torture, resuscitate the unconscious subject, and treat the subject in preparation for further torture. Afterwards, physicians are used to falsify health certificates, autopsy reports, and death certificates.[41]

Medical professionals thus become privy to sensitive information and must be monitored, perhaps coerced. In Turkey, for example, government authorities have harassed, arrested, and tortured physicians who resisted.[42] Physicians can also take the lead. Former US Navy Chief of Neuropsychiatry at Guantanamo Bay, William Henry Anderson (2004, p. 55)[43] wrote that 'There are about 1.4 billion Muslims in the world. Embedded within this healthy body are, perhaps, 100,000 people who are eager and active in their pursuit of killing us. Just as successful treatment of cancer requires killing of the malignant cells, we will need to kill this small minority,' whom he identified as having 'brains that are structurally and functionally different from ours'. American military medical personnel have at least tolerated torture of prisoners in Iraq,

Afghanistan, and Guantanamo Bay. Meanwhile, in numerous medical journals, physicians have expressed outrage at the complicity of US military medical personnel.[44] Thus deep schisms arise within medical communities and between medical communities and their governments.

### The Scientific Establishment

Torture interrogation techniques evolve in competition with counter-interrogation techniques (for spies, combat pilots, and terrorists) and with the torture detection techniques of human rights monitors. As a Palestinian released from an Israeli prison explained: 'We learned about all the types of ill-treatment and the techniques that the secret police use, and we learned to observe the behavior of enemy officers during our interrogation'[45] — thereby strengthening their resistance under torture. When the European Union Commission postponed Turkey's admission into the European Union because of the stream of refugee torture victims arriving in Europe, Turkish scientists attempted to develop torture techniques that leave no medical trace. In response, European forensic experts employed successively more refined methods of detection, such as ultrasonography and CAT scans.[46] Thus develops the scientific race between techniques of torture and techniques of resistance and detection.

Scientists working on military projects are often ignorant of the applications of their work, and may later find themselves compromised. In 1980, the medical engineer Eldon Byrd developed electromagnetic resonance as a non-lethal, humanitarian weapon for the US Navy in lieu of bullets 'that punch holes in people and have their blood leak out'. He later discovered the weapon applied to 'human experimentations on non-compliant individuals' and devoted much effort to helping victims.[47] Other scientists welcome the opportunity for secret, illegal research on human subjects to advance their own careers. In the 1950s, under CIA cover, the eminent Ewen Cameron, a president of the American Psychiatric Association, conducted criminal mind control experiments on psychiatric inpatients, then published sanitized reports of his research on 'psychic driving' in academic journals.[48] Scientific pursuit of successful techniques of torture interrogation would require a vast program of criminal experimentation. As a guide to the possible extent of scientific involvement, a 1977 Senate investigation determined that 80 major civilian universities and hospitals had covertly participated in the illegal CIA behavioural modification program MKULTRA.[49]

### The Police

As the War on Terror moves into the homeland, police will be at the forefront of terrorist detentions simply because of their numbers: as of October 2002 there were 800,000 police officers in the US, compared to 27,000 FBI agents.[50] A program of torture interrogation of terrorists would generate the impossible task of discriminating between terrorist and non-terrorist criminal suspects, because of many overlapping criminal activities (e.g. forgery, money laundering, illegal immigration). Counterterrorist units could not maintain a monopoly on the use of torture because investigators of other serious crimes would demand the privilege. Already the October 2002 *USA Patriot Act*, which suspends important civil liberties in pursuit of terrorists, has been applied broadly to serial murder, corporate fraud, blackmail, and child pornography.[51] Police departments have struggled for decades with the overwhelming bad consequences of coercive interrogation, including high rates of false confessions and false testimony; police deception and manipulation of courts; failure of systems of oversight; and involvement of organized crime.[52] Legalization of torture interrogation may be expected to revive all these problems.

## The Military Establishment

For the military, the most grievous consequences of a torture interrogation program are demoralization of personnel, destabilization of the institutional structure, and loss of honour. Military training programs have been studied through interviews with former torturers in Greece,[53] Argentina, Brazil, Chile, Uruguay,[54] Nicaragua,[55] and Israel.[56] Often the young, the poor, or the uneducated are recruited. Brutal training at the outset desensitizes trainees to their own pain, suffering, and humiliation. Confinement and initiation rites isolate them from prior relationships. They usually experience moral tension in their new roles and variously resort to denial, psychological compartmentalization, alcohol, or drugs. The efficacy of shame tactics in disorienting subjects tends to lead to sexual tortures that in turn contribute to stigmatization and corruption of torturers. Haritos-Fatouros, who has deeply researched the training of torturers, observed that 'the perpetrators of evil in the Abu Ghraib prison have also become its victims who will suffer disgrace, imprisonment, and mental disorders in the years to come'. 'Who is responsible for so many ruined lives?' she asks.[57] A study of 'violence workers' in Brazil's suppression of 'communist insurgents' showed that torturers experienced even greater job-related stress than members of death squads.[58] The moral rationale for ruination of torturers cannot be the same as sending soldiers into combat to defend their countries because the torturers and their families will not be honoured but disdained. Statements of military necessity and legalization of torture cannot remove revulsion and stigmatization.

Torture programs have been very disruptive of military organization. To save itself as an institution, the Brazilian military gradually eliminated torture practices between 1975 and 1986, under the leadership of several generals. With counterterrorist agencies working outside the law, torturers doubled as smugglers, blackmailers, and extortionists. Torturers scorned and controverted the chain of command, creating two factions and destabilizing the army.[59] Generally, torturers win not gratitude or admiration from their military colleagues but contempt. After the fall of the Pinochet regime in Chile, the navy and air force did not take back officers who had worked in the secret service but considered them to be 'defiled'.[60] After almost a half century, the torture of Algerian terrorists under General Aussaresses' still stains the honour of the French army, especially in France itself.[61]

## The Legal Establishment

Many legal experts have taken issue with Alan Dershowitz regarding his suggestion that, in very extreme circumstances, interrogators must be issued with 'torture warrants' by the judges before indulging in practices of torture. Dershowitz explains the concept of a torture warrant as follows:

I have no doubt that if an actual ticking-bomb situation were to arise, our law enforcement authorities would torture. The real debate is whether such torture should take place outside of our legal system or within it. The answer to this seems clear: If we are to have torture, it should be authorized by the law. Judges should have to issue a 'torture warrant' in each case. Thus we would not be winking an eye of quiet approval at torture while publicly condemning it. Democracy requires accountability and transparency, especially when extraordinary steps are taken. Most important, it requires compliance with the rule of law. And such compliance is impossible when an extraordinary technique, such as torture, operates outside of the law.[62]

The problems with the idea of a torture warrant are well known, and often recited in legal journals, so it will suffice to list them here in summary terms: that a torture warrant would be seen as an invitation to increase the use of torture, both in the US and abroad;[63] that no rule can cover the many different aspects of a ticking-bomb argument;[64] torturing the ticking-bomb terrorists would be prohibited by the due process standard of the Fifth and Fourteenth Amendments;[65] having judges issue torture warrants may compromise judicial integrity and the rule of law.[66]

More generally, a legalized program of torture could lead to the degeneration of the core values on which the liberal democratic state rests. A detailed legal analysis of Israeli torture in the Occupied Territories concluded that torture subverts the rule of law in a liberal democracy and erodes other democratic ideals supported by the rule of law.[67] There are also important lessons that should be learned from the war in Algeria, where torture was institutionalized as a wider, integrated system of repression. In Algeria torture contributed to a fatal corruption or erosion of the judiciary and the rule of law. As MacMaster (2004, p. 9) explains, in Algeria the use of torture had constituted an unspeakable catastrophe:

> Torture, widely referred to as 'la gangrene', was seen as a form of cancer that inexorably led to the degeneration of the liberal democratic state, its institutions (particularly the army and the judiciary), its core values and fundamental respect for human rights and dignity. The centrality of torture to the debate on the Algerian war lay not in the grim horrors of the practice as taken in isolation, but rather in the extent to which it served as a symbol of a deeper corruption, both of the state and of the structures of military, administrative and judicial power that had made it possible.[68]

Any State that sets up torture interrogation units will lose its moral legitimacy, and therefore undermine the political obligation of its citizens.

To his credit Dershowitz (2003–4) has tried to address some of the above criticisms, suggesting that these accusations are fundamentally empirical claims, even though his critics have failed to produce the empirical evidence — one of the aims of this article is to present the empirical evidence Dershowitz is calling for. As for some of the other accusations, those who support the institutionalization of torture could maintain that since torture would only be used in the most extreme circumstances, we shouldn't worry about such practice undermining the values of democratic society. Furthermore, his proposal is meant to bring accountability and transparency to torture practices that are already taking place 'under the radar'.

Yet Dershowitz fails to appreciate that the time constraints of the ticking-bomb argument work against the accountability envisioned by legalizing torture interrogation and requiring prior 'torture warrants' from judges. Because destruction is imminent, the captors of the terrorists will not want to lose time obtaining a search warrant. As explained by a former Brazilian police officer: 'It is necessary to get the information now because from now on to the future it might be too late. And to save time, everything is valid'.[69] Since capture of the ticking-bomb terrorist is entangled with ongoing operations, where lives of agents and future counterterrorist operations are at risk, intelligence officers will not submit evidence of guilt to judges, whom they consider naïve and poor security risks. The Argentine General Acdel Vilas, who was active in counterinsurgency operations in the early 1970s, later described how he circumvented judicial constraints on interrogation. He sent out plainclothesmen instead of uniformed officers to pick up suspects, then passed only the insignificant suspects into the justice system.[70] In Israel, interrogators from the General Security Service (GSS) routinely gave false testimony to the Israeli Supreme Court to conceal its methods from the enemy and to secure convictions where evidence was lacking.[71] The present US administration sought to authorize torture interrogation secretly within the judiciary, as revealed in memoranda from White House Legal Counsel Alberto Gonzales and others.[72] Judges and legal consultants selected for compatibility with the torture interrogation program do not provide accountability but cover.

Very little of current torture interrogation in the 'war on terrorism' falls into the category of the ticking-bomb argument. Legalization of torture creates no mechanism for monitoring such interrogation. At the same time it provides an institutional mandate for torture research and for recruitment and training of torturers.

Finally, there is also a problem with the moral calculus of the ticking-bomb argument. The captured terrorist and his/her intended victims are the principal parties whose welfare is at stake. This may be called the Principal Parties Premise. The ticking-bomb argument simply assumes that torturing the terrorist is the right thing to do because many innocent lives were saved with the sacrifice of one guilty person. This characterization of the principal parties though is an artifice of the stripped-down moral reasoning of the ticking-bomb argument. Under practical consideration, the very elements adduced to limit the damages of torture interrogation — only of knowledgeable terrorists, only when innocent lives are at risk, only when destruction is imminent — actually expand the scope of damages. The accuracy and speed of virtuoso torture interrogation dictate long advance preparation and coordination, and ultimately corruption, of many key social institutions. The principal parties actually include the medical establishment, the scientific establishment, the police, the military establishment, the judicial establishment, and a great many innocents falsely tortured.

It may appear that damages to democratic institutions are negligible compared to deaths of innocents because institutions can be repaired but the dead cannot be resurrected. Yet in country after country where alleged national security threats have resulted in the torture of domestic enemies — including Algeria, South Africa, Chile, Argentina, Uruguay, El Salvador, Guatemala, Ireland — human rights researchers have shown the failures of various programs of social repair. Criminal trials, truth commissions, reparations to victims, and community mourning rituals have all proved inadequate.[73] Part of the difficulty of social repair is the high proportion of innocents who are tortured. Realistically, the moral calculus of the ticking-bomb argument should weigh (a) the evil of the murders of innocent victims of the bomb against (b) the corruption of key social institutions, the evil of torture of many innocents mistakenly tortured, and the ruination of many torturers. The guilty terrorist himself might even be omitted from the equation as a minor item. It was easy to compare harm to the terrorist to harm to his intended victims. But a much grander moral theory than the ticking-boom argument is needed to weigh damages to some innocent individuals against damages to key democratic institutions and other innocent individuals.

## VII. Alternatives to State-Sponsored Torture Interrogation

In the ticking-bomb scenario, the brief period until detonation is a proxy for the premise that there are no alternative courses of action. Torture interrogation is presented as a quick fix. Any alternative would have to promise a quicker fix. Since no one has yet proposed a quicker fix, torture interrogation is considered the winning methodology by default. As we argued in Part VI above, the problem here is that the goal of swift and accurate torture interrogation requires extensive preparation and resources. Therefore other techniques that require extensive preparation and resources may compete with virtuoso torture interrogation, for example, techniques that require cultural awareness, linguistic competence, and self-mastery on the part of interrogators. For behavioural control of an unwilling subject, there is no reason to suppose one method would apply to all cases. The cultural background, motivation, counter-interrogation training, and physiology of terrorists are too diverse. Here is a sample of alternative interrogation techniques that have proved fruitful on occasion.

Many expert interrogators aspire to the elegant 'social skills method' of Hans Scharff. Scharff was the master interrogator for the German *Luftwaffe* in World War II. His cordial style drew military secrets from unwitting Allied pilots. He elicited seemingly unimportant pieces of information from many subjects and then assembled the puzzle pieces.[74] For sharp interrogators, it may not be necessary to compel the terrorist to betray the location of the bomb explicitly; apparently innocuous information may suffice. Among other examples of social skills methods, Islamic clerics have replaced official interrogators by reformulating the religious commitments of some terrorists.[75] Terrorists duped by their colleagues have cooperated with their captors when their exploitation was made evident to them. Chronically ill terrorists and badly wounded suicide bombers have become cooperative following successful medical treatment.[76] Of course, such methods are difficult to pursue after a captive has already been treated badly.

Torture interrogation of terrorists may actually defeat other counterterrorist methods, just as government conduct in one hostage situation has implications for other hostage situations. Innovative military strategists have recently stressed the need for an 'effective counter-narrative' to Al Qaeda's 'foundational myth' of 'the warriors of God' against the 'infidel West'. They decry our failure 'to come to grips with the narrative dimensions of the war on terrorism,' noting that, 'a grand narrative that was perfectly plausible before Abu Ghraib may be rendered perfectly inert afterwards'.[77]

## Conclusion

We live in an age when even some liberal democracies have no qualms about using torture to fight their enemies. The standard justification for legalizing the use of torture is on consequentialist grounds, of the ticking-bomb variety. In this article, we have argued against the frivolous consequentialism of the ticking-bomb argument, not from a deontological perspective but from a consequentialist one.

The empirical evidence clearly suggests that when it comes to torturing suspects, the record of epistemic success is, at best, unpromising.[78] From a moral and political point of view, fallibilism must be a serious concern for any argument based on consequentialist reasoning. The human and political costs of torturing the wrong person cannot be dismissed as necessary evils. Counterintuitively, actual innocence does not protect suspects against confession in interrogation but rather puts them at high risk of false confession, as has been conclusively demonstrated in criminological studies and psychological experiments. As Kassin (2005) explains, their naïve belief that truth and justice will prevail, for instance, leads them to waive precautions, and their denials of guilt evoke much more rigorous efforts from interrogators. Moreover, there is no formula for compensation or rehabilitation. Psychiatric studies show that torture survivors are plagued by self-destructiveness, failure to reintegrate with their families, and incapacity to take charge of their lives again.[79] Those who were not politically engaged against their captors — the completely innocent — tend to even greater devastation.

Furthermore the narrative simplicity of the ticking-bomb argument conceals the tremendous institutional support required for any rational hope of extracting the terrorist's plan under torture. The demands (and effects) of institutionalizing a state-sponsored program of precision torture interrogation on civilian, military and legal institutions are conveniently neglected by those who support the legalization of torture interrogations. A skilled torturer is like a skilled surgeon, requiring frequent practice. Yet proponents of legalized torture like Dershowitz fail to specify how and where these torturers will learn and maintain their trade, not to mention the risk that highly trained torturers may use their skills outside of official parameters. Institutionalizing torture will also mean that torturing will become a legitimate profession, or as Twining and Twining (1973, p. 352)[80] suggest, 'institutionalized torture may lead to the creation of a guild of professional torturers whose continued existence will constitute a serious threat to society'.

The bureaucratization of torture interrogation presents a serious problem. Holocaust historian Christopher Browning attributed the long-term Nazi success in persecution of despised ethnic groups to bureaucratization of anti-Semitism. After the Nazis revoked the policy of killing handicapped German citizens in August 1941, the scores of doctors and nurses — 'euthanasia experts' — who had killed 70,000 handicapped became available for killing Jews, Roma, and Poles.[81] The current proposals for torture interrogation do not contain any mechanism for terminating the program. This is the point at which to heed the military maxim that the long-term potential of a weapon or tactic is more important than its initial purpose.[82] Torture interrogation cannot fulfil its initial purpose as a low-cost life saver in the ticking-bomb argument, and its long-term potential is the devastation of democratic institutions and torture of many innocent victims.

## Acknowledgements

Research for this paper by the first author was made possible thanks to the support of the Irish Research Council for the Humanities and Social Sciences (IRCHSS), and the Arts Faculty Research Award at University College Cork. An earlier version of the paper was presented at the Department of Government at Dartmouth College. We are grateful to two anonymous referees, and to Anne Sa'adah, Allan Stam and Federico Varese for their helpful suggestions and comments on an earlier version of the paper. Material has been drawn from the second author's earlier paper, J. M. Arrigo, 'A utilitarian argument against torture interrogation', *Science and Engineering Ethics* 10 (2004).

## NOTES

1 D. Luban, 'The war on terrorism and the end of human rights', *Philosophy & Public Policy Quarterly* 22, 3 (2002).

2 A similar 'absolutist' position is defended by M. Strauss, 'Torture', *New York Law School Law Review* 48 (2003–4): 201–274; C. Tindale, 'The logic of torture: a critical examination', *Social Theory and Practice* 22, 3 (1996); E. Scarry, *The Body in Pain: The Making and Unmaking of the World* (Oxford: Oxford University Press, 1985).

3 There is a vast legal literature on torture in international law. For a legal history of torture, see J. Langbein, 'The legal history of torture', in S. Levinson (ed.) *Torture: A Collection* (Oxford: Oxford University Press, 2004). See also B. M. Klayman, 'The definition of torture in international law', *Temple Law Quarterly* 51 (1978): 449–517; A. Byrnes, 'The Committee Against Torture', in P. Alston (ed.), *The United Nations and Human Rights* (Oxford: Clarendon Press, 1992); A. Boulesbaa, *The UN Convention on Torture and the Prospects for Enforcement* (The Hague: Kluwer, 1999).

4 Amnesty International, *Amnesty International Report 2003*, London.

5 See J. Mayer, 'Outsourcing torture: the secret history of America's "extraordinary rendition"', *The New Yorker* February 14, 2005; S. Grey and I. Cobain 'British al-Qaida suspect's tale of US "torture by proxy"', *The Guardian* August 2, 2005.

6 E. Peters, *Torture* (Philadelphia, PA: University of Pennsylvania Press, 1996).

7 On Algeria see R. Maran, *Torture: The Role of Ideology in the French-Algerian War* (New York: Praeger, 1989); P. Aussaresses, *The Battle of the Casbah: Terrorism and Counter-terrorism in Algeria 1955–1957* (New York: Enigma Books, 2002); A. Shatz, 'The torture of Algiers', *New York Review* 21 November 2002. On Guatemala see V. Sanford, *Buried Secrets: Truth and Human Rights in Guatemala* (Basingstoke: Palgrave-Macmillan, 2003). On Argentina see G. Rogers, 'Argentina's obligation to prosecute military officials for torture', *Columbia Human Rights Law Review* 20 (1988–89): 259–308. On the responsibility of the USA for tortures in Latin America, see T. Kepner, 'Torture 101: The case against the United States for atrocities committed by School of the Americas alumni', *Dickinson Journal of International Law* 19 (2000–01): 475–529; On Iraq see M. Danner, *Torture and Truth: America, Abu Ghraib and the War on Terror* (London: Granta, 2005).

8 In Abu Ghraib, Iraqi prisoners had shit smeared on them, they were half-drowned in vats of urine, and forced to eat meals that have been dumped in the toilet; see Danner op. cit.

9 D. Sussman, 'What's wrong with torture?', *Philosophy & Public Affairs* 33, 1 (2005): 1–33.

10 D. Blatt, 'Recognizing rape as a method of torture', *New York University Review of Law and Social Change* 19 (1992): 821–865.

11 See also Amnesty International, *Amnesty International Report 1992*, London.; X. Bunster-Burotto, 'Surviving beyond fear: women and torture in Latin America', in J. Nash and H. Safa (eds.), *Women and Change in Latin America* (South Hadley, MA: Bergin and Garvey, 1986).

12 C. Sung, 'Torturing the ticking-bomb terrorist: an analysis of judicially sanctioned torture in the context of terrorism', *Boston College Third World Law Journal* 23 (2003): 193–212.

13 On rape as a form of torture, it is worth mentioning that still today the international community does not recognize rape by a public official as an act of torture, even though rape has all the characteristics of the definition of torture given by the UN Torture Convention; See Blatt op. cit.

14 A. M. Dershowitz, 'The torture warrant: a response to Professor Strauss', *New York Law School Law Review* 48 (275) (2003–4) at 227: 'Let me once again — for perhaps the dozenth time — state my actual view on torture, so that no one can any longer feign confusion about where I stand, though I am certain the "confusion" will persist among some who are determined to argue that I am a disciple of Torquemada. I am generally against torture as a *normative* matter, and I would like to see its use minimalized'.

15 For Bentham's writings on torture, as well as a detailed commentary on Bentham's justification of the use of torture, see W. L. Twining and P. E. Twining, 'Bentham on torture', *Northern Ireland Law Quarterly* 24, 3 (1973): 305–356.

16 H. Shue, 'Torture', *Philosophy and Public Affairs* 7 (1977–8): 124–143. Reprinted in S. Levinson (ed.) *Torture: A Collection* (Oxford: Oxford University Press, 2004).

17 In a more recent piece, after discrediting the thought-experiment of the ticking-bomb argument, Shue (2003) makes the point that if asked to decide what to do with a terrorist who allegedly has information of a ticking-bomb, he would say 'Let's risk it — let's gamble that we can honor our principles and that the children (and old men) will not only not die but will live in civilized countries': H. Shue, 'Response to Sanford Levinson', *Dissent* 50, 3 (2003).

18 B. Gert, 'Justifying violence', *The Journal of Philosophy* 66, 19 (1969).

19 C. Fried, *Right and Wrong* (Cambridge, MA: Cambridge University Press, 1978).

20 R. Posner, 'Torture, terrorism, and interrogation', in S. Levinson (ed.) *Torture: A Collection* (Oxford: Oxford University Press, 2004).

21 There are of course many others who defend a similar line, for example, Gross (2003–4) argues that we should consider the possibility that truly exceptional cases may give rise to official disobedience, whereby public officials may act extralegally and be ready to accept the legal ramifications of their actions: O. Gross, 'Are torture warrants warranted — pragmatic absolutism and official disobedience', *Minnesota Law Review* 88 (1481) (2003–4). See also B. Hoffman, 'A nasty business', *The Atlantic Monthly* January (2002): 49–52; A. Moher, 'The lesser of two evils? An argument for judicially sanctioned torture in a post-9/11 world', *Thomas Jefferson Law Review* 46 (2003–04): 469–489.

22 J. Parry, 'Escalation and Necessity: Defining Torture at Home and Abroad', in S. Levinson (ed.) *Torture: A Collection* (Oxford: Oxford University Press, 2004).

23 A. M. Dershowitz, 'Tortured reasoning', in S. Levinson (ed.) *Torture: A Collection* (Oxford: Oxford University Press, 2004).

24 See also J. Parry, 'What is torture, are we doing it, and what if we are?', *University of Pittsburgh Law Review* 64 (2003); 237–262; J. Parry and W. White, 'Interrogating suspected terrorists: should torture be an option?', *University of Pittsburgh Law Review* 63 (2002): 743–766.

25 Dershowitz uses different examples, from the scenario of law enforcement officials arresting terrorists boarding one of the airplanes [of the September 11 disaster] and learning that other planes, then airborne, were headed toward unknown occupied buildings ('Torture of terrorists: is it necessary to do and to lie about it?', in A. M. Dershowitz, *Shouting Fire: Civil Liberties in a Turbulent Age* (Boston: Little, Brown & Co. (2002)), to the capture of a terrorist who refuses to divulge information about the imminent use of weapons of mass destruction, such as a nuclear, chemical or biological device (Dershowitz, op. cit.).

26 R. Hardin, *Morality Within the Limits of Reason* (Chicago, IL: University of Chicago Press, 1988).

27 J. M. Arrigo, *Correspondence between a U.S. Counterintelligence Liaison Officer and Jean Maria Arrigo, September 2002 — August 2005* (Intelligence Ethics Collection, Hoover Institution Archives, Stanford University, Stanford, CA, 2005).

28 *Ibid.*

29 This distinction can be found in Shue (1977–8) op. cit.

30 Sanford (op. cit., pp. 166–7) recounts what happened in the town of Nebaj in 1981 after the army interrogated more than 300 Maya men: 'After the massive interrogation, there were daily disappearances as well as the discovery of mutilated bodies along the street each morning. "They were everywhere" says Don Leonel, "in the streets and hanging in the parks. The only thing that was certain was that each day there were more dead"'.

31 Aussaresses op. cit.

32 See A. Biletzki, 'The judicial rhetoric of morality: Israel's High Court of Justice on the legality of torture'. Electronic version. Unpublished paper. Occasional Papers of the School of Social Science, No. 9 (Tel Aviv: Tel Aviv University, 2001). That terrorism flourished in spite of the extensive resort to torture is of course a counterfactual claim that is virtually impossible to prove or disprove on empirical grounds; on this

specific question see B. Cohen, 'Democracy and the mis-rule of law: the Israeli legal system's failure to prevent torture in the occupied territories', *Indiana International and Comparative Law Review* 12 (2001): 75.

33 Personal communication to J. M. Arrigo from Harold William Rood, February 17, 2006.

34 Editorial, 'Towards a realistic interrogation policy', *Washington Times* March 11, 2005 [Electronic version].

35 The work of forensic psychologists in this field suggests that highly coercive interrogations lead to increased numbers of false confessions. See G. H. Gudjonsson, *The Psychology of Interrogations and Confessions: A Handbook* (Chichester: John Wiley & Sons, 2003); S. M. Kassin and G. H. Gudjonsson, 'The psychology of confession evidence: a review of the literature and issues'. *Psychological Science in the Public Interest* 5, Whole No. 2 (2004); S. M. Kassin, 'On the psychology of confessions: does innocence put innocents at risk?', *American Psychologist* 60, 3 (2005): 215–228; S. M. Kassin, 'The psychology of confession evidence', *American Psychologist* 52 (1997): 221–233.

36 T. B. Allen and N. Polmar, *Code-Name Downfall: the Secret Plan to Invade Japan and Why Truman Dropped the Bomb* (New York: Simon & Schuster, 1995).

37 J. B. Stockdale, 'Courage under fire', in Department of Philosophy and Fine Arts, United States Military Academy (eds.), *Moral Dimensions of the Military Profession*, 5th edn., (New York: Forbes Custom Publishing, 2001).

38 Sun Tzu, *The Art of War*, S. B. Griffith trans. (Oxford: Oxford University Press, 1963).

39 This section of the paper draws from J. M. Arrigo, 'A utilitarian argument against torture interrogation', *Science and Engineering Ethics* 10 (2004): 543–572.

40 L. Hart, 'Afghan detainee's leg was "pulpified", witness says', *Los Angeles Times* March 23, 2005 [On-line version].

41 See P. Vesti and F. E. Somnier, 'Doctor involvement in torture: a historical perspective', *Torture* 4, 3 (1994): 82–89.

42 H. Dôcker, 'Turkey continues harassment, arrests, and torture of medical doctors', *Torture* 10, 2 (2002).

43 W. H. Anderson, 'Terrorism — underlying causes', *The Intelligencer* [Journal of the Association of Former Intelligence Officers] 14, 1 (2004).

44 R. J. Lifton, 'Doctors and torture', *New England Journal of Medicine* 351, 5 (2004): 415–416; S. Miles, 'Abu Ghraib: its legacy for military medicine', *Lancet* 364 (2004): 725–729.

45 See S. Qouta, R.-L. Punamaki and E. E. Sarraj, 'Prison experiences and coping styles among Palestinian men', *Peace and Conflict* 3, 1 (1997): 19–36.

46 N. Zeeberg, 'Torture — a public health puzzle in Europe', *Torture* 8, 4a, Suppl. 1 (1998): 21–44.

47 E. Byrd, 'Moral issues related to high technology: nonleathal weapons and psychic warfare', *Pilot Workshop on the Ethics of Political and Military Intelligence. Intelligence Ethics Collection*, September 29 (Stanford, CA: Hoover Institution Archives, Stanford University, 2000).

48 H. M. Weinstein, *Psychiatry and the CIA: Victims of Mind Control* (Washington, DC: American Psychiatric Press, 1990).

49 US Senate, 'Select Committee on Intelligence and Subcommittee on Health and Scientific Research of the Committee on Human Resources', *Project MKULTRA: the CIA's Program of Research in Behavioral Modification* (Washington, DC: US Government Printing Office, 1977).

50 F. Bowers, 'The intelligence divide: can it be bridged?', *The Christian Science Monitor* 2–3, (October 8, 2002) — Statistics quoted from FBI Director R. Mueller.

51 E. Lichtblau, 'U.S. uses terror law to pursue crimes from drugs to swindling', *New York Times* September 28, 2003 [electronic version].

52 N. J. Gordon and W. L. Fleisher, *Effective Interviewing and Interrogation Technique* (San Diego, CA: Academic Press, 2002).

53 M. Haritos-Fatouros, 'The official torturer: a learning model for obedience to the authority of violence', in F. D. Crelinsten and A. P. Schmid (eds.), *The Politics of Pain Torturers and their Masters* (Leiden: Center for the Study of Social Conflicts, 1993), pp. 141–160.

54 W. S. Heinz, 'The military, torture and human rights: experiences from Argentina, Brazil, Chile and Uruguay', in F. D. Crelinsten and A. P. Schmid (eds.), *The Politics of Pain Torturers and their Masters* (Leiden: Center for the Study of Social Conflicts, 1993), pp. 73–108.

55 F. Allodi, 'Somoza's National Guard: a study of human rights abuses, psychological health and moral development', in F. D. Crelinsten and A. P. Schmid (eds.), *The Politics of Pain Torturers and their Masters* (Leiden: Center for the Study of Social Conflicts, 1993), pp. 125–140.

56  S. Cohen and D. Golan, *The Interrogation of Palestinians during the Intifada: Ill-treatment, 'Moderate Physical Pressure' or Torture?* (Jerusalem: Israeli Information Center for Human Rights in the Occupied Territories, 1991).

57  M. Haritos-Fatouros, 'Psychological and sociopolitical factors contributing to the creation of the Iraqi torturers', *International Bulletin of Political Psychology* 16, 2 (2005). On-line journal.

58  M. K. Huggins, M. Haritos-Fatouros and P. G. Zimbardo, *Violence Workers: Police Torturers and Murderers Reconstruct Brazilian Atrocities* (Berkeley, CA: University of California Press, 2002).

59  L. Wechsler, *A Miracle, a Universe: Settling Accounts with Torturers* (New York: Penguin, 1991).

60  Heinz op. cit.

61  See W. Schrepel, 'Paras and centurions: lessons learned from the Battle of Algiers', *Peace and Conflict* 11, 1 (2005): 71–90. It is also not clear how the torture interrogation program will be terminated when the War on Terrorism has been won. Military wisdom cautions that the long-term potential of a weapon or tactic is more important than its initial purpose. See T. M. Kane, 'Strategic analysis', *Military Intelligence Professional Bulletin* February-March (2002): 4–7.

62  A. M. Dershowitz, 'America needs "torture warrants"', *Los Angeles Times* November 8, 2001. For a fuller account, see A. M. Dershowitz, *Why Terrorism Works: Understanding the Threats, Responding to the Challenge* (New Haven, CT: Yale University Press, 2002).

63  Strauss op. cit.; Sung op. cit.

64  Strauss op. cit.

65  Sung op. cit.

66  Sung op. cit.

67  Cohen op. cit.

68  N. MacMaster, in 'Torture: From Algiers to Abu Ghraib', *Race and Class* 46, 2 (2004), pp. 1–21 at p. 12, also reminds us that, 'historically, whenever states started on the slippery slope of enabling a restricted or "controlled" use of duress, this inevitably deteriorated into a monstrous system of brutality'.

69  Heinz op. cit., p. 95.

70  Heinz op. cit., p. 87.

71  M. Gur-Arye, 'Excerpts of the Report. Symposium on the Report of the Commission of Inquiry into the Methods of Investigation of the General Security Service Regarding Hostile Terrorist Activity', *Israel Law Review* 23, 2 & 3, Special Issue (1989).

72  A. Lewis, 'Making torture legal', *The New York Review* July 25, 2004.

73  L. E. Fletcher and H. Weinstein, 'Violence and social repair: rethinking the contribution of justice to reconciliation', *Human Rights Quarterly* 24, 3 (2002): 573–649 at pp. 615 and 625.

74  R. Toliver, *The Interrogator: the Story of Hans-Joachim Scharff, Master Interrogator of the Luftwaffe* (Atglen, PA: Schiffer, 1997).

75  Associated Press, 'Saudi interrogators use new technique', *Washington Post* December 1, 2003 [Electronic Version].

76  'Intelligence operations: the opposite of torture at Abu Ghraib', *The Strategy Page* April 19, 2005 [Electronic Version].

77  W. D. Casebeer and J. A. Russell, 'Storytelling and terrorism: towards a comprehensive "counter-narrative strategy"', *Strategic Insights* 4, 3: [http://www.ccc.nps.navy.mil/si/2005/Mar/casebeerMar05.asp] [Center for Contemporary Conflict at the Naval Postgraduate School] April 24, 2005 accessed.

78  Shue (2003) op. cit. makes all these points: 'We imagine we have exactly the person we need-not some poor devil who looks like him to agents who have parachuted in from another culture. We imagine that the person we hold knows exactly what we need to know-not out-of-date information overtaken by events. We imagine that the person will reveal exactly what we need-not simply vomit and die, or descend into a psychotic state . . . We imagine that the information that will be revealed will be sufficient to prevent the terrible catastrophe-not that the catastrophe will simply be re-scheduled for a different time or place'.

79  R. Oravecs, L. Hárdi and L. Lajtai, 'Social transition, exclusion, shame and humiliation', *Torture* 14, 1 (2004): 4–15.

80  Twining and Twining, op. cit.

81  I. Deák, 'Improvising the Holocaust', Review of *The Origins of the Final Solution*, by C. R. Browning, *The New York Review* September 23, 2004, pp. 78–81.

82  Kane op. cit.

# Index